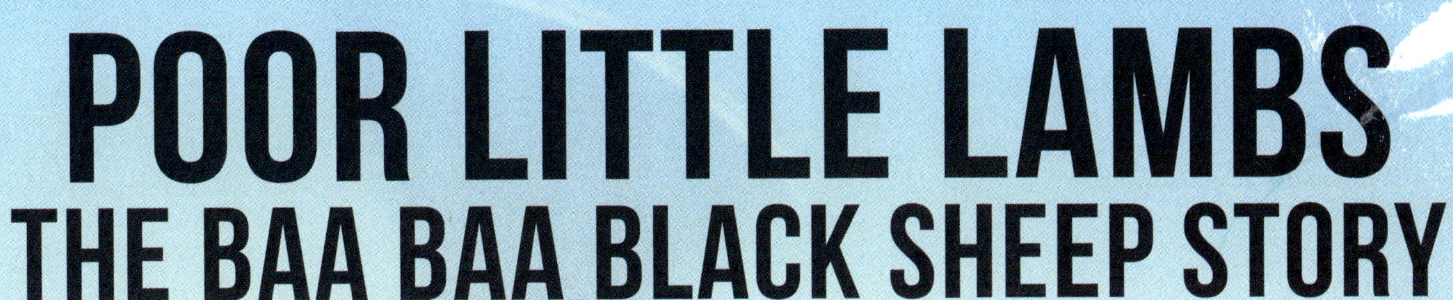

POOR LITTLE LAMBS

THE BAA BAA BLACK SHEEP STORY

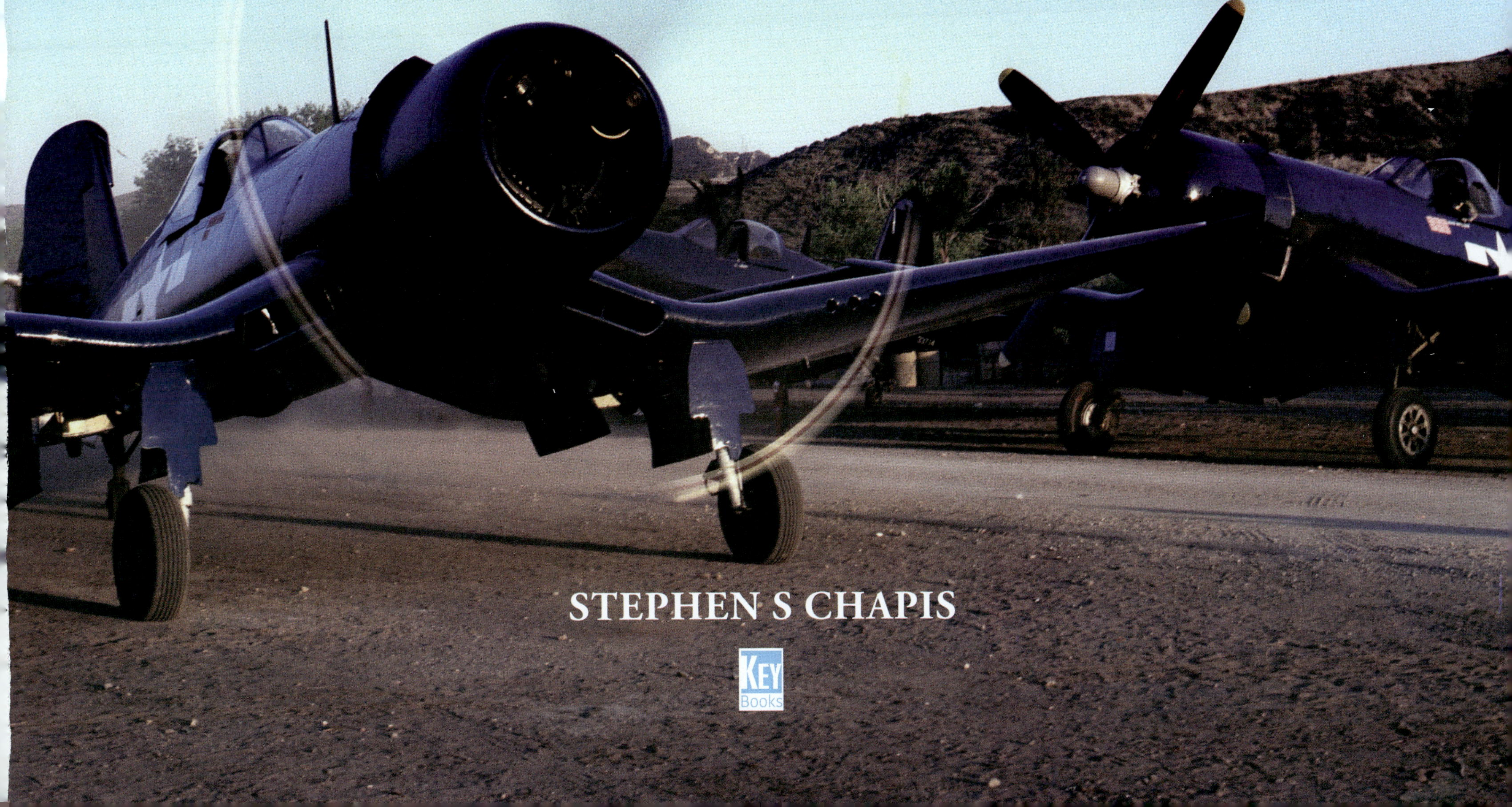

STEPHEN S CHAPIS

KEY Books

Front cover image: (Left, second left and second right, Mark Schafhausen; right, John Cassidy)

Title page image: Junior Burchinal taxies his FG-1D 92433 for a flight out of Indian Dunes. In the background are F4U-4 97359 and F4U-7 133710. (Mark Schafhausen)

Contents page image: John Schafhausen's F4U-7 133710 respendent in its "Hollywood Sea Blue" paint, which it wore until the aircraft was restored in 2017. (James Larsen)

Inside back cover image: (Greg Morehead)

Back cover image: (Mark Schafhausen)

DEDICATION

I have to thank Germaine Chapis, my best friend and spouse of 34 years; if she hadn't found and recorded "Flying Misfits" for me in 2010, this entire project would not have happened. In the past 14 years, she's learned more about Greg Boyington, the Black Sheep, and the Corsair than she ever thought possible. Her love, support, understanding, and patience was and always will be a blessing.

ACKNOWLEDGEMENTS

Zane Adams, Richard Mallory Allnutt, Joey Aresco, Alan Armstrong, Eric Boehm (Intrepid Sea, Air & Space Museum), Donald Bellisario, Chuck Bowman, Stephen Bridgewater, Mike Burke, John Cassidy, Keith Charlot, George Chung, Charles Church, JD Davis, Don "Bucky" Dawson, Robert DeGroat, Frank Dieterich, Denise DuBarry-Hay*, Fred Ellsbury, Adam Estes, James H. Farmer, Doug Fisher, Richard Flachs, Blain Fowler, Tom* and Dan Friedkin, Craig Fuller, Bruce Gamble, Steve Guilford, Dan Hagedorn, Mosely Hardy, Jason Hodge, Steve Hinton, Susan and Kenny Johnson, Erik Johnston, Ken Kaminski, Kedar Karmarkar, Ken Laird, James Larsen, Jim Laurier, Brianne Leary, John Lyles (USMC History Division), Larry Manetti, Stan Marks, Mark Mathis, Doug Matthews, Rob Mears, Greg Morehead, Frank Mormillo, Phil Myers, Obie O'Brien*, Cory O'Bryan, John O'Connor, Jerry O'Neill, Ron Olsen, Mike Patlin, Milo Peltzer, David Prescott, Frank Price, Paul Redlich, Noah Stegman Rechtin (Tri-State Warbird Museum), Phil Rogers, Steve Rosenberg, Patty Sachs (Assistant to Donald Bellisario), Jeff Sagansky, Dennis Sanders, Mark Schafhausen, Josh Shaffer, Jim Sullivan*, Sam Taber, Scott Slocum, Robert and Pam Thomas (Emil Buehler Library, National Naval Aviation Museum), Scott Thompson, Eric Trueblood, Nelson Tyler, Wally Van Winkle, Nicholas Veronico, Michael Walker, Glenn Watson, Dave Welch, Alisa Whitley (USMC History Division), James Whitmore, Jr., and Bill Yoak*.

---

* Deceased

Published by Key Books
An imprint of Key Publishing Ltd
PO Box 100
Stamford
Lincs PE9 1XQ

www.keypublishing.com

The right of Stephen S Chapis to be identified as the author of this book has been asserted in accordance with the Copyright, Designs and Patents Act 1988 Sections 77 and 78.

Typeset by SJmagic DESIGN SERVICES, India.

CONTENTS

Foreword by Chuck Bowman................4

Introduction 5

Chapter 1   *Baa Baa Black Sheep* 7

Chapter 2   The Pilot: "Flying Misfits" 27

Chapter 3   Season One: *Baa Baa Black Sheep*.................43

Chapter 4   Season Two: Black Sheep Squadron.....................70

          Epilogue.................90

          Color Profiles 101

Appendix A   The Corsairs.................132

Appendix B   The Toras 153

Appendix C   The Allies: Flyers 169

Appendix D   The Camera Ships.................198

Bibliography 205

FOREWORD

I was delighted when Stephen Chapis reached out to me in early 2019. He wanted to write a book recounting Stephen J. Cannell's *Baa Baa Black Sheep* television series. Stephen felt that my history with the production of the series from its inception would provide readers with insight as to how a television series in the late '70s was developed – from the ground up. Besides Stephen J. Cannell, huge credit rests with Frank Price, President of Television at Universal Studios, and his commitment to have Pappy Boyington's book memorialized on America's television screens. I told him I would help in any way I could.

For each of us, the journey began with the irascible Pappy Boyington's autobiography, *Baa Baa Black Sheep*. Price had read the book and felt it would make a good television show. As for me, I was in my early 20s when I read it while working in news in Tulsa, Oklahoma. I still have my copy, which Pappy graciously signed for me more than 20 years later.

Stephen J. Cannell was a close friend of mine, so when he told me he was writing a pilot script for the series I exclaimed, "Wonderful!" Over the following months, I savored his drafts with scenes that jumped off the pages.

I was naturally curious as to how Stephen Chapis would translate the history of *Baa Baa Black Sheep*, the television series, into book form. As we exchanged emails, messages, and phone calls, it became apparent that Stephen was the perfect man for the job. I began reading other aviation stories Stephen had written – discovering that they were carefully researched when it came to the aircraft and that the pilots' stories, their exciting personal and wartime experiences, came alive. That's when I felt certain that Cannell's research had been matched by Stephen in this book.

I'm not a pilot, but I always dreamed of such when I was a boy in a small town on the Kansas-Oklahoma border. Alas, it was not to happen. But as you embark on Stephen's book, you will find it's an informative, entertaining read – from cover to cover.

Chuck Bowman, Producer

INTRODUCTION

Although the work on this book began in 2010, the seed of inspiration was planted on Tuesday, September 21, 1976, when "Flying Misfits," the pilot episode for the series that became *Baa Baa Black Sheep*, premiered on NBC at 9pm. I was only five years old, but I was allowed to stay up past my bedtime to watch because in those days before VCRs were commonplace, if you were not in front of the television when your show came on, you simply missed it. Every week I would sit in our big gold lounge chair (hey, it was the '70s, after all) completely enthralled with the Corsairs that flew across the screen. I couldn't have cared less about the brawling and the drinking. As for the nurses? Well, I wasn't quite old enough to care about them just yet either.

My fascination with the Corsair increased at Christmas 1977, when my dad gave me a 1/32-scale Corsair model he'd built from the "Baa Baa Black Sheep" kit released by Revell that year. A few years later, in 1981, the first airplane book I bought with my own money was Jim Sullivan's *F4U-CORSAIR in Color*, which I read and studied cover-to-cover thousands of times. Then, in Christmas 1986, my grandparents gave me a copy of Gregory Boyington's memoirs *Baa Baa Black Sheep*, which I immediately began reading and have read several times since. These items are a little worse for wear today, but they are treasured parts of my collection. Ask any middle-aged modeler, history buff, or warbird enthusiast today and you are likely to hear similar stories of how this short-lived television show, which later developed a cult following, inspired them in so many ways.

As the decades rolled by, I earned my private pilot's license, a college degree, got married, and started a career without much thought of the influential television show from my youth. That all changed one night after work in 2010 when my wife, Germaine, showed me a movie she DVR'd on a local classic TV station. It was "Flying Misfits," and as soon as the music of the opening credits began the fascination and wonderment of my youth came rushing back. The channel ran one episode per night, so in little more than a month we'd watched the entire series.

By that time, I'd become a semi-regular contributor to *Warbird Digest* magazine, and as I watched that first episode again, I thought it would make an interesting article to trace the histories of the eight Corsairs flown in the show and talk to the pilots that flew them; and when the article "Poor Little Lambs" was published in 2013, it was quite well-received. However, in 2016, when the article was published on the magazine's website and Facebook page, it went viral, so the decision was made to repost it every year on September 21, and

The author with F4U-4 97359 during the reunion between the aircraft and its wartime pilot Charles "Obie" O'Brien in September 2012. (*Greg Morehead*)

in each successive year the response grew. Five decades after it went off the air, the show still mattered.

Given the popularity of a single narrowly focused magazine article about the Corsairs, I began to think a book about the entire series would be extremely popular. The only problem was that I was in the middle of writing my first book, *Allied Jet Killers of World War 2*, so there was no time to start a new project. However, after it was released in 2017, I took a deep breath and dived in headfirst.

From the beginning, there were certain things I wanted to include. First and foremost, I wanted to go beyond the dry histories of the aircraft and delve into the behind-the-scenes aspects of the show. How did Pappy Boyington's book become a TV show? How were the actors cast? Why did some of the main cast members leave the show? Why was it canceled? These, and more, were all questions whose answers I had always wanted to know, and I had no doubt that there were thousands of other fans that wanted to know as well. Thanks to the actors, producers, directors, executives, pilots, and crew members that graciously granted me interviews, many of those questions, and more, have been answered.

Secondly, I wanted, as much as possible, to put the "buts" about the series to rest. Whenever there is a conversation about the series, people will say something to the effect of, "I loved the show, but…." That conjunction was sure to be followed by a bevy of criticisms that ranged from generalizations – "…it wasn't realistic…" – to nit-picky comments – "…the Black Sheep didn't fly those Corsair variants during World War Two…." All valid observations of course, but they don't consider a number of realities that the writers, producers, and directors faced in 1976.

There are also those who attest there were Marine Corps fighter squadrons more deserving of Hollywood's attention than Marine Fighter Squadron 214 (VMF-214) because the *Black Sheep* did not participate in the desperate early battles of the Pacific War, was not the highest scoring squadron in the Marine Corps, nor did it produce the greatest number of aces. While these points are valid, as you will see in the pages that follow, there were a series of seemingly inconsequential and unrelated events that occurred between 1943 and 1976 that led to the creation of *Baa Baa Black Sheep*.

Then, during the course of my research, two additional elements became apparent and merited inclusion. Both have been vaguely referenced over the decades, but they have never been examined in-depth in conjunction with one another as they related to the series. The first, which predates the series by at least a decade, was the crusade against violence on television. In today's world, where nearly anything goes, this may seem rather trite, but 50 years ago, those factions were quite militant in their views of what should and should not be on television.

The second was what the real VMF-214 veterans thought of the series. The short answer has always been that they despised it, which is true, but only to a point. There were some who did not like how the series portrayed them and were distressed with Boyington for being complicit in its creation, but at the same time they understood his motivations. One veteran in particular, though, Frank Walton, who served as the squadron's intelligence officer, cared neither for the series nor for Boyington's motives, and he set out to wage a one-man war against the series. The result was a book, published a decade after *Baa Baa Black Sheep* went off the air, that was the most vivid and detailed account of 214's time in the Solomons, and it brought Boyington and his "bastards" into a limelight that has yet to fade. The irony of that fame was a ripple effect of the television series that he'd wished had never been created.

All these elements and more are presented here in chronological order in what is perhaps the most in-depth look at *Baa Baa Black Sheep*, a television series that was unlike any other the world had ever seen when it debuted in 1976 and has yet to be equaled.

CHAPTER 1

BAA BAA BLACK SHEEP
From the Mediterranean to Indian Dunes

The Actors

Frank Price, President of Television at Universal Studios

For all intents and purposes, the genesis of the *Baa Baa Black Sheep* TV series began with Frank Price (1930–) aboard USS *Coral Sea* (CVB-43) during a Mediterranean cruise in 1949. Like so many of his generation, Price's interest in airplanes came about during World War Two. "I was reading the reports on what was happening and loved to be up to date on airplanes. I wrote every aircraft manufacturer for photos, and they sent me eight-by-ten black and white pictures. I had a great collection," Price related in November 2019.

While attending high school in Flint, Michigan, Price decided he wanted to work in the newspaper industry, so he joined the staff of the school newspaper and quickly rose to editor-in-chief, and this led to his first job at the *Flint Journal* during his senior year. In 1948, with a draft still on, he and his family moved back to California. However, Price was struggling to deal with his Los Angeles City College classes and a night job when he found out about a special Navy program. Price explained, "The Navy had a special management program where you could sign up for one year and then serve six years' reserve time. I thought, I think I'll take a break and join the Navy, because one year in the Navy sounds better than two years in the Army." Price wanted to serve in the Atlantic Fleet, so he returned to Flint to enlist and went through boot camp at Great Lakes Naval Training Center. Soon after, he went to Norfolk, Virginia, and reported aboard *Coral Sea*. Frank was impressed with the sheer size of the carrier. "I stood on the empty hangar deck at the stern...and it seemed like that ship went as far as the eye could see; it seemed it disappeared in a mist," he said.

In 1949, more than two decades before he was named president of Universal Television, Frank Price graduated from Navy boot camp and went on to serve aboard USS *Coral Sea* (CVB 43) where he first saw a Corsair. *(Frank Price)*

Embarked aboard *Coral Sea* in 1949 were three squadrons of F4U-4s and a single squadron of F4U-5s. Frank Price thought the Corsair had "a graceful look" and the design had an influence on his decision to turn Pappy Boyington's memoir into a television series in 1974. (*US Navy*)

Today, there are hundreds of memoirs written by veterans of World War Two, but Greg Boyington was among the first, if not the first, to write such a book in 1958. (*Frank Walton Collection, Emil Buehler Library, National Naval Aviation Museum*)

Originally slated to join the training office, Price mentioned his journalism experience to the right people and found his way on to the ship's newspaper. Over the next nine months, *Coral Sea* sailed from Guantanamo Bay and Haiti in the Caribbean to Greece and the French Riviera in the Mediterranean. Price's duties included editing the paper, writing editorials, typing intelligence reports, and issuing press releases for local papers, when the ship made a port call. It was during that cruise that he first saw a Corsair in person. "I thought the Corsair had a graceful look. The design was just beautiful. There were other planes aboard, of course, and they looked good, but nothing looked like the Corsair," Price said. The seed had been planted.

In 1951, after a short stint at Michigan State, Price moved to New York City to enroll at Columbia University but dropped out when he landed a job as full-time reader in the CBS TV Story Department. He returned to California in 1959, where he joined Revue Productions, as Universal TV was then known. He started as associate producer and writer and quickly rose to vice-president in 1961. Just a decade later he was named president of Universal TV and vice president of MCA. While at Universal, Price developed the concept of the "made-for-TV movie" and the mini-series.

Price spoke about getting *Baa Baa Black Sheep* on the air: "As a studio, we were always looking for ideas for series." Price had owned a copy of *Baa Baa Black Sheep*, Gregory Boyington's memoirs, for some time; and in 1974, with very little on television that depicted the military in America's "last good war" in an action-adventure series, he thought it would be fresh and different. "When I was senior vice-president, I was handling the shows we made for ABC. When I became head of the studio, I took on total responsibility for the television operation, which included developing new series for all three networks. I told my business affairs lawyer, 'I'm interested in this book. Let's see if it's available and if we can pick it up.' It was available, so we bought the rights," Price related.

Stephen J. Cannell, Series Writer

Once Universal had the rights to the story, it sat on the shelf until close to the end of the 1976–77 pilot-selling television season, when Price sent the book over to one of the studio's up-and-coming writers. Having worked at his family's interior design business, Cannell & Chaffin, for four unsatisfying years, then-27-year-old Stephen J. Cannell (1941–2010) sold his first freelance script, *It Takes a Thief*, to Universal in 1968 and was quickly hired and wrote freelance for the crime dramas *Ironside* and *Columbo* until he went full-time on *Adam-12* during the show's fourth season. By 1976, Cannell had created several series, the most successful of which was *The Rockford Files*, starring James Garner (1928–2014).

Price spoke of how he met Cannell and eventually brought him into the *Black Sheep* project: "I first met Steve Cannell when he was working on *Adam-12*. While I was running Universal

Television, I had a system of putting young, promising writers with very experienced writer-producers who had a name. I put Cannell with Roy Huggins (1914–2002) because Cannell was a good writer, but he needed to be trained as a producer. There were only a few people, only a few writers who could really write action-adventure with humor well, and Cannell was one. I sent the book over to Steve, told him about it, and to my delight he was interested. I got him to write a pilot script, which I took to NBC and got them interested in it. We did more business with them [NBC] than anybody, and I thought they would be the best buyer." Price chose Cannell because he wrote male characters very well and, having a predominantly male cast in a World War Two-based action-adventure, he felt Cannell was a perfect fit.

In his book, *Stephen J. Cannell Television Productions: A History of All Series and Pilots*, Jon Abbott wrote that Cannell's characters "are…renegades, rebels who prefer to buck the system rather than just become another cog in a faulty machine." Cannell backed this up in an interview with *Entrepreneur* magazine in October 1982: "A theme of all my shows is that the heroes are not superheroes. They're the ordinary guy reacting much as any of us would react under the same circumstances." One can certainly see this personality trait in characters created by Cannell. From Jim Rockford (James Garner, *The Rockford Files*) and Tony Baretta (Robert Blake, *Baretta*) in the 1970s to Rick Hunter (Fred Dryer, *Hunter*) and Vincent Terranova (Ken Wahl, *Wiseguy*) in the 1980s, they all found themselves in seemingly dire, no-way-out situations but in the end found a way out through sheer dogged determination and a little luck. Even a cursory look at the life of Greg Boyington, from joining the American Volunteer Group in 1941 because he needed to pay off debts to conning a doctor into clearing him for active duty and ultimately creating a fighter squadron from available pilots and aircraft, one can see that if Boyington hadn't already been a real person, Stephen Cannell would have created him.

After reading the memoir, Cannell tried to contact Boyington but could only leave messages with his wife, Josephine (1927–1992), although he never received a reply. Unbeknown to Cannell, Boyington was in the middle of a binge. Time was of the essence, so without Boyington's input, Cannell got to work on the script for the pilot episode. While he kept prominent names such as Claire Chennault and Chester Nimitz, not to mention Boyington's nickname for his nemesis, Colonel (Col) Lard, he admittedly took "some pretty good liberties" with the story. Just 12 days later, as he was putting the finishing touches on the script, Cannell's phone rang. It was Boyington. When Cannell outlined the story, Boyington replied, "Oh, that's great! I love that."

When Cannell completed the script, he turned it over to Price, who took it to NBC in New York before filming even commenced. Price explained: "So many suppliers would go to the networks with an idea and then want network money to finance the script. The minute you get their money involved, they can kill a project or decide not to go ahead with it because basically they have control over the script, so my normal procedure would be to submit a well-developed script to a network. In this particular case, NBC was interested, and we worked out a deal where we needed a two-hour pilot." Cannell also sent the script to the Marine Corps Historical Center in Quantico, Virginia, hoping to receive an endorsement from the Department of Defense. However, the Center could not correlate the script with any known events in the history of the real squadron. But, as you will see, that is only partially correct.

Robert Conrad, Actor (Pappy Boyington)

It did not take long for word of the project to go around town, and one day Cannell received a call from David Shapira, Robert Conrad's (1935–2020) agent, who said the stocky star of *The Wild Wild West* would be the perfect Pappy Boyington. Cannell's response was tepid: he knew that Conrad would be perfect, but his tough-guy reputation was well known and Cannell said, "I don't need to get a new dentist." Shapira kept the pressure on until Cannell agreed to a meeting, and once he saw how similar Conrad and Boyington were in terms of height, build, and even mannerisms, he hired him.

Though Stephen Cannell balked at hiring Robert Conrad to play Pappy Boyington, the stocky actor was perfect for the part. Conrad and Boyington had eerily similar builds and mannerisms. (*Mark Schafhausen*)

A few days later, Boyington and Conrad met. Conrad had read Boyington's book, and they chatted about it while enjoying a few cocktails. Later, Josephine joined them. Not one to sit in front of the television, Jo did not know who Robert Conrad was; and when she asked him why he was drinking and smoking and not eating, Conrad replied, "I'm celebrating because I got the part of playing Pappy Boyington," to which she replied, "You're assuming the role fast." At the time, Boyington said of Conrad, "He moves like I used to move, he's built the way I used to be built, and he's almost as good-looking."

James Whitmore, Jr., Actor (Capt James "Jim" Gutterman)

With the lead role filled, Cannell got on with hiring more "fighter pilots," many of whom were struggling to get started in Hollywood. One of the first was 28-year-old James Whitmore, Jr. (1948–), who had never planned to follow his famous father into acting, as he relayed to the author in June 2019: "I wasn't even remotely interested in acting. I wanted to be a novelist, because from as young as I can remember I was a big fan of Leo Tolstoy, Mark Twain, and the other greats. That was my real passion. I ended up going to acting school because I had a girlfriend who was in there, so I quit college and went over there just to be around her. When I started acting, though, I fell in love with it." While Whitmore may have fallen in love with acting in the late 1960s, he did not immediately begin working in the industry: "I traveled around a lot, ended up down in the West Indies, met and married my wife down in Trinidad in 1972. When we got back up to the States, I was working any kind of job I could get, like selling cigarettes out of my car and cleaning sewers for flood control," he said.

Whitmore's acting career finally began moving forward when a friend of his started the L.A. Actor's Theater and he got a job as a house manager and carpenter. This led to him reading some parts, which landed him in a couple of productions. Whitmore did not have a manager but got one in a most unusual way in 1975. "I was trying to get work, and I was given the name David Graham (1924–2015), who was a casting director, and I climbed over a wall at Columbia Pictures and snuck over to see this guy in his trailer," Whitmore related. About six months after scaling that wall, Whitmore was cast as Capt. James "Jim" Gutterman, the brash executive officer who was just as quick with his mouth as he was with his fists. Gutterman played a prominent role in season one but was inexplicably absent from season two.

Larry Manetti, Actor (Lt Bobby Boyle)

Today, Chicago-native Larry Manetti (1947–) is best known as Orville "Rick" Wright on the original *Magnum, P.I.* and Nicky "The Kid" DeMarco on the new *Magnum, P.I.* and *Hawaii Five-O*, but in the early 1970s he was still an unknown. Prior to being hired for *Black Sheep*, Manetti had appeared on popular shows of the period including *Mannix*, *Starsky & Hutch*, and *Emergency!* but in 1975 then-29-year-old Manetti was struggling to find steady work.

In June 2018, Manetti spoke to the author about how he landed the part of Lt. Bobby Boyle: "At that time of my career, I was unemployed and floundering. Robert Conrad was a very good friend of mine, and I was very aware of him being in the position to be doing *Baa Baa Black Sheep*. We had the same agent, and he said to me, 'If the timing's right, you'll be in.' While I was lucky to know Conrad, I was still a little green, so I was nervous when I auditioned for Stephen Cannell. I stuttered and stammered when I did the scene, and Cannell said, 'He's a great-looking kid, but he's just not ready to be on the runway.' So that shut me out of the pilot." For the pilot then, the part of Boyle was played by Jake Mitchell.

Robert Ginty, Actor (2nd Lt T.J. Wylie)

Born in New York City in 1948, Robert Ginty (1948–2009) sought a career in music and played with various bands from the age of 16, including rock legends Jimi Hendrix, Janis Joplin, and Carlos Santana. In the early 1970s, Ginty decided to switch to acting, so he headed for Hollywood. Prior to *Black Sheep*, Ginty had a number of bit parts in B-movies and a few TV series, including Cannell's *Rockford Files*. He appeared in the latter in 1974, which may have led to him getting a shot at *Black Sheep*.

On June 23, 1976, during a "press party" hosted by actress Sally Kirkland, then-28-year-old Ginty was interviewed for the documentary *Making It in Hollywood*, which followed several actors as they attempted to break into the movie business. The libations were obviously flowing freely when Ginty spoke about getting hired to do *Baa Baa Black Sheep*: "In September, I'm going to be on NBC network television every week, for an hour." The interviewer asked if he was the lead, and Ginty said, "No, I'm number two in it. Bobby Conrad plays Boyington, and I play second banana here. There's five of us; it's called *Baa Baa Black Sheep*. It's about World War Two and Pappy Boyington, who was a famous hero in World War Two. Boyington is down there with us every day."

Ginty went on to say that the era of the big movie star, like in the 1940s, is gone when he told the interviewer, "There's no big star trips anymore, man; everybody is just trying to make a living. What are you, kidding? A month ago, I didn't even have a job – now I got a television series." The interview was interrupted when Ginty was introduced to Corinne Calvet, a French-born film star from the 1950s, who flirtatiously asked him about his part in his "new show." Ginty told her, "I play the character of a young boy in World War Two who's not a very good pilot." With that statement it is obvious that the affable nature of 2nd Lt T.J. Wylie was already firmly established.

Walter Kirk "W.K." Stratton, Actor (2nd Lt Lawrence Casey)

After high school and a six-week fling in college, Walter Kirk "W.K." Stratton (1950–) headed for New York, where he studied acting and did so professionally. He eventually came to the conclusion that there was not enough work in the city to support the number of actors, so he headed for California in January 1975. Finding work there was still tough, and he ended up with a dinner theater production in Tucson. When it was over, he headed on to Mexico and laid on a beach for a while. Then came a call for a part in Los Angeles, but it did not pan out. In August 1977, then-26-year-old Stratton told a Hollywood reporter, "I guess they must have seen how dejected I was, because they told me to go by an office to pick up a script for *Baa Baa Black Sheep*. I did and came back to read for the part and got it." The part he landed of course was for 2nd Lt Lawrence Casey.

In his memoirs Boyington mentioned a few of his pilots, including "Casey," who was allegedly based on seven-victory ace 1st Lt William Case, who did go by the nickname "Casey" in college and the service. So, with no references to Case's personality in Boyington's book, did Cannell capture the essence of the real Casey? In the summer of 1977, Case told Beth Zeigler of the *Fairbanks Daily News*, "The first time I saw *Baa Baa Black Sheep* I didn't know it was on. I was startled. There was a Casey on the show…the series has him portrayed as a straight, square type and that's probably a fair description."

John Larroquette, Actor (2nd Lt Robert "Bob" Anderson)

Among the main cast members, then-29-year-old John Larroquette (1947–) stood out, and not just because of his 6ft 5in frame. He was one of three actors in the series that served in the military, having joined the Navy Reserve in 1966, just as the war in Vietnam was heating up. Larroquette said in an interview, "I wasn't an anti-war protester or anything. I just didn't want to get shot. At 6ft-5, I thought it would be ridiculous to try and hide in a rice paddy."

Dana Elcar (far right in hat) was already an established actor when he was cast in *Black Sheep*, but for the young up-and-coming (L–R) Robert Ginty, WK Stratton, and Dirk Blocker, the series more or less served as the springboard that launched their careers. (*Mark Schafhausen*)

Dirk Blocker, Actor (1st Lt Jerome "Jerry" Bragg)

The youngest actor in the main cast was 19-year-old Dirk Blocker (1957–), son of Dan Blocker (1928–1972), who is best known for his role as Hoss Cartwright on *Bonanza*. Though his father neither encouraged nor discouraged him from becoming an actor, Blocker got into dramatics in high school and signed a seven-year contract with Universal Studios at the age of 16. After a couple of small walk-on parts, including an appearance in *Little House on the Prairie*, with his father's former *Bonanza* co-star Michael Landon (1936–1991), Blocker landed the part of 1st Lt Jerome "Jerry" Bragg. One day at Indian Dunes, someone asked him if he was happy. Blocker replied, "On a scale of 1 to 10, I'm a 12." Other than Conrad himself, Blocker and Stratton were the only cast members to appear in all 36 episodes.

Jeff MacKay, Actor (1st Lt Donald French)

Dallas-native Jeff MacKay (1948–2008), who studied three-and-a-half years of pre-med at the University of Oklahoma before switching to drama, was a friend of one famous actor and the cousin of another. While his father, an Air Force Colonel, was the Air Attaché to Chile, young MacKay befriended another Colonel while acting as a fishing guide. That Colonel was none other than Jimmy Stewart. When MacKay set off on his own, his cousin, Robert Redford, told him, "…that if your personality is made interesting by experience,

Left: Thanks to his work on *Black Sheep*, Jeff MacKay landed jobs on Stephen Cannell's *Tales of the Gold Monkey* and with Donald Bellisario's *Magnum, P.I.* (*Mark Schafhausen*)

Right: One of the three characters taken directly from Boyington's memoir was Major General Thomas "Nuts" Moore, who was instrumental in the formation of VMF-214 in the fall of 1943. (*Marine Historical Division*)

people will come to see you on stage." Redford also helped him get his SAG card with a part in the 1976 film *All the President's Men*.

Before getting his big break, MacKay worked as a night manager in a Manhattan hotel while studying acting at the Neighborhood Playhouse. He later studied under Jeff Corey in Hollywood and worked primarily in dinner theaters. After *Black Sheep*, MacKay appeared in a number of popular series in the '80s, most notably as "Mac" on *Magnum, P.I.* An avid golfer with an 18 handicap, MacKay passed away on August 22, 2008.

Simon Oakland, Actor (Maj Gen Thomas Moore)

The final original characters, Maj Gen Thomas Moore and Col Thomas A. Lard, were the only two characters other than Boyington and Case that were based on real Marines, and each bore a slight physical resemblance to the men they played on screen.

To play the part of Boyington's protector and drinking buddy, Maj Gen Thomas Moore, Cannell cast Simon Oakland (1915–83), an actor who was said to be a face that the public may recognize but don't recall his name. In Hollywood, producers often typecast him as a boss. Prior to *Black Sheep*, Oakland played Darren McGavin's high-strung, screaming boss, Tony Vincenzo, on *Kolchak: The Night Stalker*, but on *Black Sheep* he was the perfect actor to play the tough but fair Gen Moore.

Born in New York City, Oakland was a concert violinist as a child. He appeared in his first play shortly after World War Two and a part in *The Great Sebastians* led him to Hollywood, where he made his television debut in 1950. Over the next three decades, Oakland appeared in dozens of movies, including *Psycho* and *Bullitt*, and had hundreds of appearances on many of the popular television shows of the 1960s and '70s, such as *Gunsmoke*, *Twilight Zone*, and Cannell's *The Rockford Files*.

Oakland's character was based on decorated aviation officer Major General James Tillinghast "Nuts" Moore (1895–1953) of Barnwell, South Carolina. Moore was commissioned a 2nd Lt in the Marine Corps in September 1916, and when World War Two broke out, he was serving as Chief of the US air mission to Peru as well as Commanding General of the Peruvian Air Force. After a short stint with the Fourth Air Wing in Hawaii, Moore was named Chief of Staff of the First MAW in May 1943.

Unlike Gen Moore, Boyington changed the name of the real-life and much-hated Col. Joseph Smoak to Col. Lard. Fortunately, Dana Elcar made the character more likable as the series progressed. (*Marine Historical Division*)

Dana Elcar, Actor (Col Thomas A. Lard)

The part of the love-to-hate Col Lard went to 49-year-old Dana Elcar (1927–2005), whose acting career was born out of a failed attempt to run away from home at the age of 13, when he was forced to spend the night in an all-night movie theater that was showing *Citizen Kane*, which he watched four times over the course of the night. His acting career finally began in his senior year of high school in 1945, which led to decades of appearances in regional and off-Broadway plays, television, and movies. By the time he was cast as Col Lard in 1976, he'd already worked with Cannell on *Baretta* and *The Rockford Files*. Elcar was the second of three cast members that served in the military. He joined the Navy at 18 in 1945 and served several years in Newfoundland.

Lt Col Joseph Allen Smoak

In his memoirs, Boyington made a vague reference to an instructor who gave him a "down" during flight training at Pensacola in the late '30s, and when he returned from China, he and the nine other Marines that joined the American Volunteer Group (AVG) were held up in Washington by a "renowned son of a bitch" who dug up a 1939 order that anybody who leaves the Marine Corps "in time of national emergency" could be classified as a deserter. However, none of the Marines were informed of this regulation or given the opportunity to defend themselves. That "renowned son of a bitch" was none other than Lt Col Joseph Allen Smoak, and with the premier of "Flying Misfits", he would forever be known as Col Lard.

During that period of the war, when pilots rotated off a combat tour, they went down to Turtle Bay to relax, unwind, and recover from the stress of daily combat and the loss of squadron mates. The last thing they needed, or expected, was to have a demented ground officer quoting manuals and harassing them about housekeeping. When interviewed by Frank Walton for his book *Once They Were Eagles*, John Berget, who flew with the squadron on its first tour, recalled the real-life Col Lard: "Before that [Boyington assuming command of VMF-214], we sat around doing nothing. There was some idiot colonel in charge of the base; I think in the TV show he was Colonel Lard. He made us go out and pick up cigarette butts, and he was hot on using mosquito nets, poking his flashlight into every tent. He's lucky he didn't get shot." While there were a few high-ranking officers that respected Smoak's demand for rigid adherence to the Marine Corps manual, those under his command considered him a bully. Though he'd been a pilot early in his career, ever since he'd arrived in the South Pacific, Smoak had been assigned to a series of non-flying staff jobs.

The Aircraft

Having cast the pilots and supporting characters, Universal set out to "cast" the real stars of the series – the aircraft. In the days when filmmakers still used real airplanes, they were forced to use whatever aircraft were available. From P-51Ds sporting swastikas in *Fighter Squadron* and T-6s and SBDs dolled up as Japanese Zeros in *From Here to Eternity* to T-28s masquerading as Communist Yaks in *Battle Hymn*, realistically portraying period-correct combat aircraft was quite difficult, if not impossible. While these indiscretions went unnoticed by the casual moviegoer, history buffs and aviation enthusiasts were left rolling their eyes. Such would not be the case in "Flying Misfits," however, as Universal acquired an incredible collection of warbirds from both organizations and individuals.

Considering that the warbird movement was still in its adolescence in 1976, it is incredible to note that a total of 44 aircraft was used throughout the entire series. This number included 31 flyers, of which there were two camera ships, and 13 static/taxi aircraft. What follows is a summary of the 15 aircraft used in "Flying Misfits." The remainder will be introduced in the order in which they appeared in the series.

From Tallmantz Aviation came a pair of Curtiss Warhawks, P-40N USAAF #44-7983 (N9950) and TP-40N USAAF #44-47923 (N923) and Tora Val N56867. From Ed Schnepf's Challenge Publications "air force" came Tora Zero N7757 and Kate N6438D, while additional Tora replicas, Zeros N15799 and N15797, came from the then-Confederate Air Force (CAF). Reyline Aviation provided Kate N7062C, and Zero N296W came from William Childers.

Among the six Tallmantz-owned aircraft used in the series was TP-40N N923, which appeared in the opening scenes of "Flying Misfits". In its single appearance, the fighter was flown by Frank Tallman. (*Scott A. Thompson*)

To counter the seven Tora aircraft, there were six Corsairs of various models. There were four Goodyear-built FG-1Ds; BuNos. 92132 and 92106, came from David Tallichet's collection, while the second pair, BuNos. 92629 and 92433, belonged to Texans John Stokes and Isaac "Junior" Burchinal, respectively. These visually accurate Corsairs were joined by Tom Friedkin's newly acquired Corsair, F4U-4 BuNo. 97359, and John Schafhausen's F4U-7 BuNo. 133710. As the rivet counters will quickly point out, none of these variants were operated by VMF-214 between August 1943 and January 1944. My response to this is, be thankful the series featured actual Corsairs, because the six Corsairs flown in the pilot episode constituted nearly 60 percent of the world's airworthy Corsair population at that time. When you add the two additional Corsairs that appeared later in the series, that number jumps to more than 66 percent! It was a commendable feat to assemble that many Corsairs in one place at one time, regardless of the era.

Photographed during the filming of "Flying Misfits" in April 1976, David Tallichet's FG-1D 92106 leads the Challenge Zero N7757 out towards the Channel Islands during an early morning sortie. (*Mark Schafhausen*)

As for non-combatants and camera ships, the former included Joel Frieland's ill-fated Douglas C-47B USAAF #45-1059 (N63250) and a brief appearance by a mystery Beechcraft C-45. The latter aircraft included at least one Bell 206 Jet ranger (N200B), the world famous Tallmantz B-25N USAAF #44-30823 (N1042B), and Tom Friedkin's T-28A USAF #49-1587 (N28DS), which had supposedly been converted to a T-28R-2 by Hamilton Aircraft.

The cadre of pilots that flew on "Flying Misfits" and *Black Sheep* was an eclectic mix of warbird, airline, and agricultural pilots. Here aerial co-ordinator Frank Tallman (far left) briefs (L–R) Gerald Martin, John Schafhausen, Tom Friedkin, Tom Mooney, and Junior Burchinal on an upcoming filming sortie at Indian Dunes. Friedkin's F4U-4 97359 sits in the background. (*Mark Schafhausen*)

The Pilots

The pilots who flew these aircraft were a mix of well-known movie and airshow pilots as well as agricultural pilots, airline pilots, World War Two veterans, and notable personalities from within the then-fledgling warbird movement. For obvious reasons, pilots from Tallmantz Aviation made up a substantial part of the roster. In addition to Tallman himself, these included James Appleby, Junior Burchinal, James Gavin, Tom Mooney, Frank Pine, and Art Scholl. The Ag (agricultural) pilots included Fred Ellsbury, Gerald Martin, and Mack Sterling, with Steve Rosenberg being the sole airline pilot. In addition to Mooney, the World War Two veterans included Glen "Dad" Riley and John Schafhausen, who flew Corsairs and Hellcats, respectively. Warbird pilots consisted of Tom Friedkin, Steve Hinton, Clay Lacy, Dick Martin, Frank Sanders, and Bill Yoak. Sadly, far too many of these men had gone west by the time the author started this project in 2010, but I was able to interview five and the relatives of two others. In many cases, these interviews elicited stories that are being published here for the first time.

Thomas Hoyt Friedkin

By the late 1960s, Thomas Hoyt Friedkin (1935–2017) had built an impressive collection of "surplus military aircraft," as warbirds were called back then, including a T-6, P-51, and P-38. Shortly after he acquired his F4U-4, Frank Tallman called Friedkin and informed him that NBC was looking for Corsairs for a TV show about Pappy Boyington. Friedkin agreed to make his Corsair available, but only if he flew it. Tallman agreed. Prior to heading for California, Friedkin got together with a few of his friends to knock the rust off his formation skills. When speaking of this demanding type of flying in 2012, Friedkin said, "Formation flying is a very perishable skill, and if it is not done regularly, you lose your edge."

Left: By the time filming of "Flying Misfits" commenced in April 1976, Tom Friedkin had already built an impressive collection of warbirds, including the Korean War veteran F4U-4 he flew throughout the series. (*Dan Friedkin*)

Right: When Steve Hinton began flying on "Flying Misfits", he had a mere 1.2 hours in Corsairs and could not have dreamed that he would go on to become one of the most prolific warbird pilots in the world. (*John Cassidy*)

Steve Hinton

When he broke into the business of flying for movies and television, Steve Hinton was just 24 years old and had a mere 1.2 hours in Corsairs, but that didn't stop John Stokes, owner of FG-1D 92629, from giving Hinton a call from San Marcos, Texas, as Hinton related in 2012; "John called me up and said, 'How you would like to fly the Corsair for an upcoming TV show?' I said, 'Well, yeah, I have Mustang and Hellcat time, but not much in Corsairs.' He said, 'Well, why don't you come down and pick this thing up.'" Hinton went down to San Marcos and ferried the Corsair back to California via Fort Stockton, El Paso, and Tucson.

Tom Mooney

Tom Mooney (1922–78) received his commission on August 16, 1943, and went on to fly Corsairs with VMF-212 *Hell Hounds* during the Bougainville campaign in November 1944. In 1952, Tom was actually attached to VMF-214 while the squadron was in El Toro. While attached to VMF-232 *Red Devils*, Mooney flew FJ-4 Furies off USS *Bennington* (CVA-20) during the Quemoy Matsu Crisis in fall 1958. He later served three tours in Vietnam with his last as CO of H&MS-36 in Chu Lai, South Vietnam. Upon retiring from the Marine Corps in 1968, Mooney became Chief Pilot at Tallmantz Aviation, where, in addition to *Baa Baa Black Sheep*, he flew on *Catch-22*, *Charlie's Angels*, and *The Six Million Dollar Man*.

Tom Mooney's career as an aviator in the Marine Corps spanned a quarter of a century, during which he saw combat during World War Two and Vietnam. He was also a real *Black Sheep*, having served in VMF-214 in the early 1950s. (*Mark Schafhausen*)

John Schafhausen was another pilot who brought his own Corsair to California and flew it throughout the series. He joined the Navy in 1942, flew anti-submarine patrols in the Atlantic, and was slated to deploy to the Pacific when the war ended. (*Mark Schafhausen*)

John "Shifty" Schafhausen

John "Shifty" Schafhausen (1924–2003) was a student at the University of Minnesota when he was called up by the Navy in November 1942. His first two hours of flight training, at a civilian flying school in Albert Lea, Minnesota, were in a ski-equipped J-3s. After further training in Wacos, SNVs, and SNJs, John was commissioned as a 2nd Lt and immediately headed for Florida to begin fighter transition in FM-1 and -2 Wildcats. After carrier qualifications in the FM-2 aboard USS *Wolverine* (IX-64), John flew anti-submarine patrols on the East Coast. After V-E Day, he transferred to VF-5 in Klamath Falls, Oregon, and was preparing to deploy to the combat zone when the war ended.

After years of flying amphibians, John bought his first warbird, a Cavalier Mustang, in May 1972 and sold it to pilot/writer Richard Bach a year later to buy the Corsair, which he described as "the Cadillac of fighters." On July 27, 1976, Schafhausen applied for an Experimental Airworthiness Certificate for the purpose of motion-picture work for the period of one year. In this letter Schafhausen wrote, "The specific motion picture in which this airplane will be involved is entitled *Baa-Baa Black Sheep*, a production of Universal Studios." This Corsair was one of four that appeared in 35 of the 36 episodes and is easily identifiable in films and photos due to its 20mm gun barrels and silver propeller hub. The latter is important because it is the only feature that distinguishes 133710 from Bob Guilford's 133693, which featured a black propeller hub.

Like Steve Hinton, Bill Yoak's career in television and movie flying began with *Baa Baa Black Sheep*, although he missed flying in "Flying Misfits" due to injuries sustained in a motorcycle accident. (*Jerry O'Neill*)

William "Bill" Yoak

William "Bill" Yoak (1946–2013) told the author in 2012 that he got involved with *Baa Baa Black Sheep* because he was in the right place at the right time and, more important, because he knew Tom Friedkin. Friedkin told aerial director Jim Gavin, "Yoak is a good stick with great credentials." However, Yoak was not able to participate in the filming of "Flying Misfits" because he was recovering from severe injuries sustained in a motorcycle accident. Although Yoak would eventually fly every Corsair variant except the F2G, in 1976 he'd never even sat in a Corsair. This made for a very memorable check ride with Tom Mooney that will be detailed in a later chapter.

The Other Pilots

For decades, the list of pilots that flew on *Black Sheep* has more or less had the same names, but the author found that there were four names that were always missing – Clay Lacy, Frank Sanders, and CAF pilots Fred Ellsbury and Mack Sterling. Lacy could not be reached for comment, Sanders left us far too early in 1990 at the age of 52, and Sterling passed away in 2014 at the age of 79. However, I was able to interview Ellsbury in 2018 and Sanders' son, Dennis, in 2019. Sanders said the family business was based in Chino in the mid-1970s and surmised that is how his father became involved in the series: "Jim Gavin was a friend of my dad's, and I'm guessing that is how he got recruited to fly. He flew the Zeros and the T-28 camera plane, which came from Tom Friedkin's Cinema Air." While he never flew on camera, Dennis moved the Corsairs and Zeros between Indian Dunes and Oxnard.

Through the first few episodes of season one, there seemed to be just three Zeros involved in filming, but then one notices during some of the dogfight sequences that four Zeros are on screen at the same time. That being said, it took detective work to identify this fourth Zero, and it is thanks to Tora pilot Dan Reedy. When the author spoke with Reedy about which CAF/Tora aircraft were flown on the show, Reedy mentioned that Fred Ellsbury and the late Mack Sterling had flown a pair of CAF/Tora Zeros on the show.

Fred Ellsbury and Mack Sterling

In 1967, after a four-year stint in the Marine Corps, Fred Ellsbury began flight training in Angleton, Texas, under the GI Bill and attended aviation/agricultural school and started flying crop dusters for R & W Ag in 1974, the same year he joined the CAF. The following year he joined the Tora group, flying Zero AI-114 and Val AI-356, and remained on the team until 1984. In a June 2018 interview Ellsbury related how he casually became involved in the filming of "Flying Misfits:" "I was walking through the hangar, I think I was working on one of the AgCats...and I saw J.K. West on the phone and heard him say, 'Hold on, I'll ask him. Hey, Fred!

Do you want to go to California and make a movie?' I said, 'Sure, boss.' I kept on going and went back to work on the airplane. A few minutes later J.K. came out and said, 'Hey, you've got to get your stuff together – you and Mack [Sterling] have to leave the day after tomorrow.' I said, 'Wow, you were serious?'" And just like that, Ellsbury and Sterling were in show business.

Two days later, Ellsbury and Sterling took off in Zeros N15797 and N15799, respectively, and made the two-day cross-country flight to southern California. The first day they flew from Angleton to El Paso, and they made it all the way to California the next day. Before they flew for the cameras, they had to join the Screen Actors Guild; and afterward it was eight days of intense flying out over the Pacific Ocean. However, being the wingman, Ellsbury didn't have too many anecdotes about the flying: "Mack was Green One and I was Green Two, and since I was on his wing I didn't have any time to look around," he told the author.

It should be noted that, according to Tallmantz Aviation records, a majority of the air-to-air sequences were filmed in March to May and July 1976 and again in July 1977; but throughout the filming of the series, the Corsairs and a few other warbirds were ever present at Indian Dunes for static, taxi, take-off, and landing sequences. During the primary periods of air-to-air filming, particularly the filming of "Flying Misfits" in the spring of 1976, Friedkin said he and his fellow pilots flew up to three sorties a day, sometimes lasting up to 90 minutes, for nearly a week, something Friedkin thoroughly enjoyed. What he was never thrilled with was the producers keeping a couple of pilots on the set in case they needed somebody to start an engine or taxi around the strip. To that point Steve Hinton laughingly added, "We shot stuff out there [over the Channel Islands] for days, and they ended up showing the same scene 12 times."

Photographed off the coast of Oxnard are FG-1Ds 92106 and 92629, F4U-7 133710, FG-1Ds 92433 and 92132. Getting five Corsairs in the air at one time was a rarity because the fleet was often plagued with maintenance issues. (*Mark Schafhausen*)

The Location

Filming of the pilot episode took place at several locations around southern California, including Universal's backlot and Camp Pendleton, among other locations, but a majority of filming took place at Indian Dunes airstrip. Built sometime in the late 1960s, on a 600-acre ranch owned by Newhall Land & Farming Company, Indian Dunes Airport (4CA4), with its single north-east/south-west dirt runway, was located at the intersection of Route 126 and Wolcott Way in Valencia, California. Since it featured hills, plains, riverbeds, and densely wooded areas, it could, and did, portray locations from the American Southwest and Western Europe to the Middle East and Southeast Asia, not to mention famous World War Two airfields such as Munda and Vella Lavella. In addition to *Black Sheep*, the site was used in other television series such as *The Dukes of Hazzard*, *The Fall Guy*, and *The A-Team* and feature films *Escape from New York* and *The Color Purple*.

The last television show filmed at Indian Dunes was *China Beach*, and the last film was *The Rocketeer* in 1991. By that time, the property had been converted fully to agriculture. On November 9, 1990, Larry Franco, executive producer for *The Rocketeer*, told the *Los Angeles Times*, "It was a place with all kinds of freedom. You have wide open spaces, and you can easily stage pyro effects." Lindsley Parsons, Jr., who at the time had wanted to shoot his film based on the Stephen Hunter novel *The Day Before Midnight*, at Indian Dunes, said, "I sent scouts to almost every Western state…Indian Dunes worked for us." Lisa Rawlins, then-director of

Six Corsairs can be seen here at Indian Dunes, including Friedkin's F4U-4 and Tallichet's FG-1D 92629 on the left and Schafhausen's F4U-7 on the right. (*Steve Guilford*)

the California Film Commission, backed up these sentiments: "In terms of sheer size of the mesas that Indian Dunes has, you truly can't match it." Marlee Lauffer, a spokeswoman for the Newhall Land & Farming Co., said, "Our primary purpose is, and always has been, farming. We have a demand to increase our crops, and this is good land." However, she also said that the company had an additional 10,000 acres in the Valencia area that was available for filming but admitted that it doesn't have the unique appeal of Indian Dunes.

Between the collection of warbirds, the pilots flying them, and building up Indian Dunes to look like a South Pacific airstrip, the budget for the pilot episode came to a staggering $1.9 million, which equated to approximately $10.2 million in 2024. In an interview that appeared in the *El Paso Herald Post* on September 3, 1976, Conrad told Hollywood writer Dick Kleiner, "It is one of TV's most expensive shows. If this turkey doesn't fly, somebody will have lost a lot of bread."

Televison Scheduling

In early spring of 1976, while the pilot was still in production, NBC Executive Vice President of Programming Marvin Antonowsky (1929–2015) picked up the series, but shortly thereafter he was replaced with Irwin Segelstein (1925–2008), who had been the president of CBS Records Division since 1973. Segelstein knew little about the project and placed it in a slot on Tuesday nights at 8pm. This concerned Cannell because this put the show with its "drinking, fighting, and wenching" on during the so-called "family hour," but Price told him to film the show as he saw fit, and they would "fight them" (NBC) script by script. Another issue with the timeslot was that it pitted the brand new show against ABC's *Happy Days* and *Laverne & Shirley*, the number one and two shows at the time, and pulling 31.5 and 30.9 percent of the shares, respectively.

Why Segelstein placed *Baa Baa Black Sheep* in a so-called "suicide slot" is a matter for conjecture, but Chuck Bowman, who produced 24 episodes, theorized, "I think one of the problems that the boys in the conference room at NBC New York had with the show is, none of them really had an understanding of what the *Black Sheep* were, and not that all the audience had any understanding of it either – I think that was critical. They were just confused by it." Price explained, "I was delighted that we sold it, but I figured we're going to have a tough time. They saw it as counter-programming that would attract a male audience."

Courting publicity

Before the completed pilot was sent to NBC, Price had it screened by a test audience. He explained the process: "You would screen it for a selective audience, and they would have dials in their hands to indicate when they were really interested or when they weren't. Then you would have a focus group afterwards to get their reaction and input and so on.

You're looking for what scenes don't really work or any surprises that are in there that an audience might tell you or that you didn't pick up on in the projection room. All of this gives the network an idea of how well the test audience reacts to the show. *Black Sheep* tested very well, so it was screened by the network, by which time I had shifted my base from Universal in Hollywood to our New York offices, which were on 57th and Park [Ave.], while all the three networks were working on their schedules." The network's reaction to the show was referenced in a review of the show by Hollywood-based writer Paul Henniger: "When NBC saw the pilot, it was upset about the emphasis on on-camera drinking, so Cannell did a little trimming to de-emphasize that part of the show. Now, guys do a lot of talk about drinking, which still gives the series the flavor of Boyington's novel."

Meanwhile, out in Hawaii, with no knowledge of what was going on at Universal, 47-year-old Frank Walton, who served as the VMF-214 air intelligence officer, had been busy organizing the first *Black Sheep* reunion since 1945 – a time when they gathered in San Francisco to welcome Boyington home from his 20 months of captivity. Three years Boyington's senior, Walton looked after all of the men in VMF-214, including its cantankerous commander. When Boyington responded in March 1976, he told Frank he was uncertain of his schedule due to the show and excitedly told Walton about the upcoming Universal project. He told Frank it was "loaded with humor, somewhat similar to *M*A*S*H*." Walton said he would look for the show in the fall.

Shortly after NBC announced its fall schedule, Boyington started receiving interview requests. One of the first appeared in the April 26, 1976, edition of *Sarasota Herald-Tribune*, which picked up a United Press International story out of Hollywood, and right off the bat Boyington told the distorted Hollywood version of VMF-214. Described in the article as, "a nonconformist, swinger, two-fisted drinker, and brawler," Boyington, after making some rather objectionable comments about there being no war heroes after World War Two, said, "I scrounged and connived to get my flyers. I stole them from a pool of flyers who'd been dropped from other squadrons for bad behavior. Some were awaiting court-martials."

It is unknown whether Walton saw the piece in the Florida newspaper, but he did see the article filed by Barbara Zuanich in the July 22, 1976, edition of the *Los Angeles Herald Examiner*, where Boyington continued to spin the history that matched up with the script of "Flying Misfits," including the following "fact": he said of his pilots, "They were all awaiting court-martials when I found them, but after they performed well one day I threw the disciplinary files away." Walton was furious. He found Boyington's comments exaggerated, derogatory, and downright unconscionable.

Although Quantico found no historical relevance between VMF-214's combat history and the "Flying Misfits" script, it didn't keep the Marine Corps from recognizing the

Photographed at Van Nuys on August 11, 1976, are (L–R) the wingtip of the Challenge Publications Tora Zero (N7757), Bob Guilford's F4U-7 133693, David Tallichet's FG-1D 92106, John Stokes' FG-1D 92629, and Frank Tallman's J2F Duck. Eight days later, the F4U-7, with Steve Rosenberg at the controls, would suffer a catastrophic engine failure and would not fly again until 1979. (*Bill Curry via Jim Sullivan*)

new show. On September 17, 1976, MCNEWS Release No. 000-183-76 said in part, "Retired Marine Col. Gregory 'Pappy' Boyington, leading Marine Corps ace in World War Two, is flying again in a new NBC television series entitled *Baa Baa Black Sheep*. Boyington, 63, and his wife, Jo, are frequent visitors to the Universal location where filming is still in progress. The cast and crew all call him 'Pappy.' Universal purchased over 21,000 feet of color gun camera film that would be mixed with Gavin's (Gavin James, Aerial coordinator] aerial sequences."

While "Flying Misfits" may have fared well with test audiences and the network, it drew more than its share of criticism, even before it was seen by the public. In the September 21, 1976, edition of *The New York Times*, John J. O'Connor said, "*Baa Baa Black Sheep* could turn out to be one of the most objectionable projects of the new season." To that he added, "The series offers glorification of drinking and brawling" and how NBC placed a show where "bloody fistfights and breaking of rules are the behavioral norms" smack in the middle of family hour, when violence and sexual content were supposed to be kept to a minimum. Throughout the rest of his piece, he panned the show for many of the same reasons that so many did at the time and in the decades afterward – dribbling comedy with hokey dialogue and story lines, just to name a few.

Surprisingly, Sherry Woods, TV/radio editor for *The Miami News*, felt that Cannell's use of wartime newsreel footage, often cited as a favorite among fans, was distracting and "slows things down far too much." She followed up that comment with a rather backhanded compliment: "The acting in this show won't overwhelm you and the script in the hour screened wobbled a bit, but the premise is sound and there's enough situational humor and action to make it work." Woods obviously did not take into account that, other than Conrad, Elcar, and Oakland, none of the actors in the main cast had any significant television experience at the time.

One positive comment the author found was made by the television editor for *The Morning Call* out of Allentown, Pennsylvania, who said, "It's an old-fashioned macho-type show, directed at a male audience that likes its action rough (the flight combat sequences are said to be terrific), its whiskey straight, and its women incidentally. Boys, teenaged and younger, could go for it too." The latter sentence perfectly described the show's fan base and the 40- and 50-somethings that are holding this book in their hands right now.

So as one can see, from its inception, this new series was the proverbial black sheep, but thanks to the tenaciousness of Gregory Boyington and Robert Conrad and the passion and belief of Stephen Cannell, the show survived, against all odds, to run for 35 episodes over two seasons to become a cult classic in the succeeding decades.

CHAPTER 2

THE PILOT: "FLYING MISFITS"

Tuesday, September 21, 1976

"We are poor little lambs who have lost our way / Baa baa baa." This, the fifth verse of the *The Whiffenpoof Song*, was followed by an air raid siren and images of heroic pilots scrambling into the cockpits of their mighty Corsairs and roaring into the sky to meet the enemy. The visuals were backed by bold brass-infused theme music, written and composed by the dynamic TV theme duo Mike Post (1944–) and Pete Carpenter (1915–87) and performed by the Monterey Radio and TV Philharmonic Orchestra. This is how every exciting episode of *Baa Baa Black Sheep* began, and nearly five decades later it is sure to bring a smile to the face of every warbird enthusiast who is old enough to remember the days when you had to get up and walk across the room to change channels and adjust the TV antenna.

Throughout the series, a majority of the episodes opened with a newsreel-type film, which was always a clever mixture of period films and contemporary footage and essentially set the tone and the storylines for the episode. In "Flying Misfits," the film championed the China-based "valiant Americans" of the American Volunteer Group (AVG) who were leaving China to return to their respective services in the wake of Pearl Harbor. Boyington resigned from the AVG in April 1942 but the establishment of VMF-214 on Espiritu Santo in the South Pacific took until September 1943. For Boyington this was a long, arduous, and frustrating period in his life, so for brevity's sake Cannell compressed that 17-month period into approximately 45 minutes.

To be honest, Cannell's version of Pappy leaving the AVG and getting reinstated in the Marine Corps was much more exciting than real life. Instead of the six-week ocean voyage from India to the United States and several months parking cars in Seattle, Cannell had Pappy (and his bull terrier Meatball) steal a P-40 and fly to India and then con his way on to a C-47 bound for Espritos Marcos, the fictional stand-in for Espiritu Santo. During his flight to India in the P-40, he was jumped by a pair of Zeros, which he promptly shot down, right before he ran out of fuel and dead-sticked his Tomahawk in a farmer's field then completed his journey to Calcutta in the back of a truck. The P-40 used in this scene was TP-40N USAAF #44-47923 (N923), which, at the time, was owned and flown by Frank Tallman. The so-called Tora Zeros in the scene were ex-Royal Canadian Air Force (RCAF) Harvard Mk. IVs, RCAF 20380 (N7757) and RCAF 20473 (then N296W, now N60DJ), which were owned by Challenge Publications and William Childers, respectively.

When Pappy arrived on Espritos, he reported to his chief antagonist throughout the series, Col. Thomas A. Lard, who was unimpressed by the newly arrived pilot with six Zeros to his name. Lard told Pappy, "I'm up to my brass buckle in hotshots. I don't need another one, especially a rule-and regulation-breaking drunk." Lard immediately placed Pappy in hack until he could sort out just how he made it to Espritos. The mutual animosity between Pappy and Lard is an area where Cannell's script was 100 percent true to history.

While in hack, Pappy received a visit from a gentleman who claimed to be from General HQ and began to give Pappy advice on how to behave, and just as Pappy was about to physically throw him out the door, the man took off his coat to reveal a silver star on his collar and introduced himself as Brigadier General Thomas A. Moore. The general then produced a flask, poured Pappy a drink, toasted screen idol Betty Grable, and proceeded to tell Pappy that while combat pilots were needed, 35 years of age was too old for combat. In actuality, Boyington was 31 years old in September 1943, and it is unknown why Cannell added four years to Pappy's age. It is interesting to note that when *Baa Baa Black Sheep* commenced filming in the spring of 1976, Robert Conrad was 41 years old, a full decade older than Boyington was in 1943.

Whereas Boyington drew his pilots from the pilot pool at Turtle Bay, Cannell turned those combat veteran pilots into soon-to-be-court-martialed rule-breaking brawlers. At the midpoint of the pilot, Pappy met 2nd Lt. Lawrence "Larry" Casey and they discussed their mutual displeasure with their desk jobs, especially Casey, who was uncomfortably handling court-martials of fellow Marines. Pappy took the court-martials and reviewed the files and chose the pilots he wanted in his squadron. The next morning, Pappy and Casey gathered the pilots, all of whom were drunk or hungover and marched them to a warehouse, where the first of many brawls ensued. Today, a fist fight in a television show seems quite tame,

Above: When he was cast as Pappy Boyington in *Black Sheep*, Robert Conrad was at the zenith of his career. Between 1959 and 1969, he starred in two highly successful series', *Hawaiian Eye* and *The Wild Wild West*, both of which ran for four years and 104 episodes. (*John Cassidy*)

Opposite: Of the eight Corsairs flown in the series, these six, seen here at Indian Dunes in August 1976, made the most appearances (near–far) FG-1Ds 92433 (30), 92106 (35), 92629 (32), and 92132 (35), F4U-7 133710 (35), and F4U-4 97359 (35). (*Mark Schafhausen*)

but in the mid-1970s many viewers were taken aback and their opposition to that type of "violence" would hound the show throughout its existence.

Once Pappy had his pilots, he needed to form a squadron, and how he did so was not true to history, but it was true Cannell. While he conned a medical officer into believing a squadron that was about to rotate out of action was riddled with malaria and yellow fever and needed to be quarantined, Capt James "Jim" Gutterman found the island of Vella La Cava (a fictional version of Vella Lavella) to base their aircraft.

Having conned his way to Corsairs, a squadron, and an island, all Pappy needed was an official endorsement from Gen Moore, so he invited his drinking buddy to a luau with 30 nurses. After most of those in attendance were passed out on the beach, Pappy laid out his plan for Moore. While he admitted to being "a little bagged," Moore agreed that more fighter squadrons were needed, but there were none available. Pappy informed Moore that he already had aircraft and pilots. Moore laughed and asked, "Can they fly?" Pappy made a statement that is certainly true to history: "General, this is going to be the best damn squadron in the South Pacific. You gimme this squadron, and I promise you, you're going to bag Zeros." Moore reluctantly agreed and asked the number of the squadron coming out of action. Pappy gave him the number that would and has gone down in the annals of Marine Corps aviation – Two-Fourteen. Moore followed up with, "What are you going to call them?" Pappy responded with the forever-legendary name: "I'm going to call them what they are – the Black Sheep."

This version of how the squadron was formed and named was representative of Cannell's penchant for writing characters that buck the "faulty" system. While it was extremely entertaining and somewhat true on the surface, it was not entirely accurate. However, one must keep in mind that in 1976 we were decades away from the in-depth histories of the squadron, published by Frank Walton and Bruce Gamble, so Cannell was forced to rely solely on Boyington's book and its embellished "facts." It's entirely excusable, not to mention entertaining, which is Hollywood's job.

Once he got Moore's blessing, Pappy wasted no time in getting his pilots on a transport to "Munda Island" to pick up their Corsairs, where we finally, a full 75 minutes into the episode, got our first glimpse of the real stars of *Baa Baa Black Sheep* – the Corsairs. In studying the scenes from the pilot and photographs from Steve Guilford, the line up, from closest to farthest from the camera, was found to be as follows: F4U-4 BuNo. 97359 (N97353), FG-1D BuNo. 92132 (N3466G), FG-1D BuNo. 92629 (N62290), FG-1D BuNo. 92106 (N6897), and F4U-7 BuNo. 133710 (N33714). As Pappy stepped off the C-47B, he explained in the narration that the outgoing pilots had lost six Corsairs without shooting down a single Zero. Pappy introduced himself to the outgoing CO of VMF-214, Maj. Red Buell (Charles Napier, 1936–2011), who didn't understand why his pilots were being pulled out of combat for malaria when they didn't have malaria.

The elaborate, extensive, and highly detailed set that was built at Indian Dunes was one of the factors that made *Black Sheep* one of the most expensive television shows of its day. (*Steve Guilford*)

Cast and crew set up an early "Flying Misfits" scene at Indian Dunes. The aircraft line-up includes (near–far) the F4U-4 and FG-1Ds 92106 and 92629. (*Steve Guilford*)

Above: A wider photo taken at the same time as the previous one depicts John Schafhausen in the cockpit of his Corsair and the first of two C-47s that appeared in the series. (*Steve Guilford*)

Opposite: F4U-7 133710 and FG-1D 92433 pass under the Tallmantz B-25 camership (N1042B) while filming over the Channel Islands. This particular sequence was used in the scene where TJ Wiley inadvertently shot down Jim Gutterman in "Flying Misfits". (*Mark Schafhausen*)

But orders were orders, so Buell and his pilots boarded the transport while Pappy and his men prepared to fly the Corsairs up to Vella La Cava. Pappy climbed up on to the F4U-4 and informed the men that, because of their combat experience, Gutterman, Anderson, French, and Boyle would be flight leaders, even though two of them did not have rank.

As the squadron launched out of "Munda," Pappy explained that he learned in China that the Zeros could be shot down but, before they could do that, they had to learn to fly formation. This sequence, for the most part, features a four-ship consisting of 133710, 92629, 92132, and 92433. Gutterman started to close in on Wiley's wing, which got T.J. uptight and, as he urged Gutterman to back off, a burst of machine gun fire erupted from Wiley's Corsair that caused damage to Gutterman's aircraft. It is interesting to note that right after he fired the burst, Ginty reached up to the right eyebrow panel and safed his guns – something entirely accurate!

Fact meets fiction

Unlike the subsequent episodes, the two missions depicted in "Flying Misifts" were taken from Boyington's memoir and bear some resemblance to a pair of missions flown by the *Black Sheep* during their first tour. On television, the first was a strike on an airstrip on the fictitious island of San Mintos. As they approached the field there was a brief shot (with film reversed) that showed a four-ship flying up a shallow valley toward the ocean, and judging from the shadows, the Corsairs were less than 100ft off the deck! They started strafing in line abreast, and as they made repeated passes over the field, there were thrilling shots of the Corsairs on the deck coming right at the camera; these were mixed in with actual color gun camera films from aircraft strafing Japanese airfields.

As the last pair, Gutterman and Wiley, bore down on the camera, there was a palm tree in the foreground. Just as Boyington told Wiley he was too low, the second Corsair passed over the tree and the tree shuddered and lost a number of branches and leaves. It has long been debated as to whether or not the Corsair actually struck the tree, but after close scrutiny of the sequence and discussions with Steve Hinton and Bill Yoak we can now say with certainty that the FG-1D, specifically 92629, which was being flown by Bill Yoak, did not strike the palm tree. Bill Yoak said, "Tom [Mooney] was on my ass chasing me as we came over the 'Jap village'. They were going to set off explosions as we went by, and we hoped they wouldn't [expletive] it up. Setting off explosions in front of our airplanes was not a good deal." Watching the incident in slow motion confirms Yoak's statement, as one can see a small charge go off just after the Corsair leaves the frame. The charge caused a number of branches and other debris to fall.

Left: Camera crews filming repeated "strafing runs" by a pair of Corsairs. Much of the footage shot in the spring and summer of 1976 was used throughout the series. (*John Cassidy*)

Opposite: Steve Hinton brings FG-1D 92629 at treetop level for the cameras. The palm tree on the right was rigged with a small charge that would cause the tree to shudder and shed some branches thus creating the illusion that the Corsair struck the tree. (*Jim Farmer*)

Opposite: The Tallmantz B-25 cameraship leads FG-1Ds 92106 and 92629, F4U-7 133710, and FG-1D 92433 out over the Pacific. Filming around Santa Catalina Island was always preferable, but the presence of sailing boats often forced aerial co-ordinator James Gavin to move the flight out to the less-populated, albeit more distant, Channel Islands. (*Mark Schafhausen*)

This incident was based on an actual strafing mission flown by VMF-214 on September 21, 1943. Boyington led three flights of Corsairs on a strafing mission against Kahili Airfield on Bougainville. After making a number of four-abreast strafing runs on the field, the *Black Sheep* headed home, but Bill "Junior" Heier was missing. No one had seen him go down, so it was assumed he'd been lost. However, when they landed back at their field, they heard that he'd landed at their future airfield on Vella Lavella with 3ft missing from each wingtip. Boyington wrote, "Junior had been so intent on strafing Jap planes that when he finally decided to pull up it was too late, and he was forced to fly between two coconut trees at the end of the Kahili strip."

Cannell used this incident to make Wiley a Japanese fighter ace. While Lard was reading the latest list of charges against Pappy and his pilots, he spoke of the number of aircraft that T.J. had crashed in his short career. He said three, but Pappy said Wiley had since shot down Gutterman, which brought his score to four. French walked in and interjected, "It's, ah, five, sir. He crash-landed on the bomber strip on Peletau. He's okay, but he wholesaled the plane." Greg turned to Lard and said, "There, you see? Now it's five. You know that boy has only been flying for three months and he is already a Japanese ace?"

The final mission of the episode was devised by Pappy in the middle of the night while downing a bottle of scotch. On their way to the target, Pappy and his boys mimicked bombers by making radio calls, like, "Gunners, check your guns," etc. The Japanese heard the transmissions and scrambled their fighters to intercept. As the Jap pilots ran to their aircraft, we got a glimpse of five of the nine Tora replicas that were used in the show. In the line-up were the Tallmantz Val (N56867), Reyline Aviation's Kate (N7062C), Challenge Publication's Kate (N6438D), and two Zeros (N7757 and N296W). As they took off, they realized they'd been duped. We were shown a subtitle of the Japanese radio transmission, "They've tricked us. Alright, now let's teach them a lesson." A giant dogfight broke out, and the *Black Sheep* scored 18 victories, with no losses and Pappy downed five to become an "ace in a day." While many warbird enthusiasts and historians bemoan this as another piece of Hollywood hokum because VMF-214 did not engage the Japanese on its first mission, this is actually yet another case of Boyington either twisting or misremembering the facts.

This scene sounds similar to the mission flown by the squadron against Kahili on October 17. To get the Japanese up in the air for a fight, Boyington put one division down at 6,000ft as bait, while 17 other Corsairs were up at 20,000ft. The result was a huge dogfight that lasted 40 minutes and when it was over, the *Black Sheep* were credited with the destruction of 12 Japanese aircraft.

When the *Black Sheep* landed back on Vella La Cava, they were met by the press; and as they enjoyed their new-found fame, Lard scowled in the background, eager to bring down the hammer on Pappy and his "misfits." Lard hauled Greg into the ops shack and proceeded to chew him out and read off the charges he was filing against him and his men. Even when Greg reminded Lard of how bad he'd look by court-martialing a squadron of pilots that just shot down 18 Zekes, Lard said, "We'll see about that." Just in the nick of time, Gen Moore stormed in and saved the day. Moore called Pappy a national hero, but Lard called him a drunken bum and informed him he was under hack, pending disposition of the charges. Lard and Moore eventually agreed to disagree about the charges, and Lard stormed out of the shack. Moore toasted Patsy Kelley (a starlet from the 1920s), and he and Boyington threw back a shot of scotch.

The closing scene featured the Corsairs taxiing out for a mission silhouetted by the rising sun while the fifth verse of *The Whiffenpoof Song* was solemnly sung again. Up on to the screen flashed the statement, "While 214 was under the command of Pappy Boyington, it was responsible for more victories than any other Marine fighter squadron operating in the Pacific at that time" – a true statement. Finally, Conrad broke in with a narration: "Somebody once said that wherever I went, I set up my own Marine Corps. There was a reason for that: I didn't like the way it was set up when I got there. My guys stayed in more trouble on the ground and in the air than any other squadron in Marine Corps history. We were a haven for drunks, and screw-ups, and troublemakers. But that didn't seem to matter to the nurses, and God knows it didn't matter much to me. Some of us lived, and some died. But we were always Black Sheep." As a Corsair rose into the sky, the music stopped and the narration concluded with, "Just name a hero, and I will prove that he's a bum." That last quote was the last sentence in Boyington's memoir.

The crux of the pilot was that the pilots joined Boyington's squadron to avoid being court-martialed. While there is a minuscule historical basis for this, it was wildly spun by Cannell and Boyington. In the early weeks of February 1943, Boyington was placed in administrative command of a number of non-existent squadrons on Espiritu Santo, during which he handled disciplinary actions, including court-martials; and the way he handled them in 1943 was quite similar to how it was depicted on the show. Boyington wrote, "I'll bet a few Marines thanked their lucky stars a major who hated to go through channels or didn't think they had done anything he wouldn't do himself was the one to sort this paper out. The net result was that there were no court-martials, and only a few received a fatherly talking-to." While it isn't known who those "few Marines" were, it is known that they were not the pilots who would go on to serve under him in VMF-214.

Filming the aircraft

Throughout the series, the late John Schafhausen shot Super 8 home movies at Indian Dunes and Van Nuys, and during filming for the pilot in March 1976 he captured one of the Zeros and the P-40 making a couple of low passes upon returning from a filming sortie. Being so close to these aircraft made quite an impression on the folks from Hollywood, as producer Chuck Bowman vividly recalled in a June 2019 interview: "The first time I saw those airplanes we were in the middle of a scene. Boy, I'll never forget it. We heard the roar of airplanes and then we saw them coming. There was one of those T-6s that was painted up as a Jap Zero and right behind him was Frank Tallman in the P-40. They were coming right at us at high speed. As they went right over our heads, they pulled up and we all cheered and applauded as Frank did a victory roll."

Schafhausen's films were narrated, and as he filmed four Corsairs and the Tallmantz B-25 taxiing into Van Nuys for fuel and lunch, he offered insight on Second Unit filming during the pilot. In the first three days of filming, they flew a total of 17 hours: five hours on the first day, seven on the second, and five on the third. These sorties were flown over at least three of California's Channel Islands, namely, Santa Barbara and Santa Rosa off the coast of Oxnard, and San Clemente farther south near San Diego, all of which made for excellent stand-ins for the Russell Islands. There were various attempts to film around the much closer Santa Catalina, but most of the time there were too many sailboats, thus forcing Gavin to go farther out to sea.

Junior Burchinal prepares to taxi out for a flight, while F4U-7 133710, with Schafhausen's flight gear hanging from the 20mm cannons, awaits its turn in front of the Universal cameras. (*Mark Schafhausen*)

Fake news

As the series got under way in the fall of 1976, the character assassinations by Boyington in the mainstream and warbird media continued; and the Cannell/Boyington version of the *Black Sheep* had been told so many times in newspapers, magazines, and television talk shows that fiction seemed to become fact. In an interview with Challenge Publications photographer and Marine Corps Staff Sergeant Dub Allen, which took place on the set at Indian Dunes and appeared in *Air Classics Quarterly Review* (*ACQR*), winter 1976, Boyington fueled the fire he'd started with the *Herald Examiner* back in July. Having openly admitted to being a "psychopathic liar," Boyington said, "I had to go and pick out these guys who were sittin' in the pilots' pool and waiting court-martials, getting ready to be shipped back home, people who had been kicked out of squadrons. That's the only thing I had to draw from." Four decades before the term became part of society's vernacular, this was outright "fake news."

As the *ACQR* interview continued, it seemed that Boyington even had the actors convinced that the story they were acting out was true history. Boyington claimed that James Whitmore, Jr., came to him one day and asked, "Why was it that you guys fought so much between yourselves? Why did you drink so much? Was it because you were scared to death underneath it all?" Boyington replied with a cockamamie story about flying eight missions a day, sleeping on bare coral under the wings of their Corsairs, and going out on another mission before stating, "...when things would let up, our adrenalin would still be in high gear. We would have loved to have fought the neighboring squadron out in a coconut patch, but when we couldn't do that, we would just go after each other." His lies apparently knew no bounds. Other than Boyington getting drunk and wanting to wrestle everyone, nowhere in the half-dozen books used as references was there mention of brawls among the *Black Sheep* themselves.

With 92106 and 97359 as a backdrop, the *Black Sheep* pilots pose for a photo. Standing L–R: Steve Rosenberg, Fred Ellsbury, Gerald Martin, unknown, Steve Hinton, Frank Tallman, and John Schafhausen. Kneeling L–R: Glen Riley, Frank Pine, Jim Gavin, Tom Friedkin, and Tom Mooney. (*Jim Farmer*)

The stance against violence on television

The violence in the pilot and subsequent episodes put the series squarely in the crosshairs of the burgeoning anti-violence movement, which was targeting not only television shows that were perceived as violent, but also the companies that paid millions in advertising dollars during the airing of those shows. To put this movement in perspective and how it relates to *Baa Baa Black Sheep*, we must go back to 1967, when President Lyndon Johnson signed into law the Public Broadcasting Act and Thomas P.F. Hoving founded the National Citizens Committee for Public Broadcasting (NCCB). The former created a congressional charter for the Corporation for Public Broadcasting, a private non-profit corporation funded by taxpayers to disburse grants to public broadcasters in the United States. Johnson described the act's purpose: "It announces to the world that our nation wants more than just material wealth…we want most of all to enrich man's spirit."

The purpose of Hoving's NCCB was to "help develop support in all walks of life in public television." However, less than a year later, the NCCB became a self-appointed watchdog of all television programming as the *York Daily Record* reported in December, 1968: "organization appears to have broken away from its original concept of being only a quiet helpmate to educational television and to have adopted a role of a critical gadfly ready and eager to challenge the status quo in all areas of TV."

Although the NCCB endured periods of personnel changes and lack of steady financial backers, the anti-violence movement continued to have an effect on television shows, including Robert Conrad's *The Wild Wild West*. In February 1968, while the science fiction western was riding high in the ratings, CBS notified producers that the series would be canceled. Producer Bruce Lansbury would later claim that the show was a "sacrificial lamb" for the appeasement of the anti-violence activists. Later that year, the series drew its share of criticism when executives from the three major networks appeared before President Johnson's National Commission on the Causes and Prevention of Violence in December 1968 as well as a Senate communications subcommittee headed by Senator John O. Pastore (D-Rhode Island), whom Conrad called "a fool" in March 1969.

In November 1970, over two years after *The Wild Wild West* was canceled, the Foundation to Improve Television asked a US District Court to ban re-runs of the show before 9pm. In 1972, with the anti-violence movement hurting his career, Conrad told the *Oakland Tribune*, "It's ridiculous, it's nonsense, this fuss about violence. When I was a kid going to Errol Flynn movies I'd come out and pretend to sword fight, but I never stabbed anybody. How can you do an action show without action?" This and similar articles made it clear that Robert Conrad took the anti-violence movement personally.

By 1974, the widespread public criticism in regard to the amount of sex and violence on television had grown. In response, the Federal Communications Commission (FCC) established a policy under which each television network in the US had a responsibility to air "family-friendly" programming during the first hour, 8 to 9 pm, of the prime-time line-up. By the end of the year, the executives of each network agreed to endorse the Family Viewing Hour beginning in the 1975–76 season. The National Association of Broadcasters (NAB) took the gesture one step further, decreeing those local stations also air family-friendly programming in the 7pm timeslot, a time that networks were forbidden from programming, under the Prime-Time Access Rule, thus leaving programming for that timeslot in the hands of the individual stations.

In the summer of 1976, the anti-violence movement, convinced that witnessing violence on television would be harmful to the psyche of America's youth, felt that sponsors, broadcasters, and producers should be held accountable and therefore launched a multi-pronged attack on the industry. The first was a resolution from the American Medical Association that condemned a "massive daily diet of symbolic crime and violence in 'entertainment' programs" and called on parents to oppose those shows they deemed violent and boycott the products that sponsored those shows. This seemed to have a mild effect, as J. Walter Thompson Co., the largest advertising agency at the time, conducted a survey that showed eight percent of respondents were "consciously not buying a product" that advertised on what they considered violent programs.

However, according to an August 8, 1976, article in *The Times and Democrat*, the most active organization was the NCCB, which hired six trained observers from B1 Associates to analyze the prime-time programming of the three major networks over a six-week period in June and July 1976. The article stated in part: "to determine which programs were the most violent and what companies are sponsoring them. Their message to advertisers: 'We think you ought to know what you're sponsoring and you ought to be responsible for it.'" The article also quoted the executive vice-president of the National Association for Better Broadcasting, Frank Orme, who said, "Complaining to sponsors 'seems to be the only way to get any kind of action. The FCC had become a dead end and Congress says they can't do anything because they think they're blocked by the First Amendment.'" The day after "Flying Misfits" aired, *The Tampa Times* ran an article with the results of the NCCB survey. It determined that the top five most violent programs at that time were ABC's *S.W.A.T.* and *Sunday Movie*, *Friday Movie* on CBS, *The Rockford Files* and *Starsky & Hutch* on NBC. The corresponding advertisers were Tegrin shampoo, Burger King, Clorox, Colgate Palmolive Products, and Gillette Hair Products.

Although the NCCB's initial survey was conducted months before "Flying Misfits" debuted, NCCB representative Ted Carpenter told *The Tampa Times*, "NCCB plans to have similar surveys made four times a year. The fall survey has been expanded to cover 13 weeks, the typical duration of a sponsor's advertising schedule." Therefore, *Baa Baa Black Sheep* would be caught in the NCCB's next dragnet.

Another group photo, this time with Tallmantz's famous N1042B. Standing L–R: Unknown, Frank Pine, unknown, Art Scholl, unknown, Frank Tallman, unknown, John Schafhausen, and Clay Lacy. Kneeling L–R: Jim Gavin, Tom Mooney, and unknown. (*Mark Schafhausen*)

In the two days between the airing of "Flying Misfits" and the premiere of the first one-hour episode, "The Best Three Out Of Five", newspapers continued to hammer the show. The review by Bill Morrison, entertainment editor *for The News & Observer* in Raleigh, North Carolina, started out well, as he praised the aerial sequences: "They had verve and lush technical touches one associates with Hollywood epics rather than weekly television series." However, the accolades stopped there. Morrison then summarized the contents of the pilot followed by the oft-to-be-repeated comments about the show and its perceived violence being slotted during family hour. He further described Conrad as "colorless" and the supporting actors, with the exception of Simon Oakland and Jeff MacKay, as "cut from cardboard." Lastly, he predicted that "mid-season cancellation seems inevitable." There is no doubt that he was stunned to see the show run for two seasons.

While some of the VMF-214 veterans got a thrill out of seeing their story, not to mention the Corsairs, on the small screen, a majority vehemently objected to the drinking and brawling, especially Frank Walton. The *Los Angeles Herald Examiner* piece was bad enough; but to him, seeing it on the screen was beyond the pale. If Walton was going to do something to undo the damage done to the reputations of the real *Black Sheep*, he certainly had his work cut out.

Though he instantly and forever despised the show, VMF-214 Intelligence Officer Capt. Frank Walton's promotion of the squadron in its first and second combat tours in the fall of 1943 was the first of five seemingly inconsequential events that led to the creation of *Baa Baa Black Sheep* 30 years after the war. (*Frank Walton Collection, Emil Buehler Library, National Naval Aviation Museum*)

CHAPTER 3

SEASON ONE: *BAA BAA BLACK SHEEP*

September 23, 1976 – March 22, 1977

"Best Three Out Of Five" (Episode 1, September 23, 1976)

In the first season episode, "Best Three Out Of Five," Gen Moore returned to Washington, leaving Col Lard in command. While there, he wasted no time in cutting the shipment of supplies to the *Black Sheep*, in the hope of getting the unit shut down for not flying, and so he could place Maj Red Buell back in command of the squadron. This placed Pappy and Buell in a power struggle for the squadron, which they ultimately decided to settle with a boxing match. The match was broken up when Casey informed Buell that his brother, a tailgunner on a B-24, had been shot down over Bougainville. Naturally, Pappy concocted a plan to spring Buell's brother from a Japanese prison camp in a commando raid, which led to the series debut of the Tallmantz J2F-6 Duck BuNo. 35587 (N67790), which Casey had "rented" in a complicated four-way trade. The Duck appeared in four episodes, two in each season.

Joey Aresco, Actor (Sgt John David "Hutch" Hutchinson)

At the 6:22 mark of this episode, a new character, Sgt John David "Hutch" Hutchinson, a mechanic played by Joey Aresco (1949–) was introduced. Born in New York City, Aresco moved to California with his family at the age of 13 and became an avid surfer. After two years at Pierce College, where he'd read Shakespeare, Aresco attended the University of California, Santa Barbara, where upon realizing literature wasn't for him, he joined a theater company, landing a part in *The Zoo Story*, which set him firmly on a path to acting.

Prior to *Black Sheep*, Aresco appeared in a handful of television series, including Cannell's *Chase*, *Toma*, and *Baretta*. Those appearances led to Aresco getting the part of Hutch in a unique way: "I didn't have to audition for the part. My manager, Mimi Weber (1927–2007), explained that after the pilot they wanted a Fonzie-esque character…to have certain scenes where Bob Conrad could say what he was thinking. If there was a problem with the planes, or refueling, or ammunition, or whatever, he would talk to the mechanic instead of thin air," Aresco told the author in April 2022.

Four and a half decades on, Aresco doesn't remember the details of his hiring but did say that Weber worked directly with Milt Hammerman, the Head of Casting at Universal, and Pete Terranova, Head of Business Affairs at NBC, and got him a "pretty nice deal." It was well known that Conrad saw *Black Sheep* as "his" show; and since he and Cannell put the show together and hired everyone for the pilot, he apparently wasn't happy that Aresco had been hired without his involvement. Therefore, when Aresco arrived on set for his first day of filming, he received a cool reception from Conrad. Aresco explained: "We had a scene the first day, and he looked at me like, 'Yo – who are you?' I tried to be nice to him, but he never really acknowledged me." On screen, Pappy and Hutch appeared to have good chemistry – and they did – but off camera, over the course of the season, Conrad's attitude toward Aresco never warmed.

F4U-7 BuNo. 133693

Over the decades, there have been a number of "experts" who have claimed that Robert Guilford's (1933–2005) F4U-7 BuNo. 133693 appeared only in the pilot episode and never in any of the series episodes, and that when you see a -7 on-screen it's John Schafhausen's aircraft, but that was not the case. Careful examination of period photographs revealed that the -7s were nearly identical, but there was one subtle difference – the propeller hubs. The hub on '693 was black, and '710 was silver. Once that difference was identified, the author was able to determine that 133693 appeared in a total of 21 episodes – 14 in season one and seven in season two. All of the footage was shot in March and August 1976.

As mentioned earlier, Steve Rosenberg was tasked with flying Guilford's Corsair. It is entirely possible that he and '693 could have continued flying on the series, but after he flew just three filming sorties on August 12, 13, and 19, the television careers of Rosenberg and *BLUE MAX* were cut short by a catastrophic engine failure. In 2011, Rosenberg described the flight that took place on August 19, 1976: "I took off for a short flight out of Van Nuys. I pulled into a loop and simultaneously noticed a light inside the cockpit and smoke coming

Though it wasn't always easily discernable, Bob Guilford's F4U-7 *BLUE MAX* appeared in 21 episodes, but there were two episodes in which it featured quite prominently. It was front and center during a strafing attack in "High Jinx" (S1, E2, October 5, 1976), and in "Divine Wind" (S2, E1, December 14, 1977) it actually struck power lines while landing at Indian Dunes. (*Steve Rosenberg*)

down the left side of the fuselage. I rolled the aircraft upright, checked my gauges. The oil pressure was down to 25psi, and the temperature was rising through 128°C. The prop was freewheeling, but I had no power. Luckily, I was at about 7,000ft, which was enough for me to make a straight-in approach to Van Nuys' 16R. I wheeled it on and coasted off one of the high-speed turn-offs just as the R-2800 seized." Although this seems like a dramatic incident, Rosenberg's logbook entry for this flight simply reads, "VAN NUYS LOCAL 0.6HRS – ENGINE FAILURE." The engine change that followed turned into a full-fledged restoration from which the Corsair did not emerge until 1979 – a year after *Black Sheep Squadron* was canceled.

"High Jinx" (Episode 3, October 5, 1976)

When *BLUE MAX* made its debut in "High Jinx" (Episode 3, October 5, 1976), it was front and center during an airfield attack by the Tora Vals. The scene was well-documented by photographers James Farmer and John Cassidy. In June 2020, Cassidy spoke about how his father's association with Planes of Fame and his friendship with noted photographer James H. Farmer led to unique access and experiences on the set at Indian Dunes: "My dad loved to fly; he loved aviation. He was from the Lindbergh generation…he was 10 years old when Lindbergh made his flight. I don't know exactly how he connected with Ed Maloney at the museum, but I believe he was involved in getting their P-26A flying again. For three years, practically every Saturday, we drove out there from the valley to help out," Cassidy related.

One day in the summer of 1967, Cassidy and his father were fitting a windshield to a Spitfire Mk. XIV when they saw a man walking around with a camera and they asked him to lend a hand. The photographer turned out to be Jim Farmer, and he and the younger Cassidy immediately clicked. Cassidy explained, "We would just sit and talk. I remember Jim talking about this book he wanted to do about airplane movies, which became his book *Celluloid Wings*. We'd just sit and talk about that and movies and things. If a movie would come out, he'd ask, 'Did you see it?' That's what led to *Black Sheep*. I seem to recall…an announcement in the *Times* about NBC doing a series called *Baa Baa Black Sheep*. Jim knew about it and called me. Jim always had contacts and things, so he found out that it was at Indian Dunes…he asked, 'Hey, John, you want to go up and take a look?' We just wandered up one day…when they were doing the pilot…and the gate was open. I don't recall anybody saying, 'Hey, don't go there.' We pretty much just hung out at the airfield."

Radio personality and then Planes of Fame volunteer Tom Cassidy and Robert Conrad chat during a break in filming of "High Jinx". Actor Phillip Simms is seated in the cockpit of Friedkin's F4U-4. (*John Cassidy*)

WK Stratton and Robert Conrad chat with a crewmember on set at Indian Dunes. Stratton was lying on a beach in Mexico contemplating his acting future when he received the call to work on *Black Sheep*. (*John Cassidy*)

A wider shot of the set during the filming of "High Jinx". (*John Cassidy*)

F4U-7 133693 (identified by its black spinner) in the middle of the airfield attack during its series debut in "High Jinx". The sawhorse in the foreground contains the wires to set off the explosions. (*John Cassidy*)

Left: With the Vals overhead, Conrad is clearly enjoying the airfield attack in "High Jinx". (*John Cassidy*)

Opposite: Almost a half-century before *TOP GUN: Maverick*, the externally-mounted cameras on the Corsairs and Zeroes captured amazing aerial footage. (*John Cassidy*)

When Cassidy and Farmer returned to Indian Dunes in August 1976, they witnessed, and photographed, the airfield "attack" by the Tora Vals that was seen in "High Jinx" and a few other episodes. During the interview for this book, Cassidy offered a description of how the charges for the strafing runs were set up: "We got lucky that day because they were flying, and the Zeros [sic] did the strafing. Wow, that was so exciting. We saw them setting the charges in the ground and in one of the pictures…you'll see a sawhorse in the foreground with wires attached to it. That's the trigger mechanism for the strafing charges. Basically, it's got nails lined up along the top of that sawhorse and they're wired to a hot nail. When it was time to do it, the special effects guy just took the nail with the hot wire and ran it right along the other nails and every time it contacted a nail, the squibs went off."

Courting publicity

Two days after "High Jinx" aired, *The Charlotte Observer* ran an article titled "CBS Complains about NBC Show." The lead paragraph read, in part, "CBS has filed a complaint with the Television Code Authority of the National Association of Broadcasters charging that NBC violates the standards for family-viewing time with its new Tuesday night series, *Baa Baa Black Sheep*." In the complaint, which was the first time a network filed a complaint against another, CBS charged that the series "exploits violence, glorifies excessive drinking and condones dubious moral standards." The article further indicated that the family-viewing code, which required that programs airing week nights between 7 and 9pm not deal "excessively with sex and violence" or any type of "mature" content, so as to keep those hours suitable for children.

A detail showing the camera installation on the vertical fin of Tom Friedkin's F4U-4. (*John Cassidy*)

Above and below: To capture footage of a Zero chasing a Corsair, a camera was also installed on the aft fuselage of William Childers' Zero N296W. (*John Cassidy*)

Camera crews film one of the many fights that made *Black Sheep* a target for factions that sought to eliminate all violence on television. (*Frank B. Mormillo*)

The CBS letter, which was signed by the network's vice president of programming practices, Van Gordon Sauter, said that *Black Sheep* was "detrimental to broadcasters and the audience they serve" and requested that NBC be "swiftly brought into accord with the standards outlined in the Code." Robert Kasmire, NBC vice president of corporate affairs, acknowledged that "Flying Misfits" did contain drinking, brawling, and wenching, but those scenes were reduced in subsequent episodes. Regardless, the Code Authority did ask NBC to formally answer the CBS charge, and Kasmire said the network would comply.

Cannell weighed in and pulled no punches on the CBS complaint: "I find CBS' motives very questionable. Let's face it, if they were winning the time period, they wouldn't be filing a complaint." Cannell went on to say that *Black Sheep* was "clobbering" its timeslot competition on CBS, which was *The Tony Orlando and Dawn Rainbow Hour*. To the charge that *Black Sheep* glorified drinking, Cannell said, "I don't think we're stressing drinking any more than Sonny & Cher do on their CBS show in that weekly skit in which the two of them play drunks in a bar."

He also addressed CBS's charge about violence by referencing *Helter Skelter*, a two-part television movie about the Charles Manson murders, which garnered Nielsen ratings of 35.2 and 37.5 percent, respectively, on April 1 and 2, 1976. This made it clear that the general viewing public had no aversion to violence on television. Cannell's final comment was, "CBS is airing heavyweight fights during the Family Hour this month. That's real violence and real blood…."

While executives at NBC's headquarters at "30 Rock" put up a front of solidarity, there were some affiliates that seemed to agree with CBS's complaint. Jack Callaghan, manager of WSOC-TV in Charlotte, said other stations were concerned about the show as well, to the point that Callaghan had spoken to affiliates in San Francisco and Atlanta about collectively dropping the show from their schedules, but they ultimately decided against the move. The article closed by saying that there were no hard penalties for violating the family-viewing code; but if the board upheld the CBS complaint, NBC would be forced to move *Black Sheep* to a later time slot.

While *Black Sheep* seemed to have been unaffected by the family-viewing hour mandate, there were other shows that suffered as a result of a change in timeslot. The most prominent show, CBS's *All in the Family*, had been the dominant show on Saturday nights for five years, but when the network moved it to Monday nights at 9pm it took a hit in the ratings. This prompted producer Norman Lear (1922–2023) to file a lawsuit citing that the mandate infringed on creative freedom and his personal First Amendment rights.

"Prisoners of War" (Episode 4, October 12, 1976)

While the wrangling over violence continued in the courts and the boardrooms, filming episodes of the regular series proceeded without delay. In the summer of 1976, after NBC purchased the pilot and ordered 22 episodes, Cannell wondered aloud, "How the hell are we going to do 22 episodes of guys going up and flying against nameless Japanese pilots? I don't want to do a racist show and reignite hatred of the Japanese. This is an impossible show to do." He turned to writer Philip DeGuere (1944–2005), whom he'd brought onboard as a producer, and he helped Cannell style the show to Boyington's book, where he expressed more hatred for Col Lard than the Japanese. Therefore, Cannell chose to depict the Japanese as a "noble enemy," and the first episode in which he did so was "Prisoners of War".

At the beginning of the episode, Zeros conducted an early-morning strafing attack and Pappy shot one down. After failing to commit suicide, its pilot, Capt Tenyu Araki (Clyde Kusatsu, 1948–) was captured by a couple of the pilots along with a type of electronic device that was in his aircraft. At first the pilots, especially Gutterman, expressed an intense dislike for their enemy, but as time went on Araki and the pilots got to know each other and developed a mutual respect for one another. Araki even sat down to play poker with the

Opposite: Universal crews did an admirable job at turning Indian Dunes into a makeshift southwest Pacific airfield. Here, the F4U-4 sits in the outdoor maintenance shack. (*John Cassidy*)

pilots in The Sheep Pen. When the game broke, Araki retired to his cell and the pilots filed out, except for T.J., who sat down for a chat. He said, "You're a triple ace, and I am the worst pilot in the Marine Corps…every time I sit in an airplane I, um…." Araki interjected, "You sweat. You shake. You can't breathe. You can't get your stomach down out of your throat. You're scared. So am I. Every time." T.J. looked surprised and said they never talk about fear "around here." Araki said, "We're all afraid, lieutenant. Everybody in the whole world is afraid. That's why we're fighting a war." That scene humanized the Japanese more than any other in the series until the arrival of Capt. Tomio Harachi.

Early in this episode we were treated to Hutch's greatest moment. Pappy walked into the maintenance "hangar" and asked Hutch if he found anything in the Zeke. Hutch ignored the question and told Pappy, "You've got to talk to T.J.; he pushes the prop to the limit every time he flies this bird. He's gonna crack a piston on this bird. He's gotta stop treating my airplane this way!" Pappy asked, "Whose airplane?" Hutch said, "My airplane!" Pappy said, "Now I've heard everything." That sent Hutch into a tirade that goes to the age-old adage that military aircraft "belong" to the enlisted and NCO maintenance crews, and pilots simply borrow them for a couple hours a day.

Hutch ranted, "You guys, you know, you kill me. You jump in these birds, you fly them outta here, you treat them like yesterday's trash, then you limp back in here three hours later and you throw them at me. Well, that's fine, Pappy! That's fine for you! Who stays up all night picking flak out of the instrument panel? I do! Who sleeps with a wrench every night? I do! Pappy, I gotta contend with no parts. I got no oil. Then I got dumbos like T.J. that fly around with the mixture so rich, I gotta replace the points twice a week, which I don't have, which I then have to steal from the C-47, and then I have to grind them down. You trying to tell me this isn't my airplane?!" As Hutch took a deep breath, Pappy conceded that the Corsairs did indeed belong to Hutch.

By early October, the panning, griping, and criticism of *Black Sheep* had, for the most part, subsided, but on October 4, *Los Angeles Times* Television Critic Cecil Smith wrote a not-so-glowing review of the week's episode. He admitted the flying scenes were "spectacular", but that the show "…sags on the ground." The real sting however was he said that Robert Conrad was "miscast" as Pappy Boyington.

A week-and-a-half later, the latter comment drew a sharp rebuke from none other than Boyington himself, "I don't want you to think that I am in any way taking you to task, but, for the life of me, I cannot begin to imagine how you could say that Robert Conrad is miscast in playing me on *Baa Baa Black Sheep*. To begin with, we're the same weight and build, and within one-half inch in height. After the showing of "Flying Misfits", several pilots from the original Black Sheep Squadron called long-distance and commented that Conrad looked and acted so much like me that it took them back 30 years. One said: 'He uses his hands just like you,' and another said, 'The SOB even walks like you.'" It was clear early on that Boyington would champion and defend the series just as much as Conrad.

Shortly after "Prisoners of War" aired, Robert Kasmire responded to CBS's charge that "Flying Misfits" violated the family-viewing hour policy. An excerpt of the letter was published in New York's *Daily News* on October 17, which said, "In future episodes we wanted a reduction in the physical action and use of alcohol, for, although these were characteristics of the times and the people the program deals with, we wanted them handled in the manner consistent with the expectations of a general family audience. Those changes have been made to the extent that, in retrospect, the first two-hour episode was not typical of the series as a whole." In the end, the week-long squabble was rendered moot on November 4, 1976, when United States District Court Judge Warren J. Ferguson, who handled Norman Lear's lawsuit, declared the family-viewing-hour policy was unconstitutional. Ferguson said the idea was good in theory, but the FCC had overstepped its bounds in having it instituted. In addition, the NAB decree that individual stations air family-friendly programs in their 7pm timeslots was also overturned, giving stations free rein on what to air in the pre-prime-time slot. While this may have been a victory for the networks, those who sought to quell the violent and sexual content on network television weren't finished just yet.

The Black Sheep reunion

Two months into the first season, Cannell, after wondering how he was going to have enough material for 22 episodes, found his stride and was cranking out good stories – not historically correct stories, but good ones nonetheless. However, the disdain for the show among Frank Walton and a number of the pilots grew and came to a head when 16 members of VMF-214 gathered at the Surfrider Hotel in Honolulu on the evening of November 23, 1976. It was the first Black Sheep reunion since the end of the war.

While the gray-haired veterans, accompanied by their wives, enjoyed the reunion, there was no denying there was an underlying tension among them over the show and Boyington's part in it. In a May 15, 1993, interview with Bruce Gamble, Walton said, "We asked Boyington, 'Why the hell did you do this? Why did you put that crap in that TV show?' Boyington replied simply, 'Well, I needed the money.'" Walton came away from the reunion more determined than ever to correct the damage the show had done.

Due to the backlash from his boys, Boyington softened his rhetoric a little, but not by much. Just weeks later, the December 15, 1976, edition of the *Ocala Star-Banner* ran a short Associated Press piece out of Spokane in which Boyington erroneously said the former members of the squadron were "delighted" with the show but suggested that it was more fact than fiction. However, he dismissed the latter comments: "You think of history a lot differently when you're a distinguished grandfather," he told the reporter. However, he finally did brag on how well his "black sheep" have done since the war: "The unit's alumni include two judges, seven lawyers, three physicians, seven career Marine Corps officers, and a couple of stockbrokers." These stats were likely given to him by Walton, who'd kept detailed notes on the officers during the war. Lastly, with nearly five decades of hindsight, one can't help but shake one's head at his understatements, such as, "We're making dramatizations," and overstatements, such as, "This is not a documentary."

Latrobe Bulletin

Coverage of the VMF-214 reunion was not the only news about the show that particular week. In the small south-eastern Pennsylvania community of Latrobe, the *Latrobe Bulletin* ran two *Baa Baa Black Sheep*-related stories. The first covered the Whitmore family and how acting was part of the family's heritage and talked about Whitmore Jr.'s daily routine when shooting at Indian Dunes: "Jim is up at 6 every morning to report four days a week for location filming at Indian Dunes…. He prepares his own lunch and brown bags it to work…."

Meatball

The second article – on the same page, in fact – was a write-up on the show's unsung character, Pappy's bull terrier, Meatball. When asked if he had any problems working with Meatball, Conrad said he had only one: "He gets more fan mail than I do." While they may have gotten fan mail at the time, little has been written about the series' most beloved character. The dogs belonged to Aubrey Joseph Walker of Terriwood Bull Terriers, the leading bull terrier breeders in the country, if not the world. Walker was a retired Navy chief and president of the Ventura County Dog Fanciers Association, while his wife, Janet, served in several of the association's positions. They were also active members of a number of bull terrier clubs.

In November 2020, Aubrey and Janet's son, Michael, told the author, "When my dad was a child, he had a bull terrier. During one of his leaves from Vietnam, he bought a bull terrier – her name was Pud – and left it with my mom at Lemoore when he went back [to Vietnam]. At the beginning, my mom wanted to get rid of Pud. When he came home, though, he started talking about getting rid of her, but my mom said, 'Not on your life. The dog stays.' So, Pud ended up being our family dog for many years." A few years later, the Walkers purchased a bull terrier, Brooksales Dorymen, from a veterinarian in England. This dog, aka Job, was bred with a bitch named Cricket, and one of the pups from that litter was a female named Terriwoods Marshmallow, and it was she that became the primary Meatball. That's right, Meatball was a girl.

Aside from the Corsairs, the most popular character was Boyington's beloved bull terrier, Meatball. Her real name was Terriwoods Marshmallow and she was owned by Aubrey and Janet Walker of Terriwood Bull Terriers. (*Michael Walker*)

This all references who the dogs were and where they came from, but how do they connect to *Baa Baa Black Sheep*? In addition to his position as the president of the Ventura County Dog Fanciers Association and the Golden State Bull Terrier Club, Aubrey Walker was an American Kennel Club All-Breed Dog judge and was therefore heavily involved in the biannual Ventura Dog Show. In those shows, the "Best in Show" awards were given by celebrities, so Walker got to know many of the television personalities of the day, including Loretta Swit and Jamie Farr from *M*A*S*H*, Michael Cole from *The Mod Squad*, and Richard Thomas from *The Waltons*. Walker said, "Somehow my dad buddied up with some of those folks, and soon we had celebrities at our house. We had a big house with a bar, a pool table, pinball machines, ping-pong table, a pool – we had all that stuff. My parents used to entertain all the time."

While he cannot be completely sure, Walker thinks *I Love Lucy* writer/producer Jess Oppenheimer (1913–1988) is responsible for the beloved character Meatball: "This guy drove a little MG. He had salt-and-pepper hair in a big ponytail. I'm not sure if my dad met him through the dog club or if he was just a friend…but I believe it was that man that suggested that they put the dog on the TV show."

Regardless of how it happened, because the Walkers' dogs were on the show, they would often visit the set at Indian Dunes, and soon members of the cast and crew were frequent visitors to the Walker household. "My dad convinced those guys to come back to the house. The whole cast and crew from *Black Sheep* would hang out in my dad's living room, playing pool, sitting at the bar, and everything else. My dad was retired Navy, and he liked his Irish whisky, so he and Red West bonded really well right away. I remember once, while everyone was hanging out in the pool room, Red West was in the front yard, and he was playing soccer with about 30 kids from the neighborhood!" Walker recalled.

"New Georgia on My Mind" (Episode 9, November 30, 1976),

In "New Georgia on My Mind" we saw the PoF L-5G for the third time, but it was the first time we saw Conrad, who was a rated pilot, in the cockpit, which is a perfect point to relay a story from Bill Yoak: "The first time I met Bob Conrad, I almost killed him! There was an episode where I was supposed to taxi the L-5 and shut it down. So, I came in, stopped, and when I cut the mixture, they said 'action' and this dumb sumbitch started walking and went right through the prop arc as the engine was chugging to a stop…and the blade went right by his shoulder. I yelled, 'Jeeesus Christ!' … and when I jumped out of the airplane…it was Bob

Conrad! He said, 'What's wrong?' I said, 'You nearly got chopped up!' He just laughed at me and asked, 'You're Yoak, aren't you?' He always called me Yoak. I said yeah, and he stuck out his hand and said, "Pleasure meetin' ya. I'm Bob Conrad."

"The Cat's Whiskers" (Episode 10, December 7, 1976)

When "The Cat's Whiskers" aired, there were a pair of great flying sequences that were not rehashed all that often. The first showed four Corsairs, flying in trail, coming in low over the ocean and flying up a pass through some low hills. Steve Hinton remembered this scene well and told the author that this scene and a majority of the low-level scenes were filmed on the eastern and southern shores of Santa Rosa Island. The end of the episode featured the often-played shot of Frank Tallman performing the open-ocean take-off in the Duck, but the final scene was an unorthodox five-ship formation consisting of the Duck in the lead with two Corsairs – 92629, 92132, 92016, and 133693 – on each wing.

Frequent in-flight emergencies often left pilots in precarious situations if they occurred 50–75 miles off-shore. It was through luck and pilot skill that those emergencies never led to the loss of a pilot or an aircraft. (*Mark Schafhausen*)

Target audience

From the beginning of the series, Frank Price wanted to get more female viewers in front of the television, because they were always good for ratings. He explained, "We had *The Six Million Dollar Man*, and I felt that we were getting the young males; but I wanted to make sure their mothers were entertained too. So I went to Harve Bennett, the executive producer, and told him I wanted to boost ratings with a dying-girl love story, which I employed every so often. What happens in all great romances? The girl dies. It's Romeo and Juliet. So, we did a two-parter with Lindsay Wagner…and the ratings went through the roof. They were so strong that the network wanted to do a series." That series became *The Bionic Woman*, which premiered in January 1976 and ran for three seasons.

"Love and War" (Episode 11, November 14, 1976)

Given the overwhelming success of that experiment, Frank was eager to get the same results on *Black Sheep*, but Cannell's writing style did not lend itself well to that type of story. Price explained, "I was always pressing Steve to tap into the female audience. Steve didn't write women as well as he did guys. He wrote guys great, had a little blind spot with women occasionally." Cannell heard Price, and two of the next three episodes featured a love story as the main storyline. The first was "Love and War", and the crux of it was a love triangle between Casey, Bragg, and a friend from Bragg's hometown. The character was Capt. Anne Schaeffer (Leslie Charleson, 1945–2025), a gorgeous green-eyed blonde who would soon join the long-running daytime soap opera *General Hospital*.

With Tom Friedkin in the cockpit, crews deal with a collapsed tailwheel on the Tallichet FG-1D 92132. (*Mark Schafhausen*)

"The War Biz Warrior" (Episode 12, January 4, 1977)

In 2012, Tom Friedkin said that heavy rains would often leave the Indian Dunes' 3,800ft dirt runway covered in puddles that made take-off and landing "a little interesting." This statement was highlighted in a scene in the first episode of 1977, "The War Biz Warrior", which featured a backlit section take-off by a pair of FG-1Ds, believed to be 92132 and 92106; and on the roll, the latter's right wheel struck a water-filled pothole, which immediately caused the fighter to lurch to the right – but a stab of left rudder by the pilot, aided by the left wheel striking another pothole, straightened out the Corsair.

The main season one cast line-up during the filming of "The War Biz Warrior". L–R: James Whitmore, Jr., Larry Manetti, John Larroquette, Jeff MacKay, Robert Ginty, WK Stratton, Dirk Blocker, and Robert Conrad. (*Mark Schafhausen*)

F4U-7 133710 waits, while crew set-up the final scene of "The War Biz Warrior". (*Mark Schafhausen*)

Throughout the series, John Schafhausen often doubled for actors who guest starred as pilots on the series. Here he stands with James Darren during the filming of "The War Biz Warrior". (*Mark Schafhausen*)

wingman, Jason Corbett, who was making his second appearance as Patterson, pointed toward the ground. He'd noticed the C-47 had just dropped off a planeload of nurses; and as they were loading up in jeeps, he and Anderson made an excitingly low pass in tight section formation. The pass was filmed from two different angles. In the first shot, the Corsairs caused one nurse to jump out of a jeep and into the arms of a sailor. If you look closely in the background, you'll see Anne Francis (1930–2011), who played Lt Cdr Gladys Hope, standing in a jeep with her hands on her hips. In the second shot, which was filmed from ground level, Gladys was facing away from the camera watching the Corsairs bear down on her. As the Corsairs shot overhead, she whipped her head around with a huge smile that looked genuine, as if Annie Francis really was thrilled at the experience of a pair of Corsairs zipping 50ft over her head. After Patterson performed an aileron roll, Pappy said the next pilot who does that will be confined to quarters. However, in the privacy of his cockpit, Pappy could not help but chuckle at his boys' antics.

FG-1Ds 92433 (foreground) and 92629 rest on the ramp during a meal break at Indian Dunes. In this light, the over sprayed white arrow on '629's rudder is easily discernable. (*James Farmer*)

A later part of the episode featured two of the best shots of the series. The first was a quick glimpse, seen in a previous episode of the Challenge and Childers Zeros, in trail, on the backside of a split S, pursued by a Corsair believed to be 92132, with nothing but ocean in the background. The second showed the CAF Zeros, in a loose section, banking around away from the camera in a near 90-degree bank, with a tight section of Corsairs, 133710 and 92629, less than 50 yards behind them, with East Anacapa Island in the background. Say what you will about the hokeyness of the show, but these two scenes, which together accounted for less than ten seconds of screen time, are examples of what made *Black Sheep* so great.

"The Deadliest Enemy of All: Part 1" (Episode 13, January 11, 1977)

The following week, "The Deadliest Enemy of All: Part 1" opened with an equally impressive flying scene. As the Black Sheep were launching for a mission to Rabaul, Anderson and his

Bill Yoak

While it's impossible to verify, that brief scene of flat-hatting Corsairs was reminiscent of Bill Yoak's Corsair check ride, which he described to the author in 2012: "I had some formation time when we started *Baa Baa Black Sheep*, but I did not have any Corsair time; and my Corsair check ride was also my first job on the show. Once I was out of my back brace and started flying warbirds again, Jim Gavin called me and asked if I wanted the job on the show – and of course I said yes. So, he said, 'I've got a pretty simple deal that'd be perfect for you, because we've got to wrap this up. Tom Friedkin's Corsair is up at Indian Dunes. We've got about a day's worth of taxiing and then you'll do some flying, and after that you bring the airplane home.' They wanted early morning shots of start-ups and taxiing so it would look like a morning launch, so I got up at 0200hrs and Dick Martin drove me up to Indian Dunes in his old beat-up Mustang so we could be ready at sun-up.

"When we got up there, I found out I would be filming the scenes with Tom Mooney. Tom was a great guy, one of the best. He was an ex-Marine fighter pilot that had just finished a tour in Vietnam. Tom was always joking about something; everything was a joke to him, and he always kept us entertained with his stories. Anyway, after a morning of taxiing around we broke for lunch, and once we got fueled up to actually go fly, Tom came over to me: 'Do you have any Corsair time?' I said, 'No, sir, Mr. Mooney. Just P-51s, P-40s, and P-39s.' He said, 'Okay, come over here, kid.' He gave me a bunch of pointers on flying the Corsair. After that, we strapped in and went up for about 40 minutes. Tom put me in the lead, and we made a bunch of passes over the field, including two formation rolls. We came in and landed, and that is how I got checked out in the Corsair – over Indian Dunes, in front of the cameras on *Baa Baa Black Sheep*, with Tom Mooney on my wing. It's a day I'll never forget."

"The Deadliest Enemy of All: Part 2" (Episode 14, January 18, 1977)

The following week, the second part of this episode started with a party at The Sheep Pen, where Wiley was watching Anderson play checkers with a young woman. After she beat Anderson, he got up and headed for the bar, and Wiley stepped in and asked her, "Do you play strip checkers?" The woman, who was credited only as "Pretty Nurse," was 19-year-old Brianne Banigan Leary (1957–), the second future "lamb" to be introduced in the series. In 2018, Leary told the author, "I sort of always wanted to do it [act] as a kid…I moved to LA [from Tucson] by myself when I was 17. I went to an employment agency, got a job, a regular job, and then got an agent. I didn't really tell many people that I wanted to act because I never felt I was, you know, Hollywood material."

Though she had an agent, Leary fell into the catch-22 of acting, where, as she put it, "… you have to get a part in order to get in the union, but you can't be in the union unless you have a part." She went on to explain, somewhat self-deprecatingly, how she ended up

With cowl flaps open, Steve Hinton launches for an early morning sortie in 92629. The nine-victory scoreboard was seen to appear and disappear throughout the series. (*John Cassidy*)

making her acting debut on *Black Sheep*: "I was in a restaurant in Los Angeles, and Conrad walked in. He saw me and asked me out…and he arranged for the producers, Steve Cannell, and everyone, to get me one line so I could get into the union and get my SAG card. That's how I got the part. It wasn't for my acting ability." Leary and Conrad ended up dating throughout the remainder of the series and eventually went their separate ways in 1978.

"Devil in the Slot" (Episode 15, January 25, 1977)

A pivotal episode in the series was "Devil in the Slot", which introduced the two most quoted characters in the entire series, Master Sergeant (MSgt) Andrew Micklin (Robert Gene "Red" West, 1936–2017), who joined the Black Sheep as the new head of maintenance, and Capt. Tomio Harachi (Byron Chung, 1940–), who became the *Black Sheep's* most vaunted but respected opponent.

Robert Gene "Red" West (MSgt Andrew Micklin)

In 2018, Larry Manetti spoke of how West, who'd worked with Conrad on *The Wild Wild West*, joined the show. "When he [West] saw *Black Sheep*, he called Bobby and asked,

'How could I get on the show?' So, Bobby said to me, 'What do I do? Red wants to get on the show.' So, we went to Cannell, and he came up with this idea of him playing a southern redneck roughneck with no military manners who thought all lieutenants were kids and they were going to college, and they knew everything. He didn't take crap from anybody, and he portrayed this part to a T." In speaking of the latter, it should be noted that West was the third actor with military experience; he served in the Marine Corps from 1956 to 1958, which allowed him to bring a distinct air of authenticity to Micklin's character.

However cross Micklin might have been, everyone the author interviewed spoke of West in nothing but glowing terms. Producer Chuck Bowman said, "Red was a wonderful guy. I know of no other acting that he'd ever done, and I think Conrad helped him along. He had courage. He would take advice and became a very steady hand on the series. We stayed friends through his life. Every time I'd run into him, I was always eager to find out what he was doing. Conrad had him in everything that he did after *Baa Baa Black Sheep*." Manetti echoed Bowman's sentiments: "I just loved the guy. He was over six feet tall, and every inch was muscle. He was a sweetheart of a man who loved his Budweiser; and to me, I gotta tell you, besides Conrad, having Red West on that show was the best thing. He just lit the show up." West appeared in all of the series' 19 remaining episodes, but his appearance would ultimately lead to the departure of another character.

Today, Micklin's signature "college boys" quote is the most cited among fans, and it's possible that Cannell took the phrase from Boyington's memoirs. In Chapter 27, Boyington talked about a new group of guards that showed up at the Ofuna prison camp: "After we had been there a long time, four new guards came into the camp, and they happened to be college boys." This is pure speculation on the part of the author, but it is not outside the realm of possibility.

Byron Chung (Capt. Tomio Harachi)

Born in New York City in 1948 to parents of Korean descent, George Chung was just two years old when his father's job as an Office of Strategic Services agent in the US Air Force took the family to Korea in early 1950. They evacuated to Japan when the war broke out but returned to South Korea in 1956 and remained there for the next decade.

In October 2020, Chung explained how he got into acting while he was studying engineering at UCLA: "I really didn't have any aspirations [for acting] until about my junior year in college when I made a definitive decision that my career in engineering wouldn't work out. At the same time, I had a summer roommate that was an extra in the movie business. He would leave early in the morning and come back at 9 o'clock in the morning, and he told me that he had made $75 ($750 in 2023), which was the equivalent to me of about two weeks' pay. I asked him, 'How do I get in?' and he introduced me to the movie

extra business." Chung's work as an extra eventually led to a speaking part in 1970 on an episode of the ABC series *Room 222*, which of course landed him in SAG, and over the next seven years he appeared in ten television series, including 14 episodes of *Search* (where he met future *Black Sheep* directors Russ Mayberry and Barry Shear) and seven appearances on *M*A*S*H*.

Of the actors the author interviewed, Chung was one of the more difficult to locate, because I always searched for "Byron Chung." Then, thanks to Jason Hodge, a *Black Sheep* fan who found me on Facebook, I found that his first name was actually George. In March 2021, my wife and I met with Chung and his wife, Jo, at their home in Florida. One of the burning questions I had was how he got the name Byron. "When I first tried to get into the guild, they said there was already a George Chung and I would have to pick another name, and for whatever reason the poet Lord Byron came into my mind. To this day I still do not know why. I said, 'Okay, Byron Chung.' They looked it up; there was no Byron Chung, so that became my stage name," Chung explained.

When asked how Harachi's personality was developed, Chung said, "The script was going for humor between the Americans and the Japanese. I thought that it would be an interesting way to humanize the Japanese, as opposed to what history would like to record – meaning the Bushido code, where absolutely nothing but the empire would exist. I played it not as a straight Japanese ace, but more of, I thought at the time, as a human being. Conrad had a fairly good idea of how to portray his role and the role of the Japanese-American conflict. As a result, I followed his lead, in a sense that we're all human beings and each defended our country. As a result, what we do to defend that, from the Japanese standpoint it was an honor. I tried to view that along with, if you will say, the humor, but behind the humor was my desire to portray that the Japanese really were imbued to serve the emperor and, if necessary, to die for the emperor."

As the episode got under way, there was no explanation of how Pappy and Harachi's "friendship" developed – it was already established. The Black Sheep are on a patrol, they spot Harachi's squadron, and Pappy switches frequencies to talk to Harachi: "Good morning, Tommy, did you bring your life raft?" Harachi replied, "Not going swimming today, Boyington, maybe you." In quick succession Harachi shot down Boyle and Gutterman. After Gutterman bailed out of his Corsair, Pappy got on Harachi's tail, but Harachi turned the tables, took a few snap shots, and broke off with, "Not today, Boyington, maybe tomorrow." Pappy asked Wiley how Gutterman was doing after his bailout, and T.J. said he was okay, and that air-sea rescue were on their way to pick him up.

Later in the episode, Pappy and Harachi's pilots clashed for the third day in a row. During the engagement Pappy fired hundreds of rounds at his Zero with no hits. When Harachi rolled under Pappy to get on his tail, he popped up in front of T.J., who reflexively pulled

The heavy exhaust staining and extremely weathered paint on Schafhausen's F4U-7 highlights the tempo of the arduous flying schedule. In his home movies shot during the summer of 1976, Schafhausen commented that they often flew five to seven hours a day. (*Mark Schafhausen*)

the trigger and sent Harachi's down trailing smoke. T.J. yelled to Pappy that he got Harachi, while Casey said, "The phantom of east Philadelphia strikes again!" On the ground, in a scene reminiscent of the celebration on the carrier deck at the end of *Top Gun*, everybody surrounded Wiley's Corsair cheering the new hero that downed "the devil." In The Sheep Pen, T.J., embellishing as only he could, told the story of how he shot down Harachi, but he stopped when he saw Pappy and Gutterman walk in and sit down. Gutterman quietly said, "Go ahead T.J. I can't wait to hear the end of this one." Wiley paused a moment and finished his story with, "So I rolled under him and blew him away – T.J. Wiley, the new devil in the slot!" In Conrad's narration at the end of the episode, he said T.J.'s unlikely victory put him on the cover of *Time*.

"Poor Little Lambs" (Episode 19, February 22, 1977),

The 19th episode, "Poor Little Lambs" (February 22, 1977), was an oddity in that it was completely devoid of Corsair footage. The only aircraft that appeared in the series was an unidentified Twin Beech, out of which Pappy, Boyle, and Anderson had to bail after

going off course and getting hit by AAA. The island was naturally crawling with Japanese soldiers, played by Soon-Tek Oh (1932–2008), making his second of two appearances; Jim Ishida (1942–); and, interestingly enough, George Cheung, who was credited only as "First Japanese soldier." It was this actor who was already on the SAG list and forced George Chung to take the stage name "Byron."

"W*A*S*P*S" (Episode 20, March 1, 1977)

The next episode, W*A*S*P*S seemed reminiscent of the Battle of the Network Stars, a series of competitions in which television stars from the three networks competed in various sporting events at Pepperdine University, near Malibu. The episode began with the newsreel *Women Go to War*, which featured actual footage of WASPs flying various aircraft during the war while the narrator stated that women flying the various aircraft coming off the production lines was "a new age in aviation." The end of the reel stated that the WASPs' commander, Maj Deborah Watkins (Andi Garrett), would be heading to the Solomons for "transport duty." When the transport landed at La Cava to drop off the WASPs, the actor credited only as "C-47 Pilot," was 24-year-old Kin Shriner (1953–), who would get his big break, when he was cast as Scott Baldwin on *General Hospital* just six months later.

The next day the Corsairs and B-25s were en route to the Treasury Islands and naturally ran into trouble with Zeros. This fight featured the usual shots of Corsairs and Zeros mixing it up, but there was a new, never-before-seen shot from the front of the T-28 camera ship as it followed a smoking Zero through a large barrel roll with the Zero staying in the center pane of the windscreen through the entire maneuver. The T-28 wasn't available during the filming of the pilot episode, but once it was purchased by Tom Friedkin's Cinema Air in August 1976, it was used extensively throughout the remainder of the series.

During our interview in 2012, Bill Yoak spoke briefly about modifications that turned the T-28 into a versatile camera ship: "I made all the camera mounts on *Baa Baa Black Sheep*, including the camera pods that we mounted under the wings. They had optically pure glass on them, and inside they had two forward-facing and two rear-facing mounts. I also modified the canopy with sill plates and deflectors so there would be zero air movement in the rear cockpit. Frank Holgate was the primary guy that sat back there and ran that big Plantronics camera, and his hair was never ruffled. We flight-tested that thing for over a week."

The final dogfight featured a number of shots in which pyrotechnics were being set off on a few of the Zeros, including one that was rather large. In 2018, Fred Ellsbury spoke of what he witnessed the first time he saw a charge go off during a filming sortie in May 1976: "One thing they wanted was a spectacular shot of a Zero exploding. One day I was

Among the four aircraft Tom Friedkin made available for filming was his T-28-R1 (N28DS), which was extensively modified into a cameraship. Here Jim Gavin and a cameraman prepare the Trojan for a flight out of Van Nuys in August 1976. (*John Cassidy*)

watching the technicians install one of those explosives on Mack's [Sterling] airplane. I can't remember if it was on the baggage door or just back and down from the cockpit, but they built a stainless steel bracket that was about 12 by 18 inches with some bushing between it and the skin. I walked up to Mack and asked, 'Are you sure about this?' He said, 'They assure me that this is going to be alright.' So, we went up and they were giving him directions and he went ripping out across there with a Corsair on his tail, and when he was probably a mile away from me he detonated that charge. Bang! That thing went off with so much fire and smoke the airplane disappeared and I thought, 'Oh my God!', but a second later Mack flew out of the fireball unscathed, so it worked just like they said it would."

Violence on television

Shortly after this episode aired, the *Ithaca Journal* ran an article by *Washington Post* reporter Tom Shales that included the results of the 13-week survey by the NCCB mentioned in Chapter 2. According to them, *Starsky and Hutch* (ABC), *The Six Million Dollar Man* (ABC), *Hawaii Five-O* (CBS), and Cannell's *Baretta* (ABC) and *Baa Baa Black Sheep* (NBC) were the five most violent shows of the 1976–77 season.

While one might not associate the American Medical Association (AMA) with such activities, the AMA supported the survey with a $25,000 grant and urged companies that advertised on these shows to drop their sponsorship. It didn't take long for other organizations, such as the National Parent Teacher Association, Southern Baptist Convention, and the Screen Actors Guild, to join the movement, but perhaps none carried more weight than the Church of the Brethren, which owned stock in the largest advertiser on TV at the time, Proctor & Gamble, which tried to influence the company's advertising buys from within. NCCB president and former FCC commissioner Nicholas Johnson wasn't advocating boycotts, but was quoted saying, "We haven't urged people to boycott, but then, in all candor, when you publish the names of the most violent sponsors, you don't need to." There may not have been official calls for boycotts, but a Gallup poll indicated that a third of respondents said they would support a boycott of companies that advertised on the more violent programs.

While NBC initially denounced the NCCB study, it was the first network to proclaim a housecleaning when President Robert T. Howard said, "The proliferation of the program types whose plot lines heavily involve violence has become excessive." Cannell said, "There is incredible pressure on right now to eliminate violence from scripts. The problem has suddenly become a terribly hot political football. There is more pressure now than there has been in years." The pressure to reduce violence, plus an edict from the front office, would have an effect on the content of *Black Sheep's* second season.

When the filming schedule called for the Corsairs to fly at an established airfield, Chino was most often utilized. With the Planes of Fame TBM and several B-25s in the background, crews prepare to film a scene for "Last One for Hutch" in February 1977. (*Frank B Mormillo*)

"Last One for Hutch" (Episode 21, March 8, 1977)

The penultimate episode of the first season, "Last One for Hutch," began with Zeros strafing the airfield. As the Corsairs scrambled into the air, Pappy was stuck on the ground with a jammed canopy, which Hutch fixed with a crowbar. As he jumped down off the wing, Hutch then saw four Zeros bearing down and he yelled to Pappy to get going. With Micklin looking on, as another Zero lined up for a run, Hutch ran and dived into a foxhole, but the Zero's shells stitched right through the foxhole.

When Pappy returned from the mission, he checked in with Micklin on the status of the field. Micklin said, "Well, the generator is gone, so's the fuel dump. We're outta business." Pappy said, "I'll decide that." Micklin's voice then softened, "Ah, Major…Hutch got it. It was that last Zero. He was dead before he hit the ground." To make matters worse, a rear area officer showed up with orders to shut down the Black Sheep, and to bury Hutch on La Cava. Pappy said he didn't "give a damn" about his orders; Hutch would be leaving with the rest of the squadron. As the enlisted men formed a cordon, the pilots carried Hutch's body to the C-47. Micklin told Pappy that Hutch was good but "too damn young." Pappy said they are all too

damn young. Then he asked Micklin to bury whatever is useful "because the Black Sheep are coming back." Pappy made good on his promise.

The final shot of the episode was of a pair of Corsairs symbolically "going west" into a sunset. Conrad then broke in with his traditional narration: "Gutterman and I were heading back to La Cava to re-establish our base. The rest of the Black Sheep would be following

With "MAJ BOYINGTON" and 25 victory markings under the cockpit, the F4U-4 is readied for Robert Conrad during filming of "Last One for Hutch". (*Frank B Mormillo*)

in the morning once their orders were cut. The sunset that evening was one of the most beautiful I'd ever seen. My engine droned, and the red gold light danced on the wingtips. We were going home, but we were one man short – John David Hutchinson, mechanic, Flint, Michigan." As his name was spoken, Hutch's image and a cross appeared. As the picture faded to black, it marked the first departure of a main cast member.

In April 2022, Aresco explained how his role on the series ended: "Right at the end of the season, I was told to go to the producer's office. That's never a good thing. So, I went over there, and it seemed like everyone was there – Cannell was there, DeGuere was there, Bowman was there. I don't think Bellisario was there, but everyone else was…. I asked Cannell, 'Am I fired?' He said, 'Well, Joey. You're not really fired; we just ran out of stories for you. I think Red West might be doing some of what you've been doing.' So, I guess Red became the new mechanic." With Cannell's last statement, one cannot help but wonder if Conrad, with his penchant for employing friends, saw bringing Red West on board as an opportunity to get Aresco off the series.

"The Fastest Gun" (Episode 22 March 15, 1977)

The final episode of season one, "The Fastest Gun", was one of the best because it brought Pappy and Harachi face to face for the first and only time. This episode skipped over a newsreel and began with one of Conrad's narrations while we watched a Corsair five-ship wing their way over the north-eastern tip of Santa Rosa Island. "Bad luck is a funny thing. Usually when it comes, it comes in bunches. When you're due for a lot of trouble, all you can do is cover your chin and wait till your luck changes. Unfortunately, on this particular day, I didn't know I was due."

Hampered by a Corsair with a rough-running engine, Pappy was the last to return from a mission; and as he called La Cava tower, he got no answer. However, there was someone listening: "Hey, Boyington. That you? I hear your radio, Boyington. Where you hiding?" The voice was unmistakable. It was Harachi, and with the view from the tail camera he pulled in on Pappy's six, "Hey, Boyington, that you?" Harachi said with a smile. Pappy, trying to sound confident, asked, "How you been, Riceball? You dried off yet?" Harachi laughed and said, "You got some trouble. I give you more, maybe, now. What do you think? You ready to go swimming?" Pappy told him to take his best shot. Harachi replied, "You know, Boyington, you put me in the water, but I say what the heaven, I get later. You ready?" Harachi maneuvered into close formation with Pappy until finally he asked Harachi if he forgot where his guns were. Harachi said, "Hate to shoot you when you prane don't fry. Hey, Boyington! You fix. I get you later. Sayonara, Boyington, I catch you later." With that, Harachi broke cleanly out of the picture. Pappy took a deep breath while Conrad said, "My hands were shaking. Harachi had me. It was

only a respect between us that had built up over months of fighting that saved my life. I'll take it any way it comes."

When Pappy landed, he informed his boys that Harachi was alive, and he thought that Pappy had shot him down. When Wiley asked, "You didn't tell him it was me, did you?" Pappy said, "I told him, but he didn't believe me." This left T.J. extremely worried, and it was made worse when he translated what he thought was Harachi's obituary. As it turned out, the article said the 21-year-old Harachi was a hot pilot with 32 victories.

The next day, a winded Wiley barged into Pappy's tent and told him Harachi was on the radio and wanted to speak to him. As they entered the radio shack, we heard Harachi on the radio: "Hey, Boyington! You got your prane fixed? Hey, Boyington, you down there? You hiding?" Pappy keyed up: "How ya doing, Riceball?" A jovial Harachi replied, "Hey Boyington, I'm over the lagoon. You wanna come up and pray?" T.J. urged Pappy not to go, because he could hardly walk. Pappy, visibly swaying from excessive scotch intake, regrettably mumbled, "Uh…my plane won't fly." Harachi taunted, "You got utter pranes. I think you got no guts, Boyington. You Marine. You afraid of Tommy? One rittle riceball? You coming, Boyington?"

Wiley again told Pappy not to take the bait, but Pappy said this conversation was embarrassing and keyed up again and mumbled, "Harachi. I'm drunk." Tommy, with scorn in his voice, replied, "You drunk. You prane don't fry. I say you chicken, Boyington. I getch you anyway. Maybe I getch you on the ground." At that point, Harachi laid down a stitch of gunfire right in front of the shack. As Pappy stumbled back inside, he said to Wiley, "What's he trying to do, T.J.? He might have hurt us." Pappy bent over to pick up the mike and nearly knocked over the radio as he accepted Harachi's call-out, "That did it, you riceball! I'm gonna meet you tomorrow at 4 o'clock in the afternoon in the Slot! Just you and me!" Tommy's faced turned serious as he realized what he had gotten himself into. "Okay, Boyington, I be there." Wiley looked at Pappy and his face asked him why he did what he just did, and Pappy, still swaying, said, "What was I supposed to do? He was calling me out."

As the sun set, Conrad narrated about the coming duel over the Slot: "It was a good thing I'd been drinking; otherwise, I wouldn't have gotten to sleep that night. At my age, I should have known better than to let Harachi buffalo me into going up against him in a one-to-one. But what the heaven, my honor was at stake. The Slot wasn't big enough for the both of us."

At the beginning of the episode, when Pappy landed after his initial encounter with Harachi, he went to Micklin to confront him about the poor condition of his aircraft and ended up laying Micklin out cold with a sucker punch. For that, Micklin told Pappy he would have to work on his own aircraft from now on – but they came to an understanding, so on the morning of Pappy's fight with Harachi, Pappy and Micklin were working on Pappy's Corsair and ended up bickering over loose rudder cables when Pappy jumped down

Among the six Tora Zeroes to fly on *Black Sheep*, the Planes of Fame-owned SNJ-5 (N3375G), was not one of the original SNJs modified by Cal-Volair in 1968 for the film *Tora! Tora! Tora!* (*Frank B Mormillo*)

from the cockpit and told Micklin that since a truck mechanic drives a truck after he fixes it he was going to go test-fly an airplane and ordered him over to the SNJ. Micklin continually refused to fly until Greg called him out.

Once up in the air, Pappy had Micklin fly and then put the SNJ through some aerobatics until they were bounced by a flight of Zeros. The dogfight scene with Pappy and Micklin against Zeros was hilariously funny with a petrified Micklin hanging on to the canopy for dear life and an extremely animated Pappy yelling at him while calling for his boys to lend him a hand. As Pappy worked to shake the Zero that had started to score hits, Micklin, with his cigar clenched between his teeth, yelled, "Boyington, if we get out of this alive, I'ma kill ya!" Just then, he spotted Gutterman and Anderson entering the fight. He cheered, "Ha! C'mon college boys!" That unlikeliest of comments from the gruff officer-hating sergeant elicited a grin from Pappy.

On the ground, those college boys thoroughly enjoyed greeting their sickened maintenance chief as he climbed out of the SNJ. As soon as his feet hit the ground, he socked Greg right

Because of his extensive experience flying Corsairs, John Schafhausen was given the call sign "Black Sheep One" and was popular among pilots and actors. (*Mark Schafhausen*)

in the gut and ran off to toss his lunch. As they picked him up, they asked Pappy what the punch was all about, and he replied, "That's alright. He hates to fly."

The SNJ used in this episode was SNJ-5C BuNo. 905649 (N7976C), which was owned by Junior Burchinal at the time. In addition to the usual four Zeros seen throughout the series, the chief aggressor against the SNJ, was the sixth and final Zero to appear in the series and for years, its identity was a mystery. In the final weeks of writing, the author queried Tallmantz historian Scott Thompson and aircraft movie buff Jerry O'Neill and they both suspected it was T-6F USAAF #44-81819 (N7446C), which was part of the Tallmantz collection. However, when Thompson sent a 1971 photo of N7446C and a 1978 photo of the mystery Zero (parked next to Friedkin's F4U-4) sans N-number I had my doubts because there were too many minor differences. So, on January 23, 2024, as I had so many times over the years, I emailed Steve Hinton. He responded 20 minutes later, "The T6 Zero with the real Japanese A6M5 canopy is the Planes of Fame SNJ-5 N3375G." Mystery solved! A few days later, I exchanged emails with photographer Frank Mormillo in which he offered a very interesting piece of information. He wrote, "The museum had hoped to see the restored Zero fly in the *Black Sheep Squadron* TV series, but the series ended before the restoration was completed." It's appearance in the episode "The Fastest Gun" was N3375G's third of 11 in the series.

Later that afternoon, Micklin found Pappy, who was obviously contemplating the coming fight with Harachi, in his tent: "I tightened down your rudder cables, Major. I also gave it pre-flight. It shouldn't act up on ya," he said. Pappy called him by his first name when he thanked him. Micklin tried to lighten the moment: "If you let anything happen to ya, you gonna haveta answer to me. I spent too much time working on it."

When Pappy reached the designated spot over the Slot, he changed frequencies and keyed up: "Hey, Tommy, you up here?" The camera panned back behind a Corsair, and there was a Zero. When Harachi replied, "Right behind you, Boyington." Pappy broke right, and the fight, which lasted nearly three minutes and contained no dialogue, was on. Harachi drew first blood with some strikes on Pappy's wing, but it was quickly followed by a fatal blow that started Pappy's Corsair smoking. There is a quick close-up clip of the Tallichet FG-1D, 92132, spewing flame as one of the pyrotechnic charges exploded on the far side of the fuselage. Conrad broke in with the dramatic music: "Harachi had gotten me. But I'd hoped I could keep my plane in the air. I knew he'd try and finish me off, so I tried the oldest trick in the book. I chopped my power and went to full flaps to drop my airspeed and let him overshoot me. I wasn't finished yet."

Pappy fired a well-aimed burst that set Harachi's Zero afire. Pappy exclaimed, "You're all through, Tommy! Hit the drink!" From his smoke-filled cockpit, Tommy replied, "You too, I think, Boyington!" Pappy said, "Nah, I'm going to nurse mine home." Tommy knew that wasn't going to happen: "See you in the water, Major!" he cheerfully replied. Harachi jumped first, followed by Pappy a few seconds later.

Next, we saw Pappy traipsing through the jungle. He stopped to pull out his emergency radio and called La Cava and told the boys he was down on the south-east tip of Nataki Island. Casey acknowledged and said he'd contact air-sea rescue, and they arranged a pick-up time. Greg then tuned to what was apparently Harachi's personal radio frequency and asked his respected adversary if he was on the same island. Harachi replied, "I'm in a tree over your head, Boyington." Pappy looked up and laughed. "There isn't any tree over my head." The banter then continued, "Tommy, I gotcha," said Pappy. Harachi laughed and asked, "Then how come you sitting in sand now?" The two arranged a meeting on a beach on the east side of the island – a significant moment in *Baa Baa Black Sheep* history was upon us.

The scene cut back and forth to each pilot as they hiked out of the jungle and reached the beach about 20 yards apart, simultaneously. Pappy asked, "Got any rice wine?" Harachi countered with, "You got American chocolate?" Pappy had the chocolate, but Harachi was unable to reciprocate. Tommy asked, "What you think, Boyington?" Pappy said, "I think next time I'm gonna getcha." Tommy said his submarine would be arriving after dark and that they would meet again. Pappy said again he had him, but Harachi reasoned, "No, you didn't, Boyington. This time, no winner. But one day, one of us will win and the other will be very sad." Tommy lit a cigarette, took a drag, and handed it to Greg, thus ending the episode and the season.

The above scene was the only one in which Chung shared the screen with Conrad. He spoke of it in 2021: "The big thing about that, upon recollection, was because Robert Conrad and I were almost equal in height, they had to have me step into a trench so that he would look taller than me." In watching this scene since, one will notice that even after Conrad and Chung sat down to share that cigarette Chung actually sat down on the ground with Conrad kneeling next to him, thus making Conrad taller.

A month after that final episode aired, Frank Walton took his first step at clearing the names of his fellow *Black Sheep* when his article, "Baa Baa Black Sheep Is Pulling the Wool Over Our Eyes," was published in the April 23, 1977, edition of *TV Guide*. After his opening statement that the show was "phony as a three-dollar bill," he went on to make fact-versus-fiction comparisons, many of which have been made in this chapter. However, nothing was more poignant than pointing out the successes that the *Black Sheep* had after they returned to their civilian lives: "Seven are owners or presidents of business firms, two were mayors of their cities, two are airline pilots, three are lawyers. Seven are directors, executive officers or managers of companies or firms. One is a college professor, another is an artist, another a stockbroker," Walton wrote. He closed with one of the quotes from Conrad's narration: "Misfits? Screwballs? People who failed in everything they'd ever done?" To that Walton told the reader, "Don't you believe it." In the coming years Walton would have more to say, and his words would make the Black Sheep more famous than they ever thought possible. It would also bolster the popularity of the series.

CHAPTER 4

SEASON TWO: BLACK SHEEP SQUADRON

December 14, 1977–April 6, 1978

Despite competing with *Happy Days* and *Laverne & Shirley* and getting hammered by critics, veterans, feminist and anti-violence groups, not to mention lack of support from within NBC itself, *Baa Baa Black Sheep* survived its first season with a respectable 25 average share. However, just as the season finale aired, NBC canceled the show without any explanation to those involved. W.K. Stratton said in a 1977 interview, "I went to the production office a while back and got the bad news personally. I went there to talk about something or other and they said there wasn't any point in talking because the series had been canceled." Stratton figured "that was that"; but when the word of the cancelation spread, the network got an earful from fans. The author found two such letters in the May 22, 1977, edition of *The Tampa Tribune-Times*. Tampa resident Derrick Harrelson wrote, "I'm writing to say that *Baa Baa Black Sheep* is the best television show anywhere. The show is a combination of comedy and drama. The networks should take off those silly soap operas and put on more shows like *Baa Baa Black Sheep*." Another writer said, "I would like to see it kept on because it is one of the few series on television that does what television is supposed to do – it entertains."

However, *Black Sheep* had no greater champion than Robert Conrad. His first TV series, *Hawaiian Eye*, was followed by the extremely popular and now classic *The Wild Wild West*, which ran four seasons from 1964 to 1969 and was near the top of the ratings when CBS pulled the plug on the show. In rapid succession, Conrad starred in two failed series, NBC's *The D.A.* and ABC's *Assignment: Vienna*, which ran only 15 and eight episodes, respectively. Even with those failures, Conrad remained a hot commodity into the mid-1970s. That being said, it should come as no surprise that when Conrad heard that *Baa Baa Black Sheep* had been canceled, he thought it was a joke, because he'd been told that renewal was a cinch. He was not about to take it lying down, however, so the strong-willed and self-admitted "cocky little S.O.B.," Conrad, went on a crusade to save the show.

He first teamed up with Stephen Cannell and walked into the NBC affiliates convention that was held in Los Angeles in mid-May 1977. The pair had hatched a plan. Cannell knew

When *Baa Baa Black Sheep* was cancelled at the end of season one, Robert Conrad and Stephen Cannell successfully lobbied to get the show re-instated for a second season. It was a feat that was unheard of in Hollywood. For the new season, the series was renamed *Black Sheep Squadron*. (*Mark Schafhausen*)

the show was popular in the south, so he'd identify station managers from that region and steer them toward Conrad, who would start his pitch with, "Can you believe they canceled *Baa Baa*?" This angered the affiliates, and they started questioning the network's decision.

A few days later, Conrad and Cannell met with Irwin Segelstein, who listened to their impassioned arguments on why *Black Sheep* should be renewed. Cannell made it a point to tell Segelstein that *Black Sheep* was originally intended for a 10pm time slot and that it may perform better in a late-night slot. To make his point Cannell also said, "Look, *Emergency!* stayed on for two years opposite *All in the Family* and was getting 26s. During summer re-runs it got into the 30s." Segelstein said he admired people who would go to such lengths for a project and promised to do what he could for the show.

Even with Segelstein's promise, Conrad did not let up. While the series was still in production it was under constant threat of cancellation, and every time there was a meeting that affected *Black Sheep's* future Conrad was knocking on the door. So why not step up his efforts once the hammer actually fell on his show? Each time he managed to get himself in front of a boardroom full of executives, he presented figures that demonstrated how large *Black Sheep's* audience share would be were it not up against the Cunninghams and the ladies that worked in a beer plant. He also presented certain research studies that indicated that the show's viewers were more loyal than the average and it was just those kinds of people that sponsors wanted to reach. Those tactics were effective in the past, and they worked once again. In early June, Segelstein again met with Cannell and Conrad, and as they pored over the Nielsen numbers, they again reminded Segelstein that *Black Sheep* had never been tried out in the 10pm time slot that it was originally intended for. At the end of the meeting, Segelstein ordered six new episodes, placed the series on as a standby, and advised Cannell to have scripts prepared for an additional five episodes.

They had done it. Cannell and Conrad had accomplished something that was unprecedented in Hollywood. Prior to this, shows jumped networks after cancellations, and CBS and NBC had second thoughts after cancelling *The Dick Van Dyke Show* and *Star Trek*. But seldom has a show been cancelled, replaced, and then put back on the air. Conrad rightfully believed that it was his enthusiasm for the show that got it back on the air, but the grassroots support from its fans could not be ignored.

Production on the second season started in mid-July, but that was only half the battle. Whether the series actually got back on the air depended on the performance of the slew of new shows on NBC's fall schedule. It would not take long to see the results. Shows such as *The Richard Pryor Show*, *Mulligan's Stew*, and *Rosetti and Ryan* all tanked in six episodes or less. In the 9–10pm time slot on Wednesday nights, NBC's *The Oregon Trail*, a western set in the 1840s, aired opposite ABC's *Charlie's Angels*. As one might expect, Rod Taylor, Darlene Carr, and Charles Napier traveling in a wagon train was no match for the scantily clad Kate Jackson, Jaclyn Smith, and Cheryl Ladd.

Over Thanksgiving weekend, it was announced that *Black Sheep Squadron* would make its second season debut on December 14, 1977. The title change came about after Segelstein tested the original *Baa Baa Black Sheep* title and found that many thought it was a children's show. While Cannell was happy the show had been saved, he would have preferred to have been up against weaker competition – *The Redd Foxx Comedy Hour*, *Baretta*, and *Barnaby Jones* at 10pm on Thursdays – rather than the fourth-ranked *Charlie's Angels* on Wednesdays.

When the announcement of the show's return was made, Conrad went on the road to promote the series on local talk shows. While in Cincinnati during the first week of December he learned that WCKT in Miami would not air the first two episodes, opting instead for the 1968 feature film *The Devil's Brigade*, starring William Holden, on December 14, and the 1945 musical comedy *Anchors Aweigh*, with Frank Sinatra and Gene Kelly, on December 21. Conrad started making phone calls to NBC executives, from the network president Herb Schlosser down to relations chiefs at numerous affiliates, trying to encourage them to do something about his show losing a spot in one of the nation's largest markets.

When Conrad returned to Los Angeles on Thursday, December 8, for a scheduled appearance on *The Tonight Show*, he found that his calls for help had apparently fallen on deaf ears and he was incensed. During that particular week the show featured guest hosts, and on the night of Conrad's appearance the show was hosted by Gabriel Kaplan who, at the time, was starring in the lead role of teacher Gabe Kotter in *Welcome Back, Kotter*. During his segment, Conrad called out WCKT by noting that his two sisters would be unable to watch the show because the station would be carrying movies that "would hardly qualify as classics" on anybody's list. He had planned to ask the live audience directly if he should go to Miami to personally picket the station but never got the chance. He did, however, jokingly say he planned to throw a party in Palm Beach so all the fans in Miami could watch the show on Palm Beach's Channel 5.

In an interview with TV/radio editor Sherry Woods that appeared in the Sunday, December 12, 1977, edition of *The Miami News*, Allen Sternberg said when Channel 7 began looking for slots for local movies, it picked NBC's weakest night, Wednesday, and slotted the movies between 7:30 and 10pm. By the time the network announced where *Black Sheep Squadron* would be slotted, Sternberg said it was too late to move the movies, but the show would go into WCKT's schedule on December 28. Was Sternberg put off by Conrad's pressure to change his programming schedule? Not at all. He told Woods, "It shows that he really cares about the show. I never got a call from Rod Taylor when *The Oregon Trail* went off."

Television shows live and die by ratings, and as *Black Sheep Squadron* hit the air again, it entered the realm of what is the norm today but was downright scandalous in 1978 – sex. Not in the literal sense, but the suggestive sense. While occasional love interests for the pilots were introduced into several storylines in season one, the writers went over the top as season two progressed. The man responsible for bringing T&A to the small screen was Fred Silverman (1937–2020), who worked for all three big networks before starting his own company.

After graduating from Syracuse University and earning a master's degree from Ohio State University, the New York City-native was hired to oversee program development and children's programming at WGN-TV in Chicago and WPIX in New York City. While at Ohio State, Silverman wrote his master's thesis on a decade's worth of programming at ABC. The paper so impressed the heads of CBS that he was hired as an executive in 1963 at just 25 years of age. He was initially responsible for daytime programming, followed by all day and night entertainment programming; and in 1970 he was promoted to Vice-President, Programs, which placed him in charge of the CBS program department.

The four-month delay in getting *Black Sheep* back on the air allowed Steve Hinton and John Maloney to complete the restoration of Planes of Fame's F4U-1A 17799. The aircraft made its series debut in the season's first episode, "Divine Wind", and appeared in 11 of the second season's 13 episodes. (*John Cassidy*)

Beginning in 1971, Silverman organized what was known as the "rural purge," where he dumped numerous country-centric shows such as *The Beverly Hillbillies*, *Green Acres*, and *Mayberry R.F.D.* for the likes of *All in the Family*, *M*A*S*H*, and *The Sonny & Cher Comedy Hour*, which were aimed at baby boomers. In 1972, he reintroduced game shows to daytime programming, and two years later he ordered *Good Times* into the slot opposite ABC's *Happy Days* for the 1974–75 season.

These changes at CBS served only to solidify ABC's long-running and dismal third-place ranking among the big three networks. The management at ABC took notice of what had been happening across town and hired Silverman out from under CBS in 1975. One of his first jobs was to undo the damage *Good Times* had done to *Happy Days* the previous year! Not only did he succeed at sending *Happy Days* to the top of the ratings, but he generated the spin-off, *Laverne & Shirley*, in 1976, which rapidly took a solid spot as the #2 show on television.

Silverman's next move was controversial and criticized but ultimately forward-thinking. In what many called "escapist," he introduced shows such as *Charlie's Angels*, *Battle of the Network Stars*, and *Three's Company*, where the prevailing theme was young, buxom women with long legs, broad smiles, and skimpy outfits. As a jab, NBC executive Paul Klein (1929–1998) referred to ABC's new marketing and production strategy as "jiggle TV" and the shows themselves as "porn." So, much to the dismay of women's liberationists, veterans, and military historians, the boys on Vella La Cava roared on to our TV screens for another action-packed, albeit abbreviated, season.

"Divine Wind" (Episode 1, December 14, 1977)

The first episode, "Divine Wind" marked the debut of two new aircraft. The first was Planes of Fame's F4U-1A BuNo. 17799, which John Maloney and Steve Hinton had been restoring since March 1977. To the trained eye, this "new" Corsair was quite noticeable on-screen

The second season also saw the debut of a second DC-3 when NC28341 also made its series debut in "Divine Wind". This historic aircraft was the first DC-3 to carry passengers when Delta Airlines entered scheduled service in 1940. (*John Cassidy*)

thanks to its fresh paint job and bright white wheels. In the end, this combat-veteran Corsair would appear in 11 of the 13 second-season episodes.

The second aircraft was a new C-47. While C-47B NC23650 from season one continued to make appearances in the second season by way of films shot in 1976, it had moved on to a new owner and would meet an unfortunate end in 1979. The new Gooney Bird appeared in the first two minutes of the episode, when it dropped off Father John O'Reilly (Scott Hylands, 1943–), a priest struggling with his faith after seeing so much death on Guadalcanal. As he walked away from the aircraft, a dark blue cheat line between the white and gray, as well as R4D-6 28341, was visible over his left shoulder under the horizontal stabilizer. This is in stark contrast to NC23650, which carried no identification whatsoever. A quick Internet search revealed that "28341" was not a BuNo., but an N-number that indicated this aircraft was not a C-47 at all, but a DC-3 with an incredibly historic provenance.

In the opening minutes of "Divine Wind", Bob Guilford's F4U-7 received superficial damage when Steve Rosenberg struck powerlines on short final for runway 27. (*Steve Guilford*)

As mentioned in the previous chapter, Bob Guilford's F4U-7 BuNo. 133693 appeared on-screen in 22 episodes, but its most memorable scene occurred in the first few minutes of "Divine Wind." In the beginning of the episode, Pappy and his boys were returning from a mission and Boyle was the first to land. On short final he saw power lines strung across the threshold and attempted to avoid them, but it was too late. When the fighter hit the wires, the flash of sparks and smoke could have been passed off as Hollywood special effects, but it was a very real incident. Watching this sequence in slow motion, one can see that the electrical arc lit up the underside of the wings. The arc, along with smoke, traveled outward in both directions; and as the Corsair flared for landing, the power lines hit the ground in a cloud of dust. As the fighter rolled out, remnants of the wires could be seen being dragged behind the aircraft.

At the controls of the Corsair was Steve Rosenberg, and he relayed the details of the incident in 2011: "I remember the incident very well because it was quite dramatic. There were power lines on the east end of the field, but since it was my first flight into the field, I had no idea they were there. When I hit the wires, the whole cockpit lit up and the airplane slowly decelerated because the wires were pretty strong. When the wires snapped, the runway was right there, and I set it down in what turned out to be a pretty good landing. So, I'm taxiing back trailing this wire behind the airplane, and I did not feel good about it at all. Other than a ding on the right front landing-gear door, it did not really hurt the airplane much because it was such a brute. It did bang up my ego a little bit, though…it was still totally my fault."

Throughout the first season, John Larroquette's character, Robert Anderson, was not featured all that prominently – but that changed in this episode, and not for the better. In the first season, Anderson was more or less an irrepressible gambler and skirt-chaser, but in "Divine Wind" he suddenly turned to the clarinet, meditation, philosophy, and karma. According to the late Bill Yoak, this was one of the elements that started *Black Sheep Squadron* down the road to cancelation.

Shortly after the series was canceled for the second and final time, Conrad told Yoak about an exchange he had with one of the producers one night at a party: "This producer, who I guess had some money in the show, told Conrad, 'Our ratings are starting to sag a little bit, and I really think we need to start weeding those [hokey things] out.' People who were getting polled about what they like and don't like about *Baa Baa Black Sheep* [sic] were getting put off by the hokey [expletive]. They did not like John Larroquette playing the clarinet; they didn't like Conrad's daughter and all that [expletive]. How the clarinet thing got in there, I don't know; I guess Bob liked Larroquette. Boyington didn't like it. The guy told Bob that Pappy is complaining, they've got to do something with the writing.' Bob said, 'I don't see anything wrong with the writing,'" Yoak related in 2012.

During the 17 years that Bob Guilford owned *BLUE MAX*, Steve Rosenberg logged more than 350 hours in the aircraft. (*Steve Rosenberg*)

However, Anderson's fascination with karma led to a micro-storyline that was true to VMF-214 history. At the beginning of the episode, Anderson burned his feet walking across hot coals and missed a mission. Boyle ended up flying Anderson's Corsair, and when he returned Anderson met him and thanked him for taking care of his "aeroplane." Boyle sat on the canopy rail and said, "Well, I'll never complain about being five-foot-eight again. Look at this." He motioned toward a destroyed headrest. "You're pretty lucky you weren't here, Bobby boy, or you'd be wearing that 20mm right between your ears." Anderson stared in horror at the bullet-riddled headrest.

This was a definite reference to a real incident that Boyington mentioned in his memoir, which occurred during a dogfight over Kahili on October 18, 1943. Prior to each flight, Bill Case would lower his seat all the way down and then raise it up to the point where he could look directly through the Corsair's gunsight. It also gave him maximum protection from the armor plate behind the seat. On that particular day, after he'd lowered the seat, it would not go back up again. He flew the mission anyway.

The Sheep Pen, the squadron's bar, featured a removable wall in order to facilitate filming the interior of the building. (*John Cassidy*)

During the fight, his Corsair took a number of hits, including a 7.7mm round that smashed through the canopy and grazed the top of his head, which knocked his head forward, and shattered the windscreen. Case said at the time, "I would have been killed if I were sitting just a half inch higher; and if the bullet had missed me, my head would have stayed up and the glass would have come back into my eyes." That flight was Case's last combat sortie as the Black Sheep's tour ended the next day. For the rest of his days, Case said that nothing other than divine intervention caused his seat to jam.

Donald P. Bellisario, Story editor

This particular part of the story came from a new writer whom Cannell had hired in early 1977. This newcomer grew up in the western Pennsylvania coal-mining town of Cokeburg, and his introduction to aviation came at the tender age of five, when he sat in the cockpit

The third and final character, Lawrence Casey, played by WK Stratton, that Stephen Cannell took from Boyington's memoir was based loosely on 1st Lt William Case, a seven-victory ace with VMF-214. (*Frank Walton Collection, Emil Buehler Library, National Museum of Naval Aviation*)

During the second season, Cannell hired 42-year-old up-and-coming writer Donald Bellisario as a story editor. He worked on eight of the 13 episodes and went on to an incredibly successful career in Hollywood. (*Donald Bellisario*)

Diet
MAC KAY

Opposite: **The third episode of season two, "The Hawk Flies on Sunday", was the first of three episodes directed by Robert Conrad. The others were "Ten'll Get You Five" (E6) and "Forbidden Fruit" (E7). (*David Cassidy*)**

of a barnstormer's biplane in 1940. World War Two intensified his interest in aviation, and he set the goal of attending West Point so he could fly. He received an appointment, but he was second runner-up the first year and first runner-up the next year. In 1955, he was tired of waiting, so he joined the Marine Corps; but because he was married and did not have a college degree, he could not become an aviator, although he did serve in a Marine air wing.

Upon leaving the service in 1959, he enrolled at Penn State, earned a bachelor's degree in journalism, and landed a job as a copywriter in Lancaster, Pennsylvania, in 1965. He also found time to earn his private pilot's license. In 1968, he became a creative director at the Bloom Agency in Dallas, and by 1976, after having risen to senior vice president, he moved to Hollywood and started creating television commercials at 41 years of age. His ultimate goal was to get into feature films, so he wrote a spec script and sent it to an agent, who thought it was a good piece of writing and took the ex-Marine on as a client. However, upon being told that he could sell a script in a year, he had only 16 weeks of money in the bank, so decided to take a stab at writing for television. When his agent asked what he would write if he could get a show, the writer told him he'd like to do *Baa Baa Black Sheep* since he was a pilot and a former Marine. The agent sent the spec script over to Stephen Cannell, and he liked what he read. This Marine-turned-writer was Donald P. Bellisario.

In an interview in November 2019, Bellisario talked about his first meeting with Cannell: "He read the script while I waited outside his office. About a half-hour after our appointment time, he called me into his office. When he looked up, he did a double take because I was 40-something years old, and he was expecting some kid just out of college. He said, 'Where have you been?' I said, 'Well, I've been outside waiting....' He said, 'No, no, no. Where have you been hiding?' He took my script, and he dropped it on the desk. He said, 'I can shoot this just as it's written. How would you like to be my story editor?' I said, 'I don't know what a story editor does.' He said it was somebody who sits at a typewriter and turns out scripts. I said, 'That sounds good to me.' So, I was hired right on the spot." Bellisario ended up doing much more than that as he either wrote, produced, or directed eight of the 13 episodes in season two.

Capt. James Gutterman

While Bellisario's addition to the production team went unnoticed by fans, what they did notice was the absence of Capt. James Gutterman. The reason or reasons as to why James Whitmore, Jr., did not return for the second season have long been a subject of debate among the *Black Sheep* faithful. Although some rightfully point out that immediately after first season filming wrapped in spring of 1977, Whitmore left for the Philippines to film

the Golden Harvest Company production *The Boys of Company C*, where he'd been cast as Lt Archer. However, that project was completed in more than enough time for Whitmore to start shooting *Black Sheep's* second season.

In an exclusive interview for this book, Whitmore related why Gutterman was absent in season two. Whitmore said, "The script for the next season…it was all about my guy. When I came back [from the Philippines] the show had been canceled, but they were fighting to keep it on the air. Since it had been canceled, I went out looking for another job, and I ended up going over and reading for…the Lou Grant show. They wanted to hire me to play the part of Bobby Walden, which was ultimately played by Joe Rossi, but Universal said they wouldn't let me out of my contract, which ran, like, five days after Lou Grant was going to start shooting."

So, with the future of *Black Sheep* in doubt, Whitmore and his family went down to the West Indies for a vacation. While he was there, Whitmore received a phone call from Universal, and they offered to pay him what MTM was going to pay on *Lou Grant*, which was more than his *Black Sheep* castmates. Whitmore agreed. However, just a few days later he got a call from *Black Sheep* producer Alex Beaton (1933–2020), which Whitmore spoke of in June 2019: "He said, 'Hey, man, Conrad said if you don't work for the same money as

Four Corsair variants are represented in this July 1977 photograph (F4U-1A 17799, F4U-4 97359, FG-1D 92132, and F4U-7 133710. The latter sports a *Black Sheep* insignia on its vertical stabilizer. (*David Cassidy*)

the other guys, you can't do the show.' I used some expletives and told him to tell Bob what he could do and quit the show on the spot." With that, Capt. James Gutterman was resigned to television history, but James Whitmore, Jr., went on to an extremely successful career as an actor, producer and director, which continues to this day.

"The Hawk Flies on Sunday" (Episode 3, December 29, 1977)

On December 29, 1977, "The Hawk Flies on Sunday" aired and featured a number of firsts. It was the first of three episodes directed by Robert Conrad and the first appearance of another future "lamb," Kathy McCullen, who was credited as "Pretty Nurse." Like many of her castmates, McCullen was just getting her start when she appeared on *Black Sheep Squadron*, as she'd only had small parts on three TV series, including *Happy Days*.

On the aviation side, a pair of Mustangs appeared in the episode, but only as static props. Identifying these aircraft had been difficult, but according to Steve Hinton, they were Ed Maloney's USAAF #45-11582 (N5441V), which has gone by various identities including *Glamorous Glenn III*, *Spirit of Phoenix*, and *Spam Can*, and Tom Friedkin's USAAF #44-73856 (N7TF). Except in name, both aircraft remain with the same owners today, Planes of Fame and Comanche Group, respectively.

As mentioned in the previous chapter, Bill Yoak flew just about every aircraft that was involved in the series, and in "Wolves in the Sheep Pen" (Episode 4, January 4, 1978) he was at the controls of the L-5 when it towed a Schweizer SGS 2-33, dubbed "Duggie's Revenge" in honor of a young Corsair pilot who died earlier in the episode, that was supposed to be flown by French to find and sink a Japanese radar ship in the Slot. On-screen the L-5 was seen towing the Schweizer with no apparent difficulty, but as with so much in Hollywood, things were not as they seemed.

In 2012, Yoak relayed the rather precarious situation that developed as he attempted to get airborne out of Indian Dunes and tow the glider to the filming location over Oxnard: "So I'm in the L-5 with another guy and we take off with this glider…it won't accelerate, and the airplane won't climb. I'm going down the riverbed and somebody comes on the radio and said, 'You need to gain some altitude.' I said, 'Not possible.' They asked, 'Do you need to cut away?' I said, 'No.' Ross Reynolds was chasing me in a rented Gazelle with the door off, and Frank Holgate was manning the camera. Ross is on the radio telling me I need to figure out a way to get some altitude, but I had nothing. I had full power with a fixed-pitch prop, and this thing ain't going anywhere because it was hot. Ross said it'd be cooler if I can ever make it to Oxnard.

Well, we finally got to Oxnard, and I'd struggled to get to thirty-five hundred, and Ross wanted me at eight thousand. My response went down in the annals of *Baa Baa Black Sheep* history because everybody heard it on the radio. He kept telling me he wanted me at 8,000, and I finally said, 'Ross, let me put it to you this way! Every time I pull back on the stick, the only thing that goes up is the oil temperature!' So, everybody was bad-mouthing the airplane…Gavin was determined to get the shot.

Finally, I managed to get to 5,000, and the glider guy said, 'Ross, are you ready? We're at 5,000ft; I can do this from here.' I guess they had the background they wanted, and Ross asked Frank, 'Are you loaded?' Frank said, 'I've been loaded for an hour and a half! Let's do this! I've got to take a piss!' So, they filmed him over the beach, so it would look like an island, and then landed. All that work for just a few seconds of screen time!" Yoak laughed.

"Ten'll Get You Five" (Episode 6, January 18, 1978)

"Ten'll Get You Five" was the sixth and final episode Silverman ordered back in July 1977. It isn't known when Silverman ordered the five subsequent episodes, but in an interview that appeared in *The Valley News* on December 13, 1977, Conrad said that his contract was set to expire on December 27, and he had no intention of extending it if NBC didn't order more episodes. He said the network would have two chances, on December 14 and 21, to decide if it wanted more episodes and if it did not, "we'll just shake hands and go our separate ways."

The episode was marked by a number of firsts and lasts. The Tallmantz Duck made its first of two appearances in season two when it made an extremely low pass over a basketball game between the pilots and nurses. Among the nurses on the court, it was hard to miss 19-year-old Denise DuBarry (1956–2019) in a pair of very short shorts and a top that revealed her midriff. Though she was credited only as "3rd Nurse" and had one line, she was front and center in every scene in which she appeared.

DuBarry was supposed to make her debut in season one, but after unknowingly raising the ire of Conrad, she was shown the door. She explained in July 2018, "First of all, I was only 19 and this was my first really big gig, so I was nervous. When it came to the girls, they wanted to make sure everything was right, especially with the hair styles. They wanted them to be sexy, but still conform somewhat to the World War Two period. So, we spent the day in the trailer trying different hair and make-up styles. When we got to what we thought was right, I walked out of the trailer and found Bob and gestured to my hair and said something like, 'Here it is' or 'This is it,' as if to ask him, 'What do you think?' He just looked at me, nodded his head, and said 'Okay, fine.'

I did not think anything of it and went on and finished taping the show. After that, my agent called to tell me I wasn't invited back because I had apparently done something to piss Bob off. I said, 'No way. You're kidding. What could I have possibly done?' Anyway, I went on with my career, but I found out later that when I showed Bob my hair that I somehow came off as sassy, but I was just being me." Though her appearances on-screen were limited in this episode, DuBarry would be featured rather prominently in the final episodes of the series.

Above and below: **Art imitating life. A line up of Corsairs at Indian Dunes in 1977 looks very much like the flightline of VMF-214 F4U-1s at Munda in 1942. ((Above)** *Frank Walton Collection, Emil Buehler Library, National Museum of Naval Aviation,* **(below)** *Tri-State Warbird Museum)*

On the other hand, we saw Gregory Boyington, Robert Ginty, and John Larroquette for the final time in the series. Ginty's departure was due to landing a number of roles, in film and television, in rapid succession. During the break in filming, Ginty played the part of sergeant Dink Mobley in the film *Coming Home*, a 1978 movie starring Jon Voight, Bruce Dern, and Jane Fonda. This role was quickly followed by a part in the TV movie and an appearance in an episode of the short-lived series *Project U.F.O.* and a regular role in the TV series *The Paper Chase* (1978–79), where he met his first wife Lorna Patterson. After his first leading role in the 1980 vigilante crime-drama *The Exterminator*, Ginty started his own production company while playing various TV and movie roles throughout the 1980s and '90s. In addition, Ginty became a writer, producer, and director on a number of projects, the last of which was in 2002. Robert Ginty died of cancer in 2009 at the age of 63.

Larroquette's departure on the other hand was not so clear-cut; but it was no secret that Larroquette battled alcoholism early in his career, and it could be argued that *Black Sheep* played a part in his diving deeper into the bottle. In a 1985 interview he said, "*Baa Baa Black Sheep*…promoted that hard-drinking image. We lived that image off-screen." As mentioned in the previous chapter, Larroquette was one of the cast members that often hung out at the Ventura home of Aubrey and Janet Walker, the breeders of the show's bull terriers. Their son, Michael, who was in his mid-teens at that time said, "There was a lot of drinking going on in those days. It was a really convenient place because Ventura is close to Valencia, so it was an easy place for those guys to stop off for a drink before they headed back to Los Angeles. There would be times where after the filming a few would show up. In fact, John Larroquette…would hang out for hours at a time. My dad would sit up and drink with him for hours."

While the show may have contributed to Larroquette's drinking problem, it can also be argued that it was responsible for his decades of sobriety. In 1981, shortly after *Stripes*, Larroquette was pulled over for drunk driving, but instead of arresting him the female officer escorted him to his hotel, where she ensured he was safe. As it turned out, she was a fan of *Baa Baa Black Sheep*. As with their squadron mate Gutterman, there was no explanation for the sudden absence of Lts Wylie and Anderson.

"Forbidden Fruit" (Episode 7, February 22, 1978)

Perhaps the most pivotal episode of the second season, if not the series, was "Forbidden Fruit", because it marked the first appearance of Jeb Adams, a kangaroo, and the first time Nancy Conrad, Denise DuBarry, Brianne Leary, and Kathy McCullen were credited as individuals and collectively as "Pappy's Lambs" in the opening credits. Speaking to the latter, three of the four were described in an NBC press release: "Denise DuBarry is a willowy green-eyed blonde with a languorous look; Brianne Leary is a long-haired brunette

The Newhall Land and Farming Company's 600-acre ranch and Indian Dunes airstrip in Valencia made for a convincing southwest Pacific forward airstrip. (*John Cassidy*)

with a well-packed uniform; Kathy McCullen is a perky blonde with no-no on her lips and yes-yes in her eyes." During interviews with DuBarry and Leary, the author read the release, and both had a good laugh about it, which was refreshing in an epoch when everyone is offended about everything. Leary added, "I was just happy to be working."

As most reading this know, there were no nurses on any of VMF-214's forward operating bases on Guadalcanal, Munda, or Vella Lavella, but again the show was fighting for survival, especially after it was moved to a new suicide slot opposite *Charlie's Angels*. DuBarry, who appeared on an episode of *Charlie's Angels* in September 1977 said, "They were competing with a girlie show, so they needed to get some T&A on *Black Sheep*." In an interview excerpt that appeared in *The Jordan Valley Sentinel*, Conrad said, "Everyone knows the old saying 'Fight fire with fire.' We decided to adapt that to our situation and fight femmes with femmes. They've got three, so we'll go 'em one better." As it turned out, "Pappy's Lambs" had a positive effect on the show's ratings, which crept up to a 30 share; survival level according to Jeff Sagansky, an executive the author spoke with in October 2019.

One person who was not happy with the T&A twist in the series was Donald Bellisario. In 2020 he said, "Stephen came to me one day and said, 'We want to put girls in the show.' I said, 'You can't do that Steve. It's not real; it didn't happen. We've been very good with this show. We've been doing stories that are based on some real things that have happened. It's going to be silly to have girls in the show.' Steve said, 'The network wants it, so I've got to do it.' He and I wrote the script, but I was dead against it. I don't know who came up with 'Pappy's Lambs.' It could have been me, but I don't remember."

Although the word to increase the appearance of the women in the show came from, as Bellisario put it, "the network," Frank Price was always in favor of more female characters and touching storylines, so there is no doubt he was in favor of formalizing the four primary female characters under the catchy 'Pappy's Lambs' moniker. "I was always pressing Steve. I'll give you an example. We had *The Six Million Dollar Man*, and I felt that we were getting the young males; and I wanted to make sure we, again, tapped into the female audience. If the kids were watching, I wanted to make sure their mothers were entertained too. Getting women on-screen was my regular thing. I knew I was going to have to tell him, because, like I said, Steve didn't write women as well as he did guys. So, I told him I wanted to get women to watch the show; so, I was pressing him to find ways – factuality be damned – get some nurses, get some women on the goddamn screen," Price related.

In "Forbidden Fruit," Price got his money's worth, because DuBarry's character, nurse Samantha "Sam" Greene, sauntered on to the screen with her "languorous look" in the first two minutes of the episode and was on-screen for 18 minutes of the 44-minute-long episode. This was due in no small part to the spark that ignited between Sam and Pappy.

We first met Sam when she was boarding the DC-3 for the flight to La Cava. Also on that flight was 17-year-old Jeb Stuart Adams, who was playing replacement pilot 2nd Lt Jeb Pruitt, who lied about his age to join the Marine Corps. Bringing Pruitt into the series was Conrad's way of paying it forward. In the late 1950s, while Conrad was getting started in show business, he met Jeb's father, Nick Adams, in Chicago. Adams gave Conrad his phone number and said if he was ever in Hollywood to give him a call. When Conrad made that trip, Adams picked him up at the airport and introduced him to key people at Warner Bros. Studios; and those intros landed him a part in *Hawaiian Eye*. That was Conrad's proverbial "big break."

Sadly, Nick Adams passed away far too young in 1968, but Conrad stayed in touch with his family. In the March 17, 1978, edition of the *Fort Lauderdale News*, Adams said, "Last Christmas we were visiting my grandparents in Montana when he [Conrad] telephoned to see if I'd try out for a part in *The Black Sheep Squadron*. They were looking for a teenager to play a guy who lied about his age to get into the service. I was really excited about the possibility." Adams flew down to Hollywood, where Conrad introduced Adams to Cannell and producers Alex Beaton and Don Bellisario, and after a series of tests they gave him a contract.

The appearance of the kangaroo, which Boyle had brought back from R&R in Sydney, was the result of a conversation that Larry Manetti had with Conrad. In June 2018, Manetti explained how the kangaroo, Harry "The Rock" O'Shaughnessy, ended up becoming a regular character in the waning episodes of the series, "I went to Conrad and told him I was getting some fan mail, but didn't know what I could do to get more attention. So, he said, 'You want more attention, Larry? You want more attention? There is a show coming up where you guys go to Australia for some R&R. I'll fix it, so you get more attention.' So, it was Conrad's idea to get the kangaroo. He loved animals. It was a major pain because all it did was kick me in the groin! I had to wear a steel cup and pads on my legs."

Rocky eventually appeared in six of the last seven episodes, and when it wasn't being used in a shot Manetti didn't know what to do with the kangaroo, so again he went to Conrad. Manetti continued, "I said to Conrad, 'What do I do with this thing?!' Conrad said, 'I expect you to keep it with you or give it to your mom. I don't care.' I said, 'It stinks and kicks me in the groin all the time.' Conrad laughed, 'You wanted attention, didn't you? Everybody'll hate you 'cause you stink, but you'll get attention.' Oh God, it was a nightmare."

During the filming of a scene near the end of the episode, there was an incident with Conrad that left DuBarry thinking she was about to be fired off the show for a second time. DuBarry-Hay related in 2018, "During one of our scenes…I found out Bob had an issue with height. There was a long dolly shot we did at Indian Dunes, and it had been raining.

One of the storylines in "Forbidden Fruit" revolved around a radar-equipped Corsair. This was somewhat based on fact as F4U-2 night-fighters were co-located on Munda with VMF-214 in October 1943. (*Jim Sullivan*)

They had all kinds of Jeeps and heavy equipment on the set, and they would create big ruts. So, for this scene the crew had to lay the entire bridge down and all these tracks for the cameras.

"I was rehearsing and rehearsing…Bob and I go out and he said, 'I'll just shoot the rehearsal.' So, we're walking along and talking, and it's kind of an emotional scene and I'm trying to nail it in one take, to just keep things moving along, and we get halfway through, and he stops midtrack and he looks up at the camera and he said, 'Are we really gonna [expletive] do this? Are we really gonna do this right now?' I thought, Oh my God, did I blow it again? What did I do? You know, of course, this had to be my fault.

"So, the AD [assistant director] came over and said, 'All right, cut. Everything cut. Everybody just go back to your rooms. We gotta talk.' So I'm thinking, we're gonna talk…are they gonna fire me again? When we went back out an hour later, I asked, 'What happened?'…one of the guys said, since we were shooting the rehearsal, we, of course, hadn't rehearsed it…as we were walking Bob got into one of the ruts, and as we walked, he was getting shorter, and I was getting taller." Conrad was an inch taller than DuBarry, but to give the appearance that he was much taller the crew laid a platform for him to walk on when they redid the scene, which was shot from a low angle, to enhance Conrad's height.

For Bellisario, this episode was the fourth of seven that he wrote and second of eight that he produced, and he again brought real Black Sheep history, albeit unknowingly, to the series with a storyline about Japanese harassment raids on Vella La Cava to disrupt the sleep of the pilots. Bellisario related, "The episodes I wrote were mostly out of my mind. I was a young boy during the war, and I read and absorbed anything I could find on the war, especially if it had to do with flying. Some of my ideas came out of that, I'm sure. I don't remember anything specific, but I'm sure that's where the idea came from. In fact, I remember sitting in a Universal bar with Pappy Boyington having a drink. He said to me, 'Where did you get the idea from?' I said, 'I just came up with that.' He said, 'Well, that really happened.' I wish I could remember what story he mentioned." We'll never know for sure, but other than the previously mentioned instance about Bill Case's seat failure that saved his life and admitting that "The Hawk Flies on Sunday" was obviously based on Admiral Yamamoto's shoot down, this is the only episode written by Bellisario of which a story can be traced back to an actual event in *Black Sheep* history.

To combat what Micklin called "that Japanese college boy," but also Japanese bombers that were targeting US Navy ships, Lard suggested they borrow a radar-equipped F4U-2 off a nearby aircraft carrier. However, on the way to La Cava, the fighter and its pilot had been shot up badly enough to be taken out of action. Pappy ordered Micklin to take all the gear out of the damaged Corsair and install it in "his aircraft" in just a matter of hours. While Micklin, with just a cigar, a wrench, and an oily rag, performed that miraculous maintenance feat, Pappy attempted to take a radar course over the radio. When he finally realized it would be impossible, he was forced to turn to Pruitt, who he'd just banned from flying because he was underage.

Though it was apparently unintentional, bringing Corsair night fighters into the story was historically correct. The XF4U-2 took to the sky in the summer of 1942, and by October 1943 F4U-2s joined VMF-214 on Munda and their presence greatly decreased the night-time harassment raids, thus allowing the *Black Sheep* and other squadrons to finally get a good night's sleep.

As Pruitt led Pappy, Casey, French, and Boyle into the darkness, Conrad narrated: "He was out there, 200ft in front of me. If I slid slightly to the starboard, I could see his profile bathed in the light of the radar scope. He was leading a desperate flight to protect 3,000 Marines – hundreds of miles to the north. He was only 16." Not surprisingly, Pruitt led them right to the bombers, and after shooting down several, the rest turned back. Conrad closed the episode with, "And right there at 200 miles per hour at eight degrees south latitude and 158 degrees east longitude, we took him in. We adopted a little brother. Neither the Navy nor the Marines would ever take him away. He was ours. He was the littlest black sheep."

"Fighting Angels" (Episode 8, March 1, 1978)

The first episode in *Black Sheep's* penultimate month on the air was "Fighting Angels" (Episode 8, March 1, 1978), and the series was moved once again to a new time slot, Thursday night at 9–10pm, opposite *Barney Miller* and *Soap* on ABC and *Hawaii Five-O* over on CBS. This eliminated the threat from *Charlie's Angels* and supposedly the need for girls and love stories; but by then filming had wrapped on the final episodes, so there was plenty more jiggle in the offing. Speaking of the ladies, when the subject of the series' female characters comes up, it always pertains to the quartet who became Pappy's Lambs. This overlooks Capt Dottie Dixon (Katherine Cannon, 1953–), a nurse who made her debut in "Divine Wind."

In the seven episodes in which she appeared, she seemed to have tacit romantic involvement with T.J., but in "Ten'll Get You Five" there seemed to be some flirtations between Dottie and Pappy. In "Fighting Angels" it was clear that they had become quite taken with each other. The episode also featured another of Price's penchants, the tragic death of a female. The main storyline was the Japanese were invading a nearby island and the Black Sheep were needed to beat back the offensive. Normally that would not have been a big deal, but the Japanese had also landed a team of commandos on La Cava and were prepared to attack the airfield, and they would do so while the pilots were on a mission, thus leaving Lard and Micklin in charge of defending the field along with ground crews…and the nurses.

Just as Lard and Pappy expected, the commandos attacked the airfield immediately after the pilots launched their mission. The Marines staged a delaying action in hopes that the

Due to the appearance of a pair of P-38s, "Hotshot" (Episode 10, March 15, 1978) is a particular favorite among *Black Sheep* fans, and unlike the P-51s from "The Hawk Flies On Sunday," the Lightnings flew in front of the cameras. As rare as Corsairs were in the mid-1970s, Lightnings were even more so and the aircraft in this episode were John Stokes' P-38M USAAF Serial No. 44-53097 (N3JB) and John Deahl's P-38L USAAF Serial No. 44-26961 (N6961), both of which were captured on John Schafhausen's home movies on February 24, 1978. On that day, N6961 was flown by Dick Martin and N3JB by Tom Friedkin; and as they taxied out with Hinton in the PoF F4U-1A. Schafhausen was supposed to fly as well. But as he filmed the trio taxiing out from his cockpit, he said in narration, "The batteries on the APU were on backwards and it blew all the circuits, plus the reverse-circuit relay and whatnot in my plane."

As Schafhausen filmed the half-dozen low-level passes Friedkin and Martin made over the field, Gavin was directing them from a radio on the ground, asking them to make repeated passes closer, farther, lower, in relation to the cameras. As they made their final pass, Schafhausen said on the film, "After filming, the thirty-eights went back to Van Nuys for fuel, but they could not get started again because the same APU that blew the system in my plane had also blown theirs, although they were not aware of it at the time." He went on to say that it was discovered later in the day that sometime during the week a crew member had moved the cables around in order to jump-start a vintage ambulance for a scene, and when they converted it back to use on aircraft it was done backward.

For years, it was thought that FG-1D 92132 was the only Corsair that was ever "shot down" on the show. This was due to the fact that period photos show the aircraft fitted with plates on the rear fuselage where explosive charges were mounted. On the day Schafhausen filmed the P-38 sequences, he also filmed explosive technicians installing charges on his aircraft. He said, "I've been elected to get shot down today." During the aerial sequences of this and the subsequent episode, 133710 can be seen carrying a smoke generator pod and pyrotechnic packs on the rear fuselage.

Ongoing aircraft maintenance

The initial interviews with the pilots in 2011 and 2012 were focused primarily on the Corsairs, and back then Hinton and Yoak said that unlike today's meticulously maintained warbirds, the aircraft flown on the show, particularly the Corsairs, were not well maintained and suffered from frequent maintenance issues. In this episode the T-28 camera ship inadvertently captured, for just a split-second, an in-flight emergency that Bill Yoak experienced at the controls of Friedkin's F4U-4. At the 3:21 mark, the T-28 flew behind a formation that consisted of the Challenge and PoF B-25s and two Corsairs, one of which

With his pipe clenched in his teeth, John Schafhausen prepares for a late-afternoon sortie out of Indian Dunes. (*Mark Schafhausen*)

Black Sheep could get back in time to inflict heavy casualties on the commandos. They did exactly that, but not before the nurse corps took casualties. While surveying the damage Pappy checked in with Lard, Micklin, and finally Sam, and by the look on her face, Pappy could tell that a nurse had died in the attack. His boys watched as Pappy walked over to a body draped with a blanket. When he pulled it back, it was Dottie and in her hand was a cross he'd given her. Cannell was the writer for this episode, and it seemed he'd come a long way in a short time when it came to writing emotional scenes involving females.

By the time *Black Sheep* ended in spring 1978, Tom Friedkin had put almost 300 hours on his F4U-4. He kept the fighter until January 1988, when he sold it to the Old Flying Machine Company in Duxford, England. (*Frank B. Mormillo*)

had its landing gear down. Yoak related the incident in 2012: "We were filming out over the ocean near Santa Cruz Island, where we'd been farting around for a while, and were heading back for fuel. I was looking outside the airplane, and out of the corner of my eye… boom…there goes the hydraulic pressure. I called Jim on the radio, 'I just lost my hydraulic pressure.' Without hesitation Hinton said, 'Get the gear down, Yoak.' Steve knew those airplanes so well. So, I threw the gear out, but I did not have enough fluid to get the flaps down, so Jim said to take it to Oxnard, so Dick [Martin] could fix it.

"Oxnard had a great long runway, but it was always a crosswind, so I stuck it on the numbers and still managed to turn off midfield. Martin was waiting and asked what happened. I said, 'Well, why don't you take a look at it! The flaps are still up. I can't get them down, and there is hydraulic fluid all over the belly.' It turned out to be a broken hydraulic line, and Dick's guys couldn't fix it, so I ended up fixing it. I went down to another guy's place, but he didn't have any Aeroquip hose, so I took the hose…cut the

bad part off, and still had enough hose to put back on the fitting. It was stretched to the max, but we finished filming."

This was not an isolated incident. On a sortie out near the islands of San Miguel and Santa Rosa, Yoak suffered burns to his face, eyes, and throat after the battery on Friedkin's F4U-4 exploded and filled the cockpit with caustic acid. These are two extreme examples, but the Corsairs also suffered radio problems, engine problems, brake failures, and a host of other maintenance issues that kept the mechanics at Dick Martin's Marginal Aeromotive busy throughout the series.

Yoak noted one humorous incident that occurred while Corsairs were being refueled at Indian Dunes: "We'd been filming for a couple days, and the fuel kid jumps up on Burchinal's airplane and started filling it up. I was standing there with Dick Martin, who was in charge of all the airplanes. I'd worked for Dick at Marginal Aeromotive. He was a great mechanic and a great pilot. Suddenly Junior came running over yelling at the fuel kid, 'Get off the airplane! Don't fill that thing up!' Gavin walked over and asked, 'What's going on? We've got to get to work. We need all the airplanes filled up.' Junior said you can only fill it up to about half or it'll leak fuel into the cockpit! Gavin said that is not really a safe situation and I really wish you had told us this before we brought that airplane out here. After Gavin walked off, Dick said to Junior, 'Ace – he called everybody Ace – 'why don't you just fix this airplane and quit screwing around. This is dangerous.' Junior looked at Martin, and without batting an eye he said, 'Son, there is a fine line between spending money and airworthiness!' Well, Gavin heard this and came over that night and said, 'Get this piece of [expletive] outta here; we'll finish with four airplanes!' I'll never forget that as long as I live!"

"Sheep in the Limelight" (Episode 12, March 30, 1978)

At the beginning of "Sheep in the Limelight," the Black Sheep gain instant fame after they unknowingly save Eleanor Roosevelt's plane from being shot down, which Col Maurice Parker (James T. Callahan, 1930–2007) from Marine Corps Public Information got wind of and wished to exploit. Parker summoned Pappy to Espritos and laid out his plan to use the squadron's newfound fame for maximum PR value. Naturally, Pappy wanted no part of the scheme; at least he didn't until the pilots received free cases of scotch and Micklin a cache of brand-new Corsair parts. For a while all went well until Col Parker pulled strings to get the Black Sheep increasingly dangerous missions that generated good copy and Casey ended up getting shot down and Bragg shot up. In the end, Parker moved on and life in the Black Sheep returned to normal.

While it is impossible to know, this storyline could have been inspired by Frank Walton's PR campaigns that made the Black Sheep famous during their time in the Solomons in the fall of 1943. The photographers and films generated during that period made the men of

VMF-214 household names, and the fame garnered lasted well beyond the war and was tacitly responsible for the creation of the series three decades later.

Two days before what turned out to be the final episode of *Black Sheep* aired, tragedy struck the warbird community, particularly Tallmantz Aviation and the cadre of *Black Sheep* TV pilots. After nine years as chief pilot at Tallmantz, Tom Mooney left the company in 1977 to work for Antilles Air Boats in the Caribbean, flying Grumman amphibians. On April 4, 1978, Mooney was on a routine flight when his Goose suffered an engine failure, forcing him to perform an emergency water landing. One of the seven passengers aboard the aircraft said, "The front end of the plane exploded…." All seven passengers survived the ditching and were picked up by a passing pleasure boat, but Mooney and his co-pilot died in the accident.

One of the hundreds of people who worked on *Black Sheep* was Stephen Cannell's production secretary, Susan Appling Johnson. She was beloved by the actors, who gave her this personalized photo when the series ended. (*Susan Appling Johnson*)

"A Little Bit of England" (Episode 13, April 6, 1978)

In "A Little Bit of England," Boyle gets shot down and comes under the protection of English coast watcher Peter Buckley and King George, the latter a local islander played by future *Ghostbuster* Ernie Hudson. The coast watcher was played by rock legend Peter Frampton, who had been a fan of the show from the beginning. In his 2020 memoir, *Do You Feel Like I Do?* Frampton relayed how a chance meeting with Conrad in a restaurant led to his appearance on the show: "I looked over and there's Robert Conrad. I was a huge fan of *Baa Baa Black Sheep*…I loved it; it was a great show. So, I went over and said, 'Excuse me, I'm a huge fan – my favorite TV show is *Baa Baa Black Sheep*.' He said, 'You're kidding me!'

"He said sit down, so I did, and I said, 'Do you think there's any chance that I could have just a walk-on part, play some bit part on the show?' And he said, 'You want to do that?' I said, 'Absolutely! It's my favorite show.' So, he said, 'Let me see what I can do; I'll talk to the producer.'" At the time, Frampton was just wrapping up shooting the musical comedy *Sgt. Pepper's Lonely Hearts Club Band*.

A few weeks after he returned home from shooting the movie, a *Black Sheep Squadron* script arrived at his home. Frampton continued, "I opened it [the script], and it said your character is so and so. I read through it, and there's me, there's me – the whole bloody show is me!" When the time came to shoot the episode, Frampton traveled to Los Angeles with his road manager; and during the trip Frampton learned not just his part, but everybody else's part. He knew the entire script front to back! All of Frampton's preparation was for naught, though. "When we shot the first scene, I blanked because I was so nervous. That was the only time. I was petrified! This is my first actual speaking role on-screen – after having had the starring role in a big budget movie. Now, I actually had to learn some lines," he wrote.

Most of Frampton's first scenes were physical, including pushing an outrigger canoe into the ocean, "looking like I've been doing it all my life." Dressed in his fatigues, hat, etc, his first take did not go as planned: "I'm running into the water holding this outrigger. I trip, fall, and go right under the water, and everyone's laughing behind their hands." The final scene of the day involved Frampton and Hudson sitting in the outrigger waving to the Duck as it took off. Frampton wrote, "I was supposed to laugh, but I couldn't laugh. I couldn't even muster a snicker. I actually wanted to cry at that point. I was so exhausted; it was so tiring doing all this stuff on the first day." The next day, however, Frampton found his groove and thoroughly enjoyed the remainder of the time he spent on the *Black Sheep* set.

When the show aired, Frampton was thrilled that they topped the ratings for the first 30 minutes; and history showed that this, the series' final episode, was the highest-rated episode of them all. Soon after, he got a call from a perturbed Barry Gibb, who was upset that "A Little Bit of England" aired prior to the release of *Sgt. Pepper's Lonely Hearts Club Band*. Frampton told Gibb he didn't care because he was getting to do some real acting.

Though it was only one episode, in Frampton's mind his time on *Black Sheep* was well spent: "I enjoyed that one week of shooting more than any one day in six months of *Sgt. Pepper*."

In a May 6, 2018, Facebook post that included a photo of him standing in the cockpit of Tallichet's 92132, Frampton reminisced about his week on *Black Sheep Squadron*: "Fantastic experience but alas 'twas the last episode…finale series…closer! So, the moral of this story is don't have me as a guest on your series. I can close you down in one episode! So much fun talking with dear Red West RIP. Talking about Elvis with Red was so amazing. Lovely man."

As second season reruns began in summer 1978, *Black Sheep Squadron* continued its nomadic existence on NBC's programming schedule. It started out on Wednesday's 9–10pm followed by a move to Friday night 8–9pm. There was some discussion of a third season, but ultimately the series was canceled for good. But that is not to say that Robert Conrad didn't have hope for that third season. In 2012, Bill Yoak noted a conversation he had with Conrad at a party in 1978, "He [Conrad] was a great guy to me. He treated me like family and always called me Yoak. He said, 'Yoak, come on over here. I've got a gift for you.' He gave me a bunch of five-dollar bills that had *Baa Baa Black Sheep* stamped on them. He said, 'I'm gonna put 500 of these in circulation, and they are going to be worth money one of these days because we are going to get this series started again. And when we do, I'm gonna fly in it because you're gonna check me out in the T-6. You watch, we're going to get that show going again.' I said to him, 'Bob, I hope so, man. I hope so.'" As we know now, it never happened. *The Black Sheep* had flown their last mission.

Though Robert Conrad and Stephen Cannell pushed for a third season, the ratings just would not allow it. While it was not highly rated at the time, *Black Sheep* developed a cult following in the decades since it ended and remains extremely popular as it approaches its 50th anniversary. (*Kenneth Johnson*)

EPILOGUE

Ironically, the series finale was the highest-rated episode of the series, receiving a 34 share, so one has to wonder why the show was canceled just when it seemed to be hitting its stride. On January 12, 2013, Robert Conrad and Larry Manetti sat down for a Q&A session on the *Hollywood Show*, where Conrad offered the following explanation: "It was canceled for violence by Women against Violence on Television, and now it is on MeTV

Thanks to the popularity of *Baa Baa Black Sheep*, Greg Boyington, pictured here with (L–R) Mira Slovak, Ernie Gann, and John Schafhausen at the 9th Annual Lynnwood Rotary International Air Fair, in Spokane, Washington, in July 1977, enjoyed a resurgence in popularity that continued beyond his death in 1987. (*Jim Larsen*)

at four o'clock and it is the number one syndicated television show, which thrills me." The statement was met with cheers from the audience, with one member telling Conrad that it was the number one show in Australia during the early 1980s. Blaming protestors for the demise of the show may have made for a good soundbite that drew cheers from the crowd, but it was not the sole reason.

So, what was the real reason? In a nutshell, there were two reasons: cost and ratings. Conrad spoke to the former in the November 14, 1976, edition of the *Asbury Park Press*: "The budget for the pilot (film) with all the fancy flying hardware was nearly $2 million [nearly $11 million in 2024 dollars]. The entire operation, our recreated island air strip, the aerial sequences, the whole bag – it's costly." In 2019, Chuck Bowman theorized, "The new guys that had ascended into leadership roles at NBC really couldn't understand all this World War Two Pappy Boyington kind of stuff. Some of them thought what was being spent on the airplanes was a waste of money, but, of course, without the airplanes, there was no series." The late Bill Yoak touched on that point as well in 2011: "At the time, *Baa Baa Black Sheep* had the highest budget of any series ever on TV, and I think that record still stands. It did not make the most money, but it set the record because they spent more money per episode because of those airplanes, and that is what made it a hellva authentic series."

Cost was only part of the equation; ratings were another. Jeff Sagansky, who was a newly hired programming executive in 1977, told the author, "It was just ratings. Back in those days the shares had to be above 30, and as I recall they were at 27 or 28. Today, that kind of share would be the most-watched show on TV, but back then it wasn't survivable." Frank Price said, "I left in '78 to take over Columbia Pictures, and there wasn't anybody around who was able to do what I could on the sales front. I think I could have gotten the renewal [for a third season], but unfortunately the ratings were anemic. We had an enthusiastic audience, but that was not enough." There you have it; ratings are what sheared the sheep.

From the summer of 1976 to the present day, much has been written about the show in various aviation history magazines, most of which have regurgitated the same statements about how well the flying scenes were done while twisting or outright fabricating aspects of VMF-214's time under Boyington from August 1943 to January 1944. With the advent of the internet, message boards, and ultimately social media, new critics have emerged. They scoff at the series' hype of Two-Fourteen, claiming that within the Marine Corps there were far more august and higher-scoring squadrons and more revered commanding officers that saw action in the Pacific and therefore more worthy of praise than Boyington and his Black Sheep. These claims are valid and worth touching upon.

In every theater of the war, particularly in the Pacific, the press ballyhooed the aerial victories scored by each squadron and its pilots, especially the aces because it boosted morale for the folks back home. At the end of the war, VMF-214 ranked sixth among Marine Corps squadrons in total victories with 127, and fourth among number of aces with 11. On the list of the 118 Marine Corps aces, Boyington is ranked third with 24 victories behind fellow Medal of Honor recipients Joe Foss with 26 victories and top Corsair ace Robert Hanson with 26. In addition, five Marine aviators carried the rare and exalted title of ace-in-a-day, including James Swett, who achieved the feat twice.

Therefore, with so many pilots and squadrons to choose from, why was Greg Boyington and VMF-214 singled out for a television show? The author believes there were five events that took place over the course of three decades that ultimately led to the series' premiere in September 1976. The first was the perfect storm of circumstances that led to Boyington forming a squadron using unassigned pilots and available Corsairs and being sent into combat in the middle of the Bougainville campaign. The second factor was Frank Walton's talent for utilizing the power of the press. Walton orchestrated four distinct media events that helped make the Black Sheep famous under Boyington's command. The first took place at Turtle Bay on September 11, 1943, just before they moved up to Guadalcanal. Walton arranged for a series of staged photo and filming opportunities showing pilot briefings, a mock scramble, and pilots strapping into their Corsairs, as well as taxi and take-off sequences. Many of the images from this session are among the most famous to come out of the Pacific War.

Three weeks later, Walton was on the flight line at Henderson Field, waiting for his boys to return from the morning mission, when he happened upon *Chicago Daily News* war correspondent George Weller. Seeing another opportunity to garner some media attention for the Black Sheep, he supplied Weller with personal information on the trio of Chicago-native pilots, how the squadron was formed, and the number of victories the squadron had scored up to that point. As a result, Weller wrote a series of articles on the squadron that appeared not only in the United States, but around the world. The name Black Sheep was well on its way to becoming a household name, especially when considering that shortly after this visit, Boyington went on a scoring spree and it began to appear as though he might be able to break the 26-victory record shared by Joe Foss and World War One ace Eddie Rickenbacker.

On December 23, 1943, Boyington downed four Zeros to bring his score to a well-publicized 24, only two behind Joe Foss. Within 24 hours the news spread across the US; it was even covered by Ed Sullivan in a radio broadcast. On December 27, Boyington scored a single victory, and thanks again to Walton he was interviewed by a radio correspondent immediately after he climbed from the cockpit. That afternoon, the media blitz continued with another series of now-famous photographs.

Back on October 6, the New York Yankees and St. Louis Cardinals played Game 1 of the 1943 World Series at Yankee Stadium. Days before the Black Sheep had pledged that they would trade aerial victories for baseball caps from the winning team. The Yankees won the

Capt. Frank Walton (seated second from left) was officially VMF-214's Intelligence Officer, but he was also a master at public relations. In the fall of 1943, he arranged four media events that resulted in some of the most popular photographs of the Pacific War. (*Frank Walton Collection, Emil Buehler Library, National Museum of Naval Aviation*)

series 4–1; but it was the Cardinals that responded to the *Black Sheep*, and on December 27, a series of photographs were taken of Chris Magee and Boyington, the top-scoring pilots in the squadron at the time, exchanging "caps for Japs." In addition, images were captured of the squadron's aces standing in front of F4U-1A BuNo. 17740 holding baseball bats, with the remainder of the pilots standing on the wings. All of them were wearing St. Louis Cardinals baseball caps.

For the next eight days, correspondents milled about the airfield on Vella LaVella waiting for Boyington to return from his missions, hoping that he'd broken the record. On January 3, 1944, Boyington and his wingman, George Ashmun, failed to return. They were last seen heading down into the clouds with almost a dozen Zeros on their tails. Though his boys, the Marine Corps, and the country hoped for the best, it seemed the hard-charging "Gramps" was dead. Four days later, the squadron completed their tour and once again headed to Sydney on R&R, but when they returned, they found the squadron would be broken up. In March 1944, President Roosevelt awarded Boyington a "posthumous" Medal of Honor.

With Boyington gone and the squadron broken up, the fame that had been cast upon the *Black Sheep* could very well have faded in 1944; however, on August 20, 1945, the news broke that Boyington had been found alive in a POW camp. The details were scarce, but they were soon confirmed, and the news soon made headlines across an already jubilant United States. While Boyington was recuperating in Hawaii, the Commandant of the Marine Corps arranged for a huge welcoming celebration and officially ordered all Black Sheep on the West Coast to San Francisco to meet Boyington's plane, where they literally carried him off the plane and into the throngs of reporters and photographers.

That evening, Chance Vought hosted a party at the St. Francis Hotel, essentially fulfilling Boyington's prophetic promise that he made to his boys on Christmas Eve 1943, "If you guys ever see me going down with 30 Zeros on my tail, don't give me up. Hell, I'll meet you in a San Diego bar six months after the war and we'll have a drink for old-times' sake." The evening of revelry was photographed by *LIFE Magazine*; and when the photos appeared in the October 6, 1945, issue of the magazine it marked the first time alcohol consumption appeared in the magazine, and for a brief moment, amid the euphoric celebrations at the end of the war, Boyington and his bastards were back in the limelight.

In October 1945, Boyington stood at attention on the White House lawn while President Harry Truman placed the not-so-posthumous Medal of Honor around his neck. In the months that followed, Boyington, accompanied by Walton, went on a nationwide tour, and received a war hero's welcome in every town and city he visited. In 1946, the publicity surrounding Boyington began to turn negative as the alcohol once again took control of his life, and in the coming years he had numerous run-ins with the law, jumped from job to job,

The *Black Sheep* offered to exchange "Caps for Japs" with the winner of the 1943 World Series. While the Yankees beat the Cardinals, it was the latter team that sent VMF-214 a boxful of caps. (*Frank Walton Collection, Emil Buehler Library, National Museum of Naval Aviation*)

Boyington told his pilots if he was ever shot down, he'd return to throw them a blowout party after the war. With the assistance of the Marine Corps and Vought, he delivered on that promise in September 1945 after 20 months as a POW. (*Frank Walton Collection, Emil Buehler Library, National Museum of Naval Aviation*)

and had a series of torrid affairs, broken marriages, and bouts with cancer due to his endless smoking. Although mostly negative, this publicity kept Boyington's name in the papers long after the war, thus prolonging his celebrity well after his fellow Marine aviators assimilated back into society and got on with their postwar lives.

The final cog in the machine that led to the creation of the series was Boyington's memoir. Today, there are hundreds of books dedicated to squadron histories and an equal number of autobiographies and biographies about individual veterans, but in the 1970s such an easily accessible proliferation did not exist. So, when Boyington originally published *Baa Baa Black Sheep* in 1958, he was way ahead of the power curve. The fact that his motivations were primarily monetary is beside the point, because it was excellent, it sold very well, and thus kept him in the public spotlight. One of the thousands of people that bought the book was Frank Price, whose affinity for the Corsair, not necessarily Greg Boyington, led him to turn it into a television series. The rest is not only television history, but Marine Corps and warbird history as well.

At the time, the show no doubt had a loyal following, which has grown stronger with the passage of time. But when *Black Sheep Squadron* failed to appear on NBC's schedule for the 1978/79 season, the veterans of VMF-214 could not have been happier, though for them the damage to their collective reputations, be it real or perceived, had been done and the feeling of betrayal by Boyington lingered. However, they had Frank Walton in their corner. As soon as *Baa Baa Black Sheep* hit the air, the former patriarchal figure of VMF-214 made it his personal mission to defend his men and set the record straight that the pilots of VMF-214 were not drunks, screwballs, and misfits, but honorable and accomplished men who put their lives on hold in order to take the fight to the Japanese. He took his first small step in 1978 with the previously mentioned three-page article in *TV Guide*. He wrote several additional pieces and submitted them to various magazines, but they were rejected. It was at that point that he began work on what became *Once They Were Eagles: The Men of the Black Sheep Squadron*, which was published in 1986. This is a treasured piece of history, and a valuable resource used in the production of this book. Though it mostly detailed the day-to-day operations of the squadron while under Boyington's command, the final chapters relayed the postwar lives of each officer and when the subject of the TV series came up, several took the opportunity to express their disdain for it.

Harry Johnson, who lost a draw of straws to be Boyington's wingman the day he was shot down, was the most succinct in his comments: "It was BS." Rufus Chatham, who was section leader in Boyington's division when he was shot down, said, "It's a shame about Boyington — he was a great leader who hasn't had much success with his personal life. He betrayed his former comrades by allowing that TV show to present such a distorted image of them. I resent the characterization of us as 'misfits' and 'screwballs.' Actually, Boyington was the only one of us who ever had any trouble."

However, other than Walton himself, none had more scathing remarks for the show than Denmark Groover, a veteran of both tours under Boyington. His first tour was cut short when his Corsair was severely shot up, leaving his right arm and leg paralyzed and his Corsair nearly unflyable. However, he managed to make it back to Guadalcanal and eventually recovered from his wounds in time for the Black Sheep's second tour. After the war, Groover went to the University of Georgia and earned a law degree. He also served in the state legislature and the Georgia Farm Bureau. In his book, Walton wrote, "One of the swiftest ways to get his [Groover's] blood boiling is to mention the TV series about the Black Sheep." Groover said, "It amounted to mass character assassination. I thought about suing them when it came out, but that would have just given it more publicity. The show brought down and deprecated men of considerable bravery and valor, and for them…I resent it." Even with those harsh words, Groover could see the situation from Boyington's point of view: "I feel some compassion for Greg; I am sure he participated because he needed the money. I am delighted, of course, that he is able to get something of a financial reward based on his combat record. It does seem a shame, however, for the others who contributed so much to the squadron's record, and indeed made possible Greg's record, to have been vilified – that was unnecessary, as well as completely ridiculous."

For some veterans, the passage of time did nothing to lessen the resentment. In an interview that appeared in the May 1997 issue of *Aviation History*, Fred Avey, a replacement pilot who joined the squadron in November 1943 during their second tour, told John Wukovits, "Television made it look like all we did was party, but that was in no way true. We never went up drunk. The only thing accurate about the show was that we flew Corsairs." He also referenced the 1976 reunion in Hawaii mentioned in Chapter 3: "We gave him [Boyington] hell for allowing them to do what they did, and he realized how upset we were and apologized to us, and he was not one to apologize very often."

There seems to have been one Black Sheep, Ed Harper, who didn't really care one way or the other about the show. When the show premiered, he told his kids, "It would have been nice to have all of those nurses there…it was not what their life was like at all, but it didn't really bother him because he knew the truth."

While his men rightfully blamed Boyington for the poor image the series cast upon them, one could argue that they also had Boyington and the series to thank for the fame that was bestowed upon them for the rest of their golden years. Because of the overwhelming popularity of *Baa Baa Black Sheep*, the book and the series, the members of VMF-214 were constantly sought out for interviews, public appearances, and autographs up until the last plank owner of the squadron passed away in 2014. In his 2003 memoir, *On Boyington's Wing: The Wartime Journals of Black Sheep Squadron Fighter Ace*, Robert McClurg acknowledged this fact: "Although our wartime exploits had already gained us notoriety among historians, I think the TV show did a great deal to establish us firmly in the minds of the masses, even those who didn't necessarily have a firm knowledge or interest in WWII history."

In the final years of his life, Boyington remained a public figure, particularly at airshows, where he could often be seen selling autographed copies of his book, which by 1986, when the author received his copy as a Christmas gift, was in its 17th reprint. At these airshows and speaking engagements at schools and civic organizations, Boyington no longer pushed the false narrative that the men in his squadron were misfits but added that the embellishment was necessary because "no one ever wanted to make a movie about Boy Scouts." Boyington further defended "his" series when he would tell gatherings that the series wasn't embellished any more than any other television show and backed up the claim by saying, "I've been thrown into enough jails in this country and abroad to know that TV police shows, for example, are not more than ten percent accurate."

He also echoed Robert Conrad's sentiments that the show was not canceled because it wasn't a good show and that they got more mail from their fans than any other show on television at the time, many of which were from teenagers claiming that the show had inspired them to join the military. While the author could not corroborate Boyington's claims from 40-plus years ago, there are a multitude of warbird pilots who are today flying Corsairs and other warbirds who aspired to become aviators as a result of the series that arguably made the Corsair the most famous fighter of World War Two.

While the Wildcat had been the hero of the Pacific in the first year and a half of the war, it was soon relegated to secondary duties aboard escort carriers while the Hellcat and Corsair took over front-line duty, including combat air patrols and fighter sweeps, where pilots were sure to rack up huge numbers of aerial victories. Looking at simple numbers, the Hellcat was built in greater numbers and therefore is credited with more victories than any other fighter in the Pacific Theater of Operations. However, thanks to its distinctive inverted gull-wing, massive propeller, unmatched performance, and a protracted military career that lasted until the late 1960s and included combat operations in Korea, Indochina, Nigeria, Egypt, and Central America, the fighter that won the hearts and minds of yesteryear's combat pilots, today's warbird pilots, and tens of thousands of ground-bound enthusiasts was the Corsair. In the case of the latter group, *Baa Baa Black Sheep* contributed greatly to that popularity.

The former group, those who have been fortunate enough to experience the rush of acceleration provided by the 2,000hp Double Wasp and have whipped the stick against their leg and watched the horizon spin wildly past that elegant inverted gullwing from the cockpit speak highly of the legendary fighter. When he first flew a Corsair in June 1943, Boyington said, "The Corsair was a sweet-flying baby if I ever flew one. No longer would we have to fight the Nips' fight, for we could make our own rules." On the set at Indian Dunes in 1976, Boyington's enthusiasm for the fighter hadn't diminished: "When those Corsairs taxied one by one on to the field and started giving it the old gun to take off…that peculiar howl of those engines…a little shiver went up my spine. It was just like 35 years ago and almost as if I was taking off with them." Steve Rosenberg, who flew Bob Guilford's F4U-7 133693 on three filming sorties in August 1976 and logged 350 hours in the aircraft, said in 2012, "The Corsair really was a Cadillac – simply a wonderful airplane. It rolls much better than a Mustang, which made it a great airshow airplane." In 2012, the late Tom Friedkin told the author his favorite airplane was whichever one he was sitting in, but he echoed Rosenberg's statement: "The Corsair is simply a very lovely and smooth airplane."

Between 2002 and 2023, there were five Corsair-centric gatherings that added to the Corsair's already immense popularity. The first was the "Gathering of Corsairs and

Boyington (in blue leisure suit) was ever present on the set at Indian Dunes where the sight and sound of the Corsairs never failed to thrill him. (*John Cassidy*)

Legends," which took place at the Indianapolis Air Show in September 2002. At that time there were approximately ten to 15 airworthy Corsairs worldwide, and the event featured seven examples, including F4U-4 97359. Also, in attendance were more than a dozen Corsair veterans, including former Black Sheep Glen Bower, Tom Emerich, Ed Harper, William Heier, and Allan McCartney. The event was also attended by Robert Ginty, Jeff MacKay, and Red West. In an article that appeared in the January 2003 *AIR&SPACE*, Larry Lowe wrote, "Ginty made no attempt to vindicate the television series; 'I think everybody knew that the show was kind of unrealistic,' he said. 'It was really meant as a kids' show. It was not meant to show anything about war.' However naive the character of T.J. was, Ginty is no dilettante. He holds a deep regard for the original Black Sheep."

In summer 2005, the Connecticut Air & Space Center in Stratford, Connecticut, where more than 7,800 Corsairs were built, hosted Corsairs Over Connecticut, a multi-faceted event that celebrated the 60th anniversary of the end of World War Two and honored the

Above: In April 2011, original Black Sheep members Ed Harper, Harry Johnson, and Jim Hill, gathered at MCAS Yuma, Arizona, for what was likely the last reunion of squadron plank-owners. Dan Friedkin, son of Tom Friedkin, contributed his F4U-4 62940, which wears Korean War-era *Black Sheep* markings, as a backdrop with a VMA-214 AV-8B Harrier II. (*Phil Myers*)

Opposite: In the mid-2000s, nearly 30 years after *Baa Baa Black Sheep*, the popularity of the Corsair hadn't waned as evidenced by five examples that gathered in Bridgeport, Connecticut for "Corsairs Over Connecticut" in June 2005. Here, FG-1D 67089 leads F4U-4 97388 and FG-1D 95208. (*Richard Mallory Allnutt*)

men and women who worked on the home front and served in the military during the war. The highlight of the event was the gathering of five Corsairs, which participated in an air-to-air photo flight and a missing-man flyover. A second event held in 2011 was just as successful with five Corsairs again in attendance.

The Corsair is held in reverence by aviation enthusiasts around the world, and also by members of today's Black Sheep, most of whom are veterans of combat over Afghanistan, Iraq, Libya, and Syria. At what was perhaps the last reunion attended by original members of the squadron held at MCAS Yuma, Arizona, in April 2011, more than one of those young Harrier pilots were seen standing singularly and in small groups looking up in awe at the mighty Corsair that was positioned next to one of their Harriers. During a 60-minute panel discussion in the Black Sheep briefing room, the veterans were asked, "What made the aviators of the Black Sheep unique?" Harry Johnson replied, "There were a lot of good

squadrons in the Pacific that did a lot of great work. They just didn't get the publicity or a bad tv show named after them."

The Connecticut gatherings were well attended and praised by those who were there, but the 2019 Thunder Over Michigan (TOM) Air Show stands out, for it featured a Gathering of Corsairs that attracted 11 Corsairs, thus making it the largest since 1964, when the Aeronavale marked the type's retirement from service with a 16-plane flyover at Cuers AB in Toulon, France. The show in Michigan was to feature a pair of Corsairs from the show, Vintage Wings of Canada's FG-1D 92106 and John O'Connor's F4U-7 133710, but just weeks before the event, both aircraft were involved in separate incidents that thankfully did not result in any fatalities but inflicted damage on both aircraft that will take several years to repair.

Thanks to the release of the film *Devotion*, starring Glen Powell and Jonathan Majors, in 2022, Oshkosh Air Venture 2023 would also feature a gathering of Corsairs. With seven in attendance, it was not as large as TOM four years prior, but among the aircraft and pilots it was a direct connection to *Baa Baa Black Sheep*. Among the former, it was obvious, as the Florida-based American Honor Foundation had brought F4U-4 97359 to the show. The pilot connection, however, was not so obvious for throughout the week Jim Tobul's combat veteran F4U-4 97143 and the Warbird Heritage Foundation's FG-1D 82050 were flown by Scott Yoak, son of the late Bill Yoak, who was among the pilots that flew in the show nearly 50 years ago.

Among those who attended these events were Generation Xers who remember watching the show as children and eagerly purchased the series on DVD when it was released in 2005 and 2016. Then there were the younger generations that became fans of the show by way of the DVDs and/or MeTV. All the drinking, brawling, jiggling, hokey storylines, and historical inaccuracies aside, the overall story brought to our living rooms by Stephen Cannell was one of how a seemingly washed-up old man against all odds gathered a group of unknown pilots, molded them into an effective fighting unit, unleashed them on the enemy, and made them famous – the ultimate underdog story, for which Americans love to cheer. However, the stories would have meant nothing if they weren't backed up by what are arguably the most incredible flying scenes ever filmed, which left the staccato roar and silhouette of the Corsair forever burned into our psyche and still captivate us to this day.

Therein lies the legacy of the series – that if you show me a Corsair aficionado, I'll prove to you they're a fan of *Baa Baa Black Sheep*.

Oshkosh 2023 featured another gathering of Corsairs to commemorate the release of the film, *Devotion*, which told the story of ENS Jesse Brown and Lt(jg) Thomas Hudner. At the controls of this FG-1D from the Warbird Heritage Foundation was Bill Yoak's son, Scott. (*Stephen Chapis*)

Among the seven Corsairs that gathered at Oshkosh 2023, was *Baa Baa Black Sheep* star F4U-4 97359. Owned by the American Honor Foundation and flown by Zach McNeill, the aircraft is finished in the markings it wore in combat with VF-44 *Hornets*. (*Stephen Chapis*)

Pictured off the coast of Virginia Beach on October 24, 2021, is F4U-4 97359 and FG-1D 92508 from the Military Aviation Museum. The flight was in honor of Charles "Obie" O'Brien, CDR, USN (Ret), who flew '359 off the decks of USS *Boxer* & *Lake Champlain* during the final six weeks of the Korean War. (*Stephen Chapis*)

BAA BAA BLACK SHEEP COLOR PROFILES

(Flyers only. Shown in order of appearance)
Illustrations by Jim Laurier

Curtiss TP-40N, 44-47923 (N923), Tallmantz Aviation. First episode: "Flying Misfits" (season 1, episode 0), September 21, 1976. Total episodes: 1.
Oddly enough, the first aircraft to appear on screen in "Flying Misfits" was not a Corsair, but a P-40. The fighter was owned by Tallmantz Aviation at the time and flown by Frank Tallman.

Canadian Car & Foundry Harvard Mk.IV, RCAF 20380 (Zero replica–N7757), Challenge Publications. First episode: "Flying Misfits" (season 1, episode 0), September 21, 1976. Total episodes: 31.
The Challenge Zero appeared in more episodes than any other Tora aircraft. It was seen in various paint schemes throughout but could always be identified by its red wingtips. The scheme depicted here is from the pilot episode.

Canadian Car & Foundry Harvard Mk.IV, RCAF 20473 (Zero replica–N296W), William Childers. First episode: "Flying Misfits" (season 1, episode 0), September 21, 1976. Total episodes: 31.
This second Zero to appear in the series almost always appeared in formation with the Challenge Zero. It was distinguished by its round wingtips and lack of a tailhook and anti-glare panel. In "Meatball Circus" this Zero appeared with flashing lights in the machine gun barrels. It was also fitted with a camera on the rear fuselage to capture a Zero on the tail of a Corsair. Footage obtained during those sorties was used throughout the series.

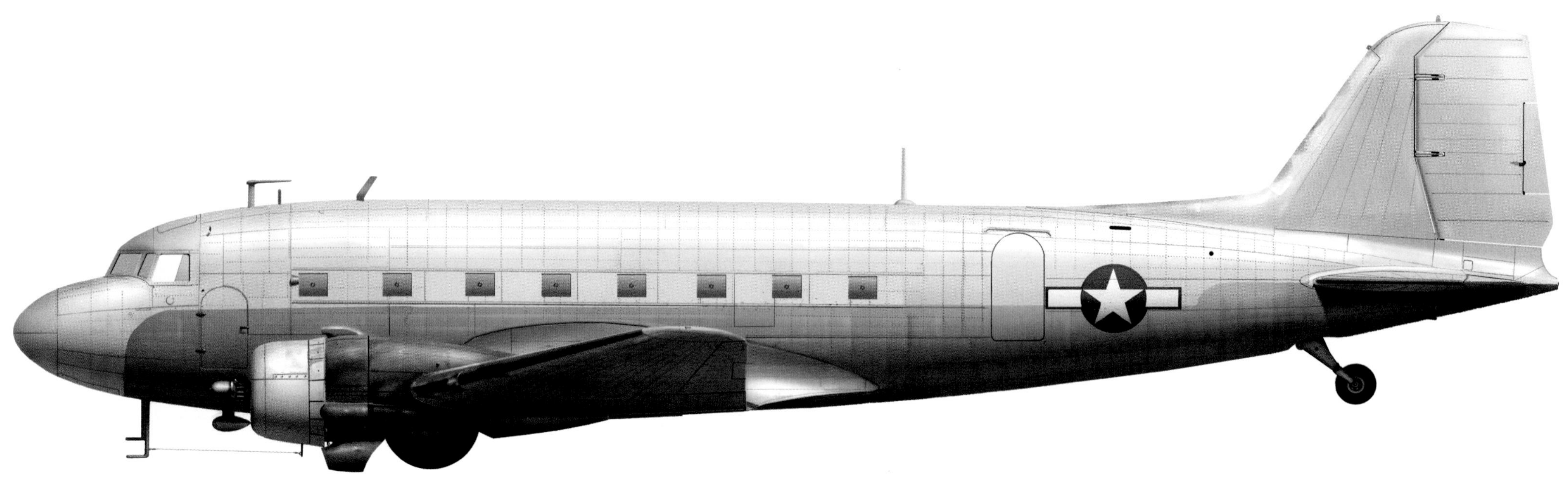

Douglas C-47B, USAAF #45-1059 (NC23650), Joel Friedland. First episode: "Flying Misfits" (season 1, episode 0), September 21, 1976. Total episodes: 25.
This aircraft was only involved in first-season filming but made numerous appearances in the second season due to canned footage obtained in the first season. It was lost at sea during a ferry flight to Hawaii on July 29, 1979.

Vought F4U-4, BuNo. 97359 (N97353), Thomas Friedkin. First episode: "Flying Misfits" (season 1, episode 0), September 21, 1976. Total episodes: 35.
The series' sole F4U-4 wore a variety of markings throughout its 35 episodes. It is shown here as it looked in August 1976 when a camera was fitted to the vertical stabilizer. This aircraft saw combat in Korea, won a grand champion award at Oshkosh, and competed at the Reno air races.

Goodyear FG-1D, BuNo. 92132 (N3466G), David Tallichet. First episode: "Flying Misfits" (season 1, episode 0), September 21, 1976. Total episodes: 35.
The pair of Tallichet-owned FG-1Ds appeared in 35 episodes of the series. Unlike its sister ship, which went on to fly once more as an award-winning warbird, this aircraft suffered an engine failure while taxiing at Chino in 1978 and has not flown since. It's currently under restoration to airworthy condition at the Tri-State Warbird Museum near Cincinnati.

Goodyear FG-1D, BuNo. 92629 (N62290), John Stokes. First episode: "Flying Misfits" (season 1, episode 0), September 21, 1976. Total episodes: 32.
Throughout the series, this aircraft was alternatively seen with and without a nine-victory scoreboard. The same holds true for the white arrow on the upper right wing. It was often seen fitted with a smoke generator under the fuselage.

Goodyear FG-1D, BuNo. 92106 (N6897), David Tallichet. First episode: "Flying Misfits" (season 1, episode 0), September 21, 1976. Total episodes: 35.
This was the only Corsair in the series that was equipped with a framed bubble canopy. In 2003, after an extensive 13-year restoration, this aircraft won Grand Champion WWII Trophy at AirVenture, Gold Wrench Award for Airpower Unlimited at AirVenture and Rolls-Royce Aviation Heritage Invitational Trophy of People's Choice Trophy at Reno. It was severely damaged in a landing accident in 2019 and is currently being restored to flying condition.

Vought F4U-7, BuNo. 133710 (N33714), John Schafhausen. First episode: "Flying Misfits" (season 1, episode 0), September 21, 1976. Total episodes: 35.
This aircraft, which often was on screen as the personal aircraft of Pappy and Gutterman, is an apparent Aéronavale combat veteran, having seen action in Algeria and the Suez Crisis. After spending 31 years in Canada and Virginia, it was acquired and restored by John O'Connor but suffered damage in a take-off accident in 2019 and is currently undergoing restoration.

Goodyear FG-1D, BuNo. 92433 (N3440G), Junior Burchinal. First episode: "Flying Misfits" (season 1, episode 0), September 21, 1976. Total episodes: 30.
This FG-1D was easy to identify thanks to the ADF football under the fuselage. It was also seen on occasion with the tailwheel extended. This aircraft was lost in a hangar fire in 1979.

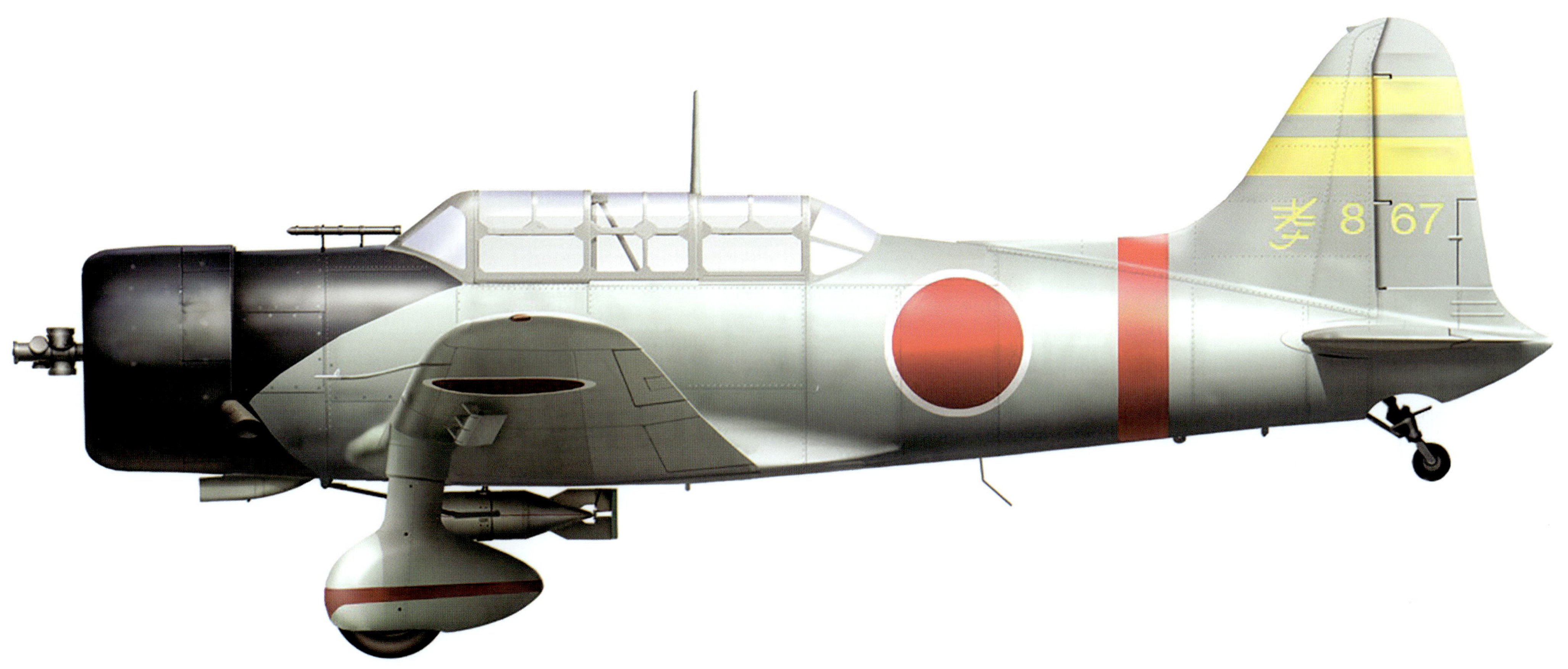

Vultee BT-13B, 42-90263 (Val replica, N56867), Tallmantz Aviation. First episode: "Flying Misfits" (season 1, episode 0), September 21, 1976. Total episodes: 11.
The Tora Vals that appeared in the series could only be told apart by the stripes on their wheel pants. The Tallmantz aircraft had red scallops.

North American SNJ-4, BuNo. 27675 (Kate replica, N7062C), Reyline Aviation. First episode: "Flying Misfits" (season 1, Episode 0), September 21, 1976. Total episodes: 8.
Just prior to *Black Sheep*, this Kate appeared in the Universal film *Midway*.

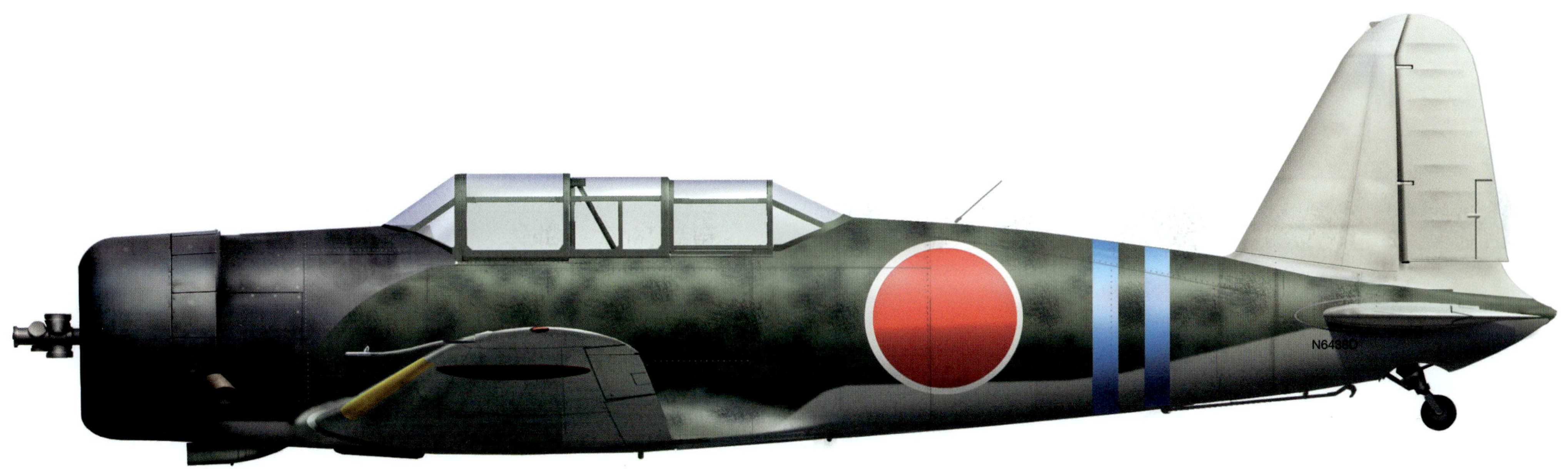

North American SNJ-4, BuNo. 90654 (Kate replica, N6438D), Challenge Publications. First episode: "Flying Misfits" (season 1, episode 0), September 21, 1976. Total episodes: 7.
When filming of *Tora! Tora! Tora!* concluded, this Kate sat derelict for three years before being acquired by Challenge Publications.

Canadian Car & Foundry Harvard Mk.4, RCAF 20326 (Zero replica, N15799), Confederate Air Force. First episode: "Flying Misfits" (season 1, episode 0), September 21, 1976. Total episodes: 29.
Four years after *Baa Baa Black Sheep*, the two "green" Zeros from the CAF gained notoriety for their dogfight with F-14s in *The Final Countdown*. This specific Zero is also famous for its participation in the first Tora airshow in 1972.

Canadian Car & Foundry Harvard Mk.4, RCAF 20408 (Zero replica, N15797), Confederate Air Force. First episode: "Flying Misfits" (season 1, episode 0), September 21, 1976. Total episodes: 29.
Four years after *Baa Baa Black Sheep*, the two "green" Zeros from the CAF gained notoriety for their dogfight with F-14s in *The Final Countdown*. This specific Zero is also famous for its participation in the first Tora airshow in 1972.

Grumman J2F-6, BuNo 35587 (N67790), Tallmantz Aviation. First episode: "Best Three Out Of Five" (season 1, episode 1), September 23, 1976. Total episodes: 4
Prior to *Baa Baa Black Sheep*, Frank Tallman made this Duck famous by performing an aerobatic routine in the aircraft at the Reno Air Races. This aircraft appeared in four episodes, two in each season. Today, it hangs in the Cold War Gallery at the National Museum of the United States Air Force in Dayton, Ohio.

Stinson L-5G, 45-34950 (N60552), Planes of Fame Museum. First episode: "Small War" (season 1, episode 2), September 28, 1976. Total episodes: 10.
This L-5G was one of seven aircraft from the Planes of Fame collection to participate in filming. It was acquired by Ed Maloney in 1961 and remains with the museum today.

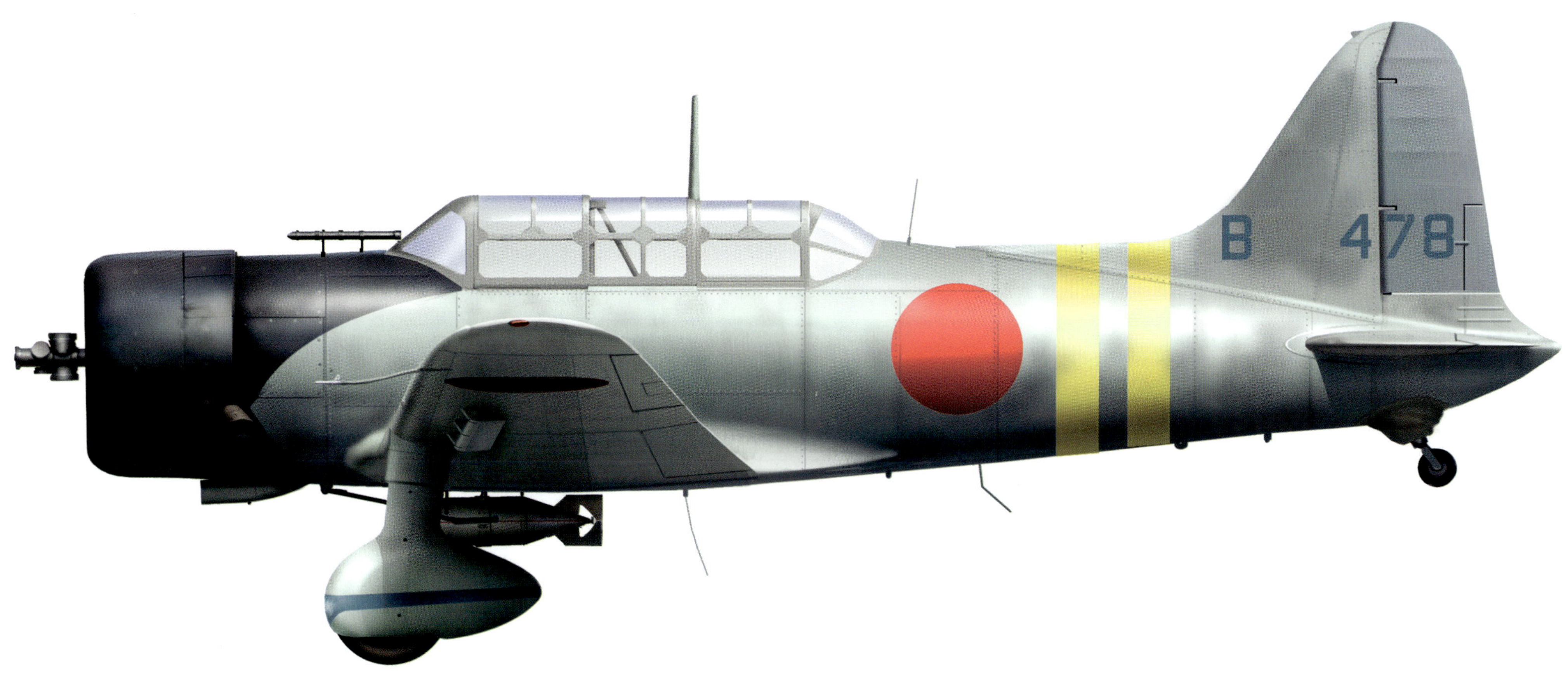

Vultee BT-13A, 41-22926 (Val replica, N56478), Challenge Publications. First episode: "High Jinx" (season 1, episode 3), October 5, 1978. Total episodes: 8.
Shortly after its time on *Baa Baa Black Sheep*, this aircraft joined the CAF in 1983 and has been flown by two generations of Tora pilots. Its movie career extended into the 21st century when it appeared in *Pearl Harbor* in 2001 and *Letters from Iwo Jima* in 2006. It is currently based in Conroe, Texas, with Zeros N15796 and N15799.

Vought F4U-7, BuNo. 133693 (N33693), Robert Guilford. First episode: "High Jinx" (season 1, episode 3), October 5, 1976. Total episodes: 21.
This aircraft, the 41st of 94 F4U-7s to roll off the Grand Prairie, Texas, production line, only flew three filming sorties in August 1976. However, there was enough film in the can for it to be seen in 22 episodes, including "War Biz Warrior" where it was seen carrying a pair of 500lb bombs.

North American B-25J, 44-30801 (N3699G), Challenge Publications. First episode: "Meatball Circus" (season 1, episode 6), November 9, 1976. Total episodes: 5.
After serving most of its military career as a VIP transport and hack, this B-25J became an agricultural sprayer. In addition to its appearance on *Baa Baa Black Sheep*, the Mitchell also appeared in the 1969 film *Catch-22* and is known today as *Executive Sweet*.

North American B-25J, 44-30423 (N3675G), Planes of Fame Museum. First episode: "Up For Grabs" (season 1, episode 7), November 16, 1976. Total episodes: 7.
This B-25 has been part of the Planes of Fame collection since 1960. In addition to *Baa Baa Black Sheep*, it has made a half-dozen other film and television appearances.

Canadian Car & Foundry Harvard Mk.4 20225 (N15796), Tallmantz Aviation. First episode: "Trouble at Fort Apache" (season 1, episode 18), February 15, 1977. Total episodes: 5.
This Zero appeared late in season one and was seen in five episodes by way of recycled footage. In addition to *Baa Baa Black Sheep*, its film resume includes *Tora! Tora! Tora!*, the tv movie *Shack*, and *Aces: Iron Eagle III.*

North American SNJ-5, BuNo. 90790 (N3375G), Planes of Fame. First episode: "W*A*S*P*S" (season 1, episode 20), March 1, 1977. Total episodes: 11.
This SNJ-5 from the Planes of Fame Museum appeared near the end of the first season. It was identifiable by its standard SNJ wing and pronounced stinger on the rudder. The canopy came from the museum's original A6M5 Zero.

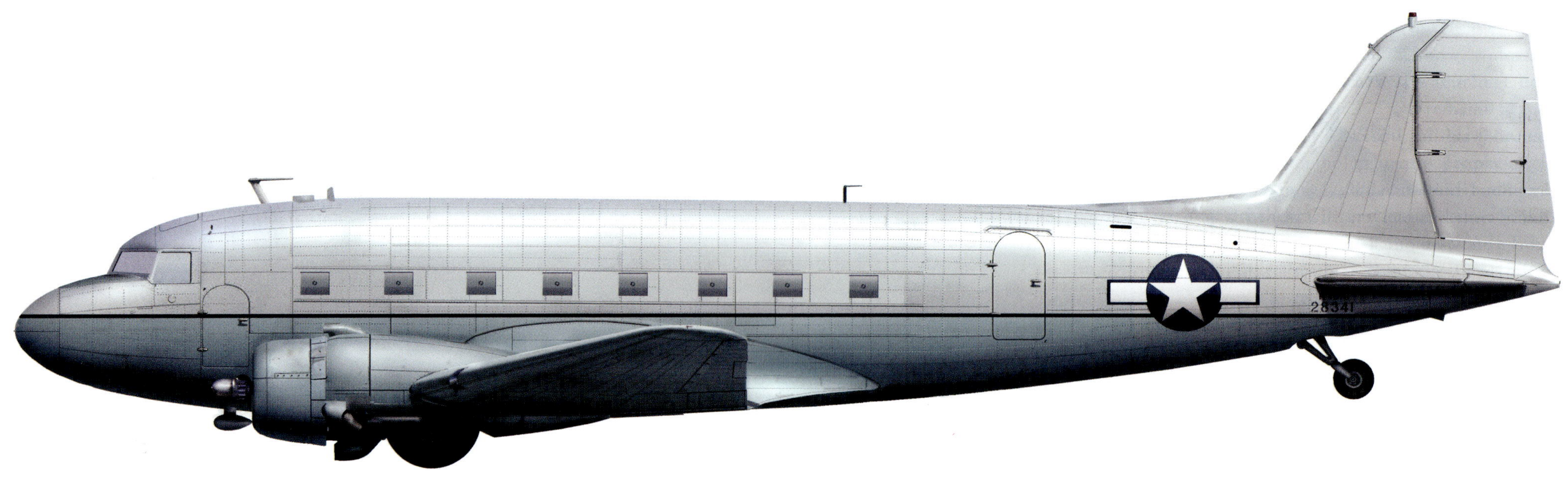

Douglas DC-3, c/n 3278 (N28341), Joel Grundy. First episode: "Divine Wind" (season 2, episode 1), December 14, 1977. Total episodes: 11.
This aircraft, which appeared only in the second season, became the first DC-3 to carry paying passengers with Delta Airlines.

Vought F4U-1A, BuNo. 17799 (N83782), Planes of Fame Museum. First episode: "Divine Wind" (season 2, episode 1), December 14, 1977. Total episodes: 11.
Aside from in "Wolves In The Sheep Pen" (E4, January 4, 1978), when it appeared as the Corsair assigned to VF-28 pilot Ensign Duggie Ibold, this aircraft was always seen in basic markings.

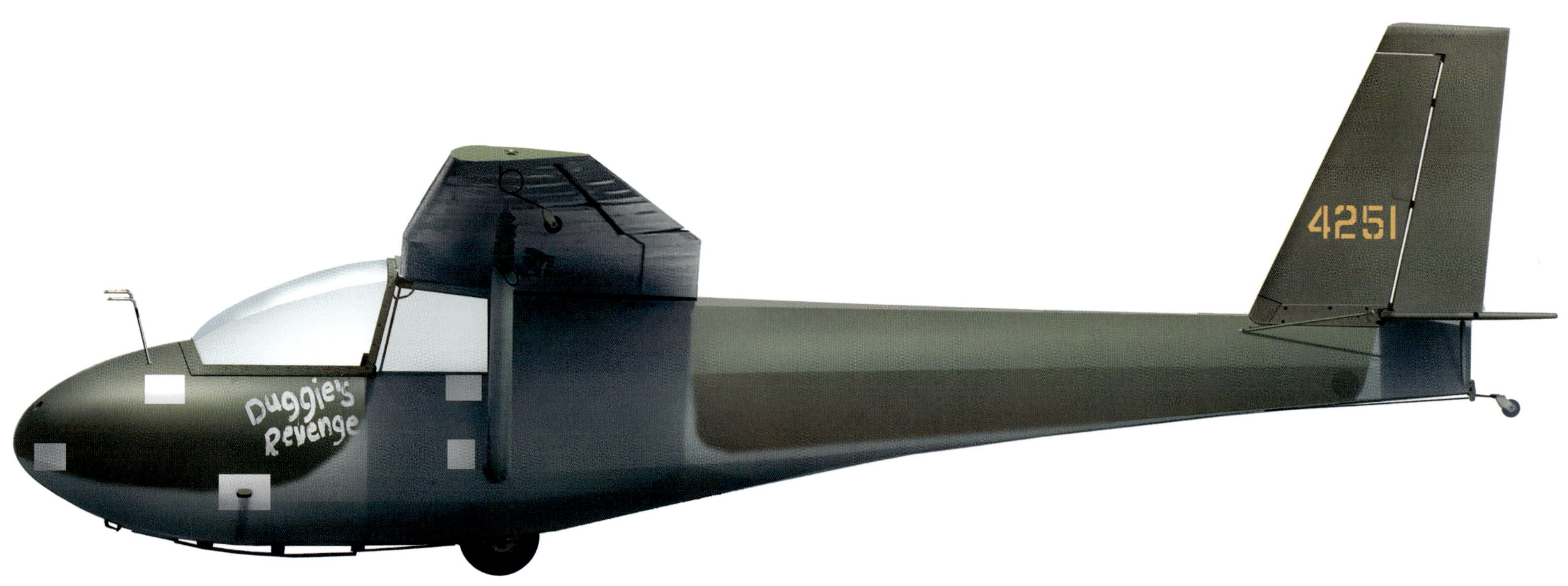

Schweizer SGS 2-33. First episode: "Operation *Stand Down*" (season 2, episode 5), January 11, 1978. Total episodes: 1.
The identity of this glider remains unknown.

North American SNJ-5C BuNo, 90649 (N7976C), Junior Burchinal. First episode: "The Iceman" (season 2, episode 9), March 8, 1978. Total episodes: 1.
Among the quintet of converted Harvards flown in the series, this solitary stock SNJ appeared in the second season.

Lockheed P-38L, USAAF #44-53097 (N3JB), John Stokes. First episode: "Hotshot" (season 2, episode 10), March 15, 1978. Total episodes: 1.
Originally built as a P-38L in April 1945, this aircraft was converted to an F-5G in June of that year and subsequently flown into storage. After a year as a gas station attraction, the aircraft entered service with the Honduran Air Force in 1948 and returned to the United States in the early 1960s. Shortly after *Baa Baa Black Sheep*, this aircraft and John Deahl were lost in a fatal crash.

Lockheed P-38L, USAAF #44-26961 (N6961), John G. Deahl. First episode: "Hotshot" (season 2, episode 10), March 15, 1978. Total episodes: 1
Upon leaving the Lockheed's Burbank facility, this P-38L was converted into a P-38M night fighter, but never saw service. After two decades with the Honduran Air Force, where it rarely flew, the aircraft returned to the United States in the late 1960s and passed through a number of owners before being ensconced in Seattle's Museum of Flight, where it remains to this day.

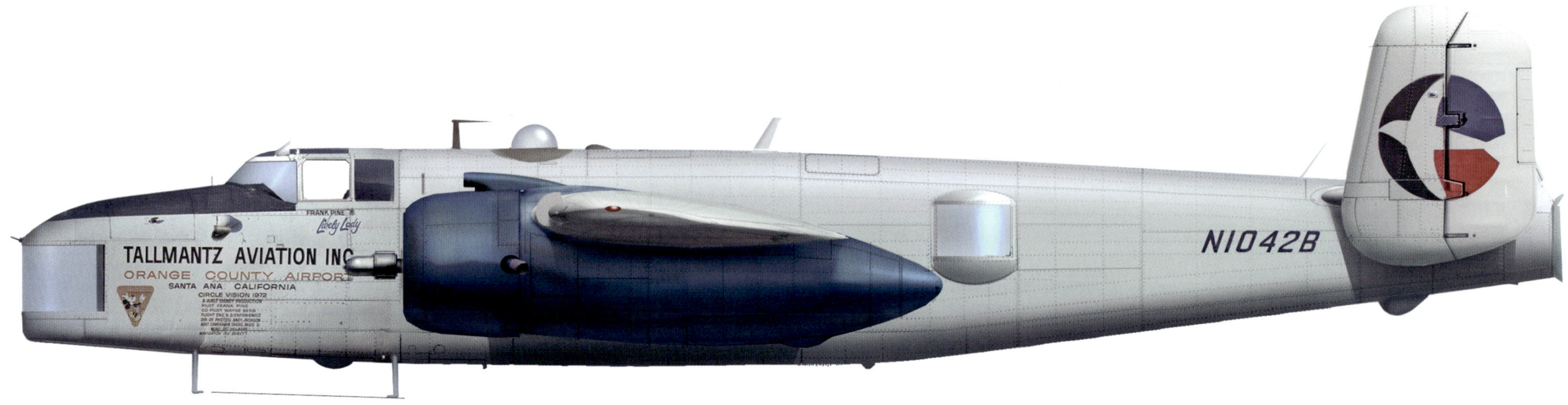

North American B-25J, USAAF #44-30823 (N1042B), Tallmantz Aviation.
After a 13-year military career, this B-25 was acquired by Tallmantz Aviation in 1962 to serve as a motion picture camera ship. The first film in which the aircraft was used was *How The West Was Won* (1962) and by the time it began work on "Flying Misfits", it'd been used in more than a dozen motion pictures. Today, it flies with the Mid America Flight Museum as a standard B-25J, but the famous camera nose has survived.

North American T-28R-1, USAF #49-1587 (N28DS), Thomas Friedkin.
Built as a T-28A in 1950, this aircraft was purchased by American Compressed Steel just five months after it was retired from the Air Force. After its time on *Baa Baa Black Sheep*, this aircraft saw action around the pylons at Reno and Phoenix.

THE CORSAIRS

Regardless of what the actors thought, the Corsairs were the real stars of *Baa Baa Black Sheep*. The motley octet of bent-wing birds included four FG-1Ds, two F4U-7s, one F4U-1A, and one F4U-4, and all have quite diverse histories both prior to and after the series: Five are combat veterans, two have turned hot laps at Reno, and two are Oshkosh Grand Champions. Since the conclusion of *Black Sheep Squadron* in 1978, two of the Corsairs have been lost, an FG-1D in a 1979 hangar fire and an F4U-7 in an unfortunate dual-fatality crash in 1984.

Of the remaining six aircraft, two are actively flying, one is maintained in airworthy condition but not flown, and three are currently under restoration to airworthy condition. All are pristine, well-maintained, pampered even, warbirds that are cherished by their owners and enthusiasts alike. However, as we will hear from four of the pilots that flew on the show, that was not always the case.

When the Corsairs began flying on camera, some had only flown a few hours since they had been retired from military service decades before and had only received enough maintenance to get them airworthy. There were many problems – engine problems, fuel leaks, hydraulic and electrical issues, and bad radios, just to name a few. These issues were often compounded by hard flying, as a majority of the sorties were flown at slower-than-usual speeds in close formation, often at low altitude, through canyons and sometimes 40-plus miles out to sea. Regardless, Steve Hinton said in 2012, "The airplanes were in less-than-ideal shape, but as worn out as they were, they got the job done."

What follows is a brief history of each Corsair, presented in order of appearance, and recollections of the men who flew them in front of the cameras of *Baa Baa Black Sheep*. You will notice with several of these aircraft that they are not merely inanimate objects, but conduits that have brought people together from across decades and generations. That is the real magic of warbirds.

The Corsairs that "served" together on *Baa Baa Black Sheep* came from varied military backgrounds. John Schafhausen's F4U-7 reportedly saw extensive combat in Algeria and the Suez Crisis with the Aéronavale, Junior Burchinal's FG-1D 92433 was one of the first Corsairs attached to VF-101 when the squadron was formed in 1952, and David Tallichet's FG-1D 92132 served in no fewer than three active Marine Corps squadrons. (*Mark Schafhausen*)

The pilots that flew the Corsairs were equally varied. Steve Hinton was just starting his career at Planes of Fame, while World War Two veterans John Schafhausen, Tom Mooney and Glen Riley followed up their military careers with success in commercial aviation. (*Jim Farmer*)

Vought F4U-7 BuNo. 133710 (N33714/C-GWFU/N965VC)

First episode: "Flying Misfits" (pilot, season 1, episode 0, aired September 21, 1976)
Total episodes: 35
Identifying features: Overall blue paint; four-blade propeller with silver hub and yellow tips; chin scoop; thick blue antenna behind cockpit; four 20mm cannons; white wheels; and "33714" under horizontal stabilizer.

This first of two F4U-7s used on the show was the 58th of 94 F4U-7s produced for the French Navy (Aéronavale) at the Chance-Vought plant in Grand Prairie, Texas. This aircraft arrived at NAS Karouba, Tunisia, in November 1953, and by the turn of the decade the aircraft was assigned to 15 Flottille (15F) at Hyères, where it was involved in a landing accident on July 15, 1960. Although there are no records to confirm it, there has long been speculation that '710 saw action in France's long-running Algerian War (1955–62) and in Operation *Mousquetaire* during the Suez Crisis. During the former, it is believed that '710 flew its missions from the deck of CVL *Bois Belleau* (formerly USS *Belleau Wood*, CVL-24), the only carrier to have launched strikes in Algeria.

By the time the Aéronavale marked the retirement of the F4U-7 with a 16-plane flyover at Cuers AB on September 28, 1964, our subject Corsair had gone to Quantico, Virginia, where it was restored over a number of years by the Marine Corps Aviation Museum. While it was impressive looking in a basic USMC scheme complete with rockets, it simply seemed out of place since the Marine Corps never flew the F4U-7. In 1971, Dean Ortner traded FG-1D BuNo. 92013, ex-N1978M, to the museum for the F4U-7 and placed the French fighter on the US register as N33714. Though it may have seemed trivial at the time, that registration number led to decades of confusion, some of which continues to this day, that this aircraft was actually BuNo. 133714. So, to set the record straight, the Corsair on these pages is 133710, not 133714. The latter aircraft ceased to exist a long time ago.

Ortner sold the Corsair to John Silberman in January 1973, but his stewardship was short-lived, as he sold it to Spokane resident John "Shifty" Schafhausen less than two months later. In preparation for its appearance in *Baa Baa Black Sheep*, the aircraft was painted in overall dark blue with the star-and-bar insignia, but there were minor variations in the scheme throughout the series. In "Flying Misfits", it was Capt. James Gutterman's assigned aircraft and sported five Japanese kill markings under the windscreen on the right side of the nose and "CAPT GUTTERMAN" under the canopy rail.

Schafhausen flew the Corsair until 1983, when he sold it to Blain Fowler of Camrose, Alberta, Canada. Fowler registered the aircraft as C-GWFU, named it *Alberta Blue*, and flew it extensively over the next 21 years. Fowler sold the fighter to Philip Rogers of Manassas, Virginia, and owner of Optical Air Data Systems (OADS), a high-technology firm that specializes in high-power fiber optics. There were plans to turn the aircraft into a technology testbed, but those plans never came to fruition and Rogers put less than six hours on the -7's clock during his 14 years of ownership.

In 2014, John O'Connor purchased the fighter and, while performing the pre-buy inspection in Manassas, Sam Taber, owner of TAB Air, discovered metal in the engine; so, the QEC was pulled and sent to Anderson Airmotive with the nose bowl, side cowls, accessory cowls, etc. By November 2015, the engine had been reinstalled and the aircraft ferried to Tab Air's shop at East Troy, Wisconsin, where a thorough IRAN was performed, during which original factory paint was found in the hellhole and tail cone.

Once TAB Air completed work, the Corsair was delivered to Ken Kaminski's Flying Colors Aviation, in Benton Harbor, Michigan, in March 2017, where it was cosmetically

Seen here at MCAS Quantico, Virginia in 1964, F4U-7 133710 spent seven years at the Marine Corps Museum before it was traded to Dean Ortner for FG-1D 92013 in 1971. (*Jim Sullivan*)

converted to represent the gray-over-white AU-1 Corsair BuNo. 129378, which had been flown by former *Black Sheep* Col John S. Bolt, the only Marine Corps pilot to make ace in two wars, the only Marine Corps jet ace, and the Marine Corps' last ace. The scheme paid homage to Vought's AU-1, a Corsair variant that has been all but forgotten by all but the most ardent Corsair aficionados and tied in nicely with this F4U-7's television star power as one of the *Baa Baa Black Sheep* Corsairs.

The aircraft was scheduled to appear at the Gathering of Corsairs at the 2019 Thunder Over Michigan, but it was involved in a take-off accident at Jerome County Airport on May 16, 2019. O'Connor suffered minor contusions and abrasions, but the Corsair received substantial damage to the landing gear, wings, and propeller blades, which damaged the engine mount and the internals of the R-2800. Sadly, it'll be many years before the aircraft takes to the sky again.

Canadian Blain Fowler cared for 133710 for 21 years and flew it extensively during that time. During the next 14 years, while based in Manassas, Virginia, it was rarely flown. When John O'Connor purchased the aircraft in 2014, it was refurbished by Sam Taber's TAB Air in East Troy, Wisconsin, and painted as an AU-1 by Ken Kaminski's Flying Colors Aviation in Benton Harbor, Michigan. (*Ken Kaminski*)

John O'Connor chose to paint his Corsair as the Marine Corps AU-1 flown by two-war Marine Corps ace and VMF-214 veteran John Bolt. (*Scott Slocum*)

Vought F4U-4 BuNo. 97359 (N97353/N240CA)

First episode: "Flying Misfits" (pilot, season 1, episode 0, aired September 21, 1976)
Total episodes: 35
Identifying features: Overall dark blue; four-blade propeller with yellow tips; silver propeller hub; chin scoop; one blue spike antenna and one white whip antenna behind the cockpit; six 50-caliber machine guns; camera mount on vertical stabilizer; silver wheels; and "97353" under horizontal stabilizer.

After F4U-4 BuNo. 97359 was accepted by the Navy on March 12, 1946, and delivered to NAS Tillamook, Oregon, it was placed in storage until October 1947. It was flown to another storage facility in Santa Ana, California, in November, followed by a four-month stint in the pool and FASRON 7 at NAS North Island in San Diego. Its first actual squadron assignment came in April 1948, when it was attached to the North Island-based VA-13A *Hellrazors*. Upon leaving the *Hellrazors*, '359 went through a period of maintenance and storage, after which it was flown to MCAS El Toro, California, where it flew with VMT-2 and Headquarters Squadron (HEDRON), which was part of Fleet Marine Forces Pacific (FMPAC). During this period, the aircraft flew an additional 167 hours.

On January 28, 1953, after passing through O&R shops in San Diego and Jacksonville, 97359 was assigned to a brand-new squadron, VF-44 *Hornets* at NAS Jacksonville, Florida, and soon made its way to Korea, where it saw extensive combat while flying from the decks of USS *Lake Champlain* (CV-39) and USS *Boxer* (CV-21). In the final years of its career, '359 served with VF-74 at NAS Quonset Point, Rhode Island; VX-2 at NAS Chincoteague, Virginia; and reserve squadrons in San Diego and Olathe. It was stricken at Litchfield Park in July 1956 with 1,798 hours. In November 1957, Bob Bean purchased the fighter for $1,500.99 ($16,265 in 2024 dollars) and stored it outside for 19 years.

Tom Friedkin purchased the Corsair on November 19, 1975, and it was in front of the Universal cameras just a few months later. The Corsair remained in the Friedkin collection until January 1988, when he sold it to the Duxford-based Old Flying Machine Company, where it flew in Royal New Zealand Air Force markings. It returned to the US in 1992 and passed through several owners over the next 20 years, including Norm Lewis, who briefly repainted the aircraft in VF-44 markings, and Max Chapman. In 2006, it was briefly reunited with its former *Black Sheep* co-star FG-1D 92106 at Vintage Wing of Canada (VWC) in Gatineau, Québec, Canada. In March 2008, it was purchased by Doug Matthews, who repainted the fighter to represent the Corsair flown by VF-32 pilot Lt(jg) Thomas Hudner on his Medal of Honor mission of December 4, 1950.

In 2010, it was discovered that retired Navy Commander Charles "Obie" O'Brien, a pilot flying with the Virginia Beach-based Military Aviation Museum (MAM), had flown this Corsair

After being saved from the smelter by Bob Bean, F4U-4 97359, photographed here in May 1970, spent nearly two decades sinking into the dirt at Moseley Field, Arizona, until Tom Friedkin acquired the aircraft in November 1975. (*Hank Rappone via Jim Sullivan*)

on three combat missions over North Korea in June 1953. At the time, Obie, then 83 years old, was the last pilot in the world who flew the Corsair in combat and still actively flew the type six decades later. When Doug, also a Naval Aviator, heard about Obie, he said without hesitation, "Well, he has to fly it again." It took more than two years to accomplish, but on Saturday September 22, 2012, Obie climbed aboard 97359 and took off on a reunion flight like no other.

Shortly after Obie's flight, Matthews sold the Corsair to Oklahoman Trent Latshaw. After flying the fighter less than 100 hours in a decade, Latshaw sold it to the newly formed American Honor Foundation (AHF). Upon learning about Obie's connection to the fighter, the foundation immediately had the aircraft repainted exactly as it appeared when Obie flew it in the summer of 1953. It made its public debut in its new VF-44 markings at Warbirds in Review at AirVenture 2021 in Oshkosh, Wisconsin.

In October 2021, AHF officials arranged to fly the fighter up to Virginia Beach, Virginia, to present it to 93-year-old Obie at a special event at the Military Aviation Museum. During the event Obie answered questions from spectators and was interviewed by Erin Miller from WTKR Channel 3. The event culminated in a flight demonstration of '359 and the MAM FG-1D that Obie had flown for ten years.

Less than five months after Friedkin saved it from oblivion, 97359 was hard at work in front of the Universal cameras. In the nearly five decades since *Baa Baa Black Sheep*, this aircraft has remained fairly active, with nearly a dozen owners in three countries. (*John Cassidy*)

Today, 97359 is in the collection of the Florida-based American Honor Foundation and is one of the finest F4U-4s flying today. (*Stephen Chapis*)

Goodyear FG-1D BuNo. 92106 (N6897/C-GVWC)

First episode: "Flying Misfits" (pilot, season 1, episode 0, aired September 21, 1976)
Total episodes: 35
Identifying features: Overall royal blue; three-blade propeller with blue hub and red/white tips; framed canopy; antenna ahead of cockpit; no national insignia on wings; short brown antenna behind cockpit; dark blue wheels; and "6897" visible under horizontal stabilizer.

Accepted by the Navy on May 17, 1945, FG-1D BuNo. 92106 was among the last Corsairs sent to the Pacific Theater of Operations, but it never saw combat and returned to the States in early 1946. Throughout the remainder of the 1940s, the aircraft was based in Norfolk, Jacksonville, New Orleans, and Seattle. In the '50s, the aircraft saw steady flight time while flying from air stations Grosse Ile, Dallas, and Spokane. On September 4, 1954, while still in Spokane, the aircraft was retired with 1,437 hours total time.

Len Berryman purchased the Corsair in 1958 and placed it in his amusement park/playground in Bridgeport, Washington. The fighter sat in the park until 1973, when the late David Tallichet saved the aircraft and returned it to flying condition just in time for *Baa Baa Black Sheep*. After the show's conclusion, Tallichet flew it to a number of VMF-214 reunions before placing the Corsair in storage.

In 1989, Gary Kohs purchased 92106 and enlisted John Lane's Airpower Unlimited to restore the fighter to factory-original condition. The project, which took 17,000 man-hours and 13 years to complete, set a new benchmark in Corsair restorations. At AirVenture 2003, it earned the Grand Champion WWII Trophy, and the Airpower Unlimited team received the Gold Wrench Award. Later that year, it was awarded the Rolls-Royce Aviation Heritage Invitational and People's Choice Trophies at Reno.

In 2007, VWC purchased the fighter and, using specialized vinyl decals, VWC applied markings to represent Fleet Air Arm Corsair KD568 (#115), the Corsair flown by Lt Robert Hampton Gray on the fateful August 9, 1945, mission over Japan, for which he was posthumously awarded the Victoria Cross. Like its co-star 133710, this Corsair was slated to appear at the Gathering of Corsairs, but on July 3, 2019, the aircraft was involved in a landing accident at Gatineau Executive Airport. Thankfully, the pilot recovered quickly from his injuries, but the Corsair incurred substantial damage that will take years to repair.

Before being acquired by David Tallichet, FG-1D 92106 spent 15 years in a playground in Bridgeport, Washington. After *Baa Baa Black Sheep*, the fighter was placed in storage until it was acquired by Gary Kohs in 1989, who had the aircraft restored to factory-original and award-winning status by John Lane's Airpower Unlimited. (*Jim Larsen*)

In 2007, 92106 was purchased by Vintage Wings of Canada in Gatineau, Ontario, Canada. Using vinyl decals, the fighter was transformed into Robert Hampton Gray's Corsair #568. On July 3, 2019, the FG-1D was damaged in a non-fatal landing accident. It has since been purchased by another owner and is undergoing restoration to airworthy status. (*Richard Mallory Allnutt*)

Goodyear FG-1D BuNo. 92132 (N3466G)

First episode: "Flying Misfits" (pilot, season 1, episode 0, aired September 21, 1976)
Total episodes: 35
Identifying features: Overall royal blue; three-blade propeller with silver hub and white/red/white tips; blue antenna ahead of cockpit; white whip antenna behind cockpit; dark blue wheels; and "3466G" in white under horizontal stabilizer.

Delivered on May 28, 1945, FG-1D BuNo. 92132 had a longer history with the Marine Corps than any of the other Corsairs in the show, having served with VMF-114, VMF-512, and VMF-323. From early 1947, the Corsair flew from Livermore, Oakland, New York, San Diego, Cherry Point, Jacksonville, and Columbus. At the latter field, '132 shared the ramp with its future co-star FG-1D BuNo. 92629. In December 1954, the fighter was flown into storage at Litchfield Park and stricken from Navy records on January 7, 1957, with 1,533 flying hours.

On October 20, 1959, the aircraft was purchased by Alu-Net Smelters for $485.67 ($5,078 in 2024 dollars) but was saved by Planes of Fame founder Ed Maloney, who placed it in storage. When Maloney first saw the aircraft at Litchfield Park in 1958, it was still wearing its NART Columbus markings and it more or less remained in that scheme until David Tallichet's Military Aircraft Restoration Group (MARG) purchased the Corsair on June 17, 1971, and brought it to airworthy status in April 1975. When it began flying on *Baa Baa Black Sheep*, 92132 had flown only 16 hours since being retired by the Navy 19 years prior. An additional 30-plus hours were put on the aircraft during filming.

The fighter remained in the MARG collection until Henry "Butch" Schroeder and the Midwest Aviation Museum in Danville, Illinois, acquired it on February 3, 1994. On April 1, 2003, the Corsair was acquired by the Tri-State Warbird Museum (TSWM) in Cincinnati, Ohio, where it has been undergoing on-again/off-again restoration. When complete, the Corsair will wear the historically correct markings of its former Columbus Reserve unit.

After two years in the Marine Corps, FG-1D 92132 went to the Navy Reserve for ten years. While assigned to Columbus the fighter served with FG-1D 92629. It was retired to Litchfield Park, Arizona, and was saved from the smelter by Ed Maloney in 1959. (*Jim Sullivan*)

In 1978, during the final weeks of *Black Sheep Squadron*, 92132 reportedly suffered an engine failure while taxiing at Chino and has not flown since. Today, it is being restored to airworthy condition at the Tri-State Warbird Museum in Cincinnati, Ohio. (*Stephen Chapis*)

Goodyear FG-1D BuNo. 92629 (N62290)

First episode: "Flying Misfits" (pilot, season 1, episode 0, aired September 21, 1976)
Total episodes: 32
Identifying features: Medium-blue upper surfaces; light-blue lower surfaces; dark-blue overspray on cowl, under cockpit, and vertical fin; three-blade propeller with gloss-blue hub and yellow tips; nine Japanese flags under windscreen; white arrow on upper right and lower left wing; white wheels.

This Corsair was in the last batch of 2,302 FG-1Ds produced by Goodyear. After acceptance on August 18, 1945, it spent the next five years at Alameda, Glynco (storage), Jacksonville, Norfolk, and Litchfield Park. Upon being pulled from storage in July 1951, it was sent to Jacksonville for maintenance and afterward it served in Seattle and Alameda; on June 12, 1952, it was assigned to MCAS Moffett Field, California, where it joined VF-713 *Vultures*. In January 1953, the aircraft departed Moffett for its new assignment with NART Columbus, where it joined the aforementioned 92132.

After another period of maintenance in Jacksonville, it was flown north to New York in October 1953. Three months later, '629 was joined by 92433, and the two Corsairs would serve together until '629 departed for Litchfield Park for the second and final time. It was stricken on January 7, 1957, having flown just 778 hours during its 13 years in the service.

In late 1957, it was one of 20 FG-1Ds pulled from storage and sold to Fuerza Aérea Salvadoreña (Salvadoran Air Force, FAS), where it saw action in the July 1969 Soccer War, where it ironically engaged F4U-5s and P-51Ds of the Fuerza Aérea Hondureña (Honduran Air Force, FAH) in what were the last aerial engagements between piston-

FG-1D 92629 was one of the five combat veterans to fly on *Baa Baa Black Sheep*. The fighter spent 17 years with the Salvadoran Air Force where it saw combat in the 1969 Soccer War and was one of the final Corsairs to be retired from active service. (*Dan Hagedorn*)

In the aerial scenes in the series, 92629 is easily identifiable by its over-sprayed markings and light blue underside. (*Jim Sullivan*)

engine fighters. Shortly after the Soccer War, three of the still-flyable Corsairs were donated to Sikorsky Memorial Museum in Bridgeport, Connecticut, but '629 was not among them. It and the other Corsair (BuNo. unknown) continued to serve in the FAS until October 1974.

The purchase from El Salvador was facilitated by Terry Randal of Har-Ran Aviation in Tulsa, Oklahoma. On October 28, 1974, Dr. Bill Harrison took off from El Salvador and delivered the aircraft to Tulsa a few days later, where it was on the US Register as N62290 by Bixby Aircraft Sales. On February 8, 1975, it was sold to John Stokes of San Marcos, Texas. In April 1977, just as the first season wrapped, Stokes sold the fighter to Robert Friedman of Highland Park, Illinois, after which it passed rapidly through a number of owners until its purchase by Business Aviation Services in Spring Park, Minnesota. In July 1983, the aircraft suffered extensive damage in an off-airport landing following an engine failure while taking off from Crystal Airport (KMIC) in Minneapolis. The wreckage was loaded on to a truck and sent to Fighter Rebuilders in Chino, California. On July 1, 1984, Steve Hinton made a successful test flight, after which it was ferried to Eden Prairie, Minnesota, as part of the Planes of Fame East. In summer 1986, Hinton returned the Corsair to California and the Palm Springs Air Museum in California. It is maintained in airworthy condition but has not flown since 2006.

Goodyear FG-1D BuNo. 92433 (N3440G)

First episode: "Flying Misfits" (pilot, season 1, episode 0, aired September 21, 1976)
Total episodes: 31
Identifying features: Overall royal blue; three-blade propeller with silver hub and red/white tips; antenna ahead of cockpit; blue-tinted windows behind canopy; large ADF football under fuselage; tailwheel is extended in some episodes; red bars on national insignia can be seen under faded white paint; silver wheels; and "N3440G" under horizontal stabilizer.

The Navy accepted this FG-1D on July 11, 1945, and immediately sent it to the pool in San Diego for almost two years. From October 1946, it served in Jacksonville, Dallas, Squantum, and a second stint in Dallas. In May 1952, it headed east to Oceana where it was among the first Corsairs assigned to the newly formed VF-101 *Grim Reapers*. However, by the end of the year the squadron transitioned to F2H-2 Banshees and 92433 served out its years in Minneapolis, Jacksonville, and New York. In November 1955, it was flown to Litchfield Park and stricken from Navy records on January 7, 1957, with 2,307 flying hours.

In April 1959, it was one of 40 Corsairs listed on an invoice/shipping document from Alu-Net Smelters of Long Beach, California. Frank Tallman purchased the aircraft from Alu-Net on May 7, 1959, and returned it to flight in 1962, at which time it had flown only three hours since its retirement. On September 16, 1969, the late Isaac Newton Burchinal (aka Junior) of Paris, Texas, bought the Corsair for his Flying Tigers Air Museum, where it was modified with a rudimentary second cockpit and flight controls, which were covered by a crude piece of Plexiglas canopy. Sadly, shortly after the end of *Baa Baa Black Sheep*, this Corsair was consumed by flames in a hangar fire at Addison Airport in Dallas, Texas, in 1979.

Junior Burchinal's so-called TFG-1D dual-control Corsair was the first of two *Baa Baa Black Sheep* Corsairs to be lost when it was destroyed in a hangar fire in 1979. (*Jim Sullivan*)

Vought F4U-7 BuNo. 133693 (CF-VUM/N693M/N33693)

First episode: "High Jinx" (season 1, episode 3, aired September 28, 1976)
Total episodes: 22
Identifying features: Glossy sea-blue with heavy dark blue sprayed over on cowling, ahead and behind national insignia, and vertical fin; four-blade propeller with black hub and yellow tips; chin scoop; four 20mm cannons, wide gray antenna behind cockpit; and white wheels.

The second F4U-7 to appear on *Baa Baa Black Sheep* rolled off the Grand Prairie production line 17 aircraft ahead of Schafhausen's Corsair. Delivered to the Aéronavale through the Military Assistance Program (MAP) '693 arrived at NAS Karouba, Tunisia, in spring 1953, where it served with Flottille 12F and later Flottille 15F. There is circumstantial evidence that while aboard CVL LaFayette (formerly USS *Langley*, CVL-27) in 1956, the Corsair saw combat over Indochina and Egypt. Later in its career, '693 was attached to Flottille 14F, where it may have seen action in Algeria. Its final assignment was a target tug with Escadrille 10S.

The Corsair returned to the United States in early 1967 and was refurbished at NAS Norfolk, Virginia. After a short stint with Lynn Garrison in Canada the -7 was purchased by Robert Guilford (1933–2006) in April 1970, who named it *BLUE MAX* and raced it quite extensively, albeit with Steve Rosenberg at the controls. After its engine failure in

Fresh off the production line in Grand Prairie, Texas, in 1953, F4U-7 133693 awaits delivery to the Aéronavale. The fighter saw combat in Indochina, Egypt and Algeria. (*American Aviation Historical Society*)

Lynn Garrison leads a trio of brand new A-7A Corsair IIs from VA-147 *Argonauts* in July 1967. Five months later, the squadron was launching strikes against North Vietnam from the deck of USS *Ranger*. (*U.S. Navy*)

August 1976 (*see* Chapter 3), *BLUE MAX* was completely refurbished over a three-year period and returned to flight in April 1979.

Once it was repainted in its former paint scheme, Rosenberg continued to race the fighter and perform his aggressive aerobatic routine until tragedy struck on May 10, 1987. On that day, Morris M. Moss, 62, and CAF member and airshow volunteer, 48-year-old Joyce D. Matthews, were killed when the fighter crashed, allegedly inverted, in a grain field near the Lower Otay Reservoir. It has long been said that Moss had been performing low-level aerobatics just prior to the crash. However, an article in the *Imperial Beach Star-News* reported that an FAA spokesman said there were reports to the contrary as several eyewitnesses stated there were no aerobatics and that the aircraft was "right-side up" when it crashed. Matthews' 29-year-old son Timothy flew with Moss before his mother and told reporters that on his flight there were only "straight fly-bys." Gary Danforth said Moss "was very safety conscious and it would not be consistent for him to perform risky, low-level aerobatics with a passenger on board."

Following its engine failure on August 19, 1976, Bob Guilford's Corsair, seen here prior to a test flight, went through a three-year restoration. From 1979 to 1987, when it was lost in a dual-fatality accident, it was active on both the airshow and air-racing circuits. (*Steve Guilford*)

Vought F4U-1A BuNo. 17799 (N83782)

First episode: "Divine Wind" (season 2, episode 1, aired December 14, 1977)
Total episodes: 11
Identifying features: Overall dark blue; three-blade propeller with silver hub and yellow tips; spike antenna behind cockpit; white wheels; and "N83782" under the horizontal stabilizer.

Due to its five-decade association with the Planes of Fame (PoF) Museum in Chino, California, Vought F4U-1A BuNo. 17799 is arguably the most well-known of the *Baa Baa Black Sheep*

Corsairs. It rolled off the Chance-Vought production line in Stratford, Connecticut, on August 31, 1943, making it one of the oldest surviving Corsairs in the world. For decades it was well known that 17799 served with VF-84, VFB-14, CASU-33, and VBF-84 before it was stricken from Navy records. However, PoF officials had long suspected that the Corsair saw combat with VBF-14 and/or VBF-98, but evidence was non-existent. Or was it?

In 1946, the Corsair was purchased by MGM Studios and had deteriorated into disrepair when Ed Maloney saved it and placed it in storage in 1970. The aircraft had deteriorated so much while at MGM, so Maloney acquired quite a cache of parts over the next few years. In early 1977, allegedly due to the departure of Burchinal's FG-1D, Steve Hinton and Jim Maloney began a program to get the Corsair airworthy, and on June 24, 1977, the F4U-1A received its Airworthiness Certificate and promptly joined the merry band of planes and pilots at Indian Dunes airport in time for filming of the second season.

In 2016, PoF's belief that '799 was a combat veteran was confirmed, thanks to a chance meeting between children's book author Michele Spry and 94-year-old Corsair veteran Ferrill A. Purdy, who'd flown with VMF-441 *Blackjacks*. While studying Purdy's logbooks, Michele found that of all the Corsairs

Left: In 1946, F4U-1A 17799 was purchased by MGM Studios, but the fighter sat derelict on the lot until Ed Maloney purchased the aircraft in 1970. The Corsair returned to flight in late 1977 and has been incredibly active for the last five decades at Planes of Fame. (*Jim Sullivan*)

Opposite: The long-held belief that '799 was a combat veteran was confirmed in 2016, when hard evidence proved that the fighter had seen action in the Pacific with VMF-441 *Blackjacks*. (*Frank B. Mormillo*)

Purdy had flown, one only survived to the present day – 17799. On June 15, 2016, Michele informed PoF historian Cory O'Bryan of her discovery, and they were both thrilled. At the same time, it was discovered that another *Blackjack* veteran, the late Edward Potter McAleer, had flown 17799 on six combat sorties against bypassed Japanese outposts in the Marshalls.

Since the early 2000s, when John Maloney performed a mild restoration on '799, it has worn a beautiful tri-color paint scheme. In 2020, however, the fighter was repainted in Korean War-era VF-32 markings for its big screen debut in the 2022 feature film *Devotion*, the story of Thomas Hudner and Jesse Brown. The aircraft remained in its movie digs until it was repainted in its current scheme during the winter of 2023/24.

The Planes of Fame Corsair (foreground) has appeared in numerous tv shows and commercials during its life, but it wasn't until the Columbia Pictures film *Devotion* in 2020, that it made its big screen debut. (*Wally Van Winkle*)

APPENDIX B

THE TORAS

When it came to providing a nemesis for Boyington and his *Black Sheep*, James Gavin and Frank Tallman had a ready-made Japanese Air Force available to them, thanks to the aircraft that had been built for the 1970 film *Tora! Tora! Tora!* Over the decades, the identity of the Kates and Vals was clear, but determining what Zeros flew in the series proved difficult. During the various interviews over the years, it was determined that a total of five Zeros flew on the show. However, in late 2023, a sixth Zero came to light, but its identity remained a mystery for months. Then, just weeks before the deadline, the author received a key photo from Tallmantz historian Scott Thompson. It showed a Zero on the ramp at Chino and it matched an aircraft seen late in season one and throughout season two, but the photo did not show an N-number. An email to Steve Hinton solved the mystery of the elusive sixth *Baa Baa Black Sheep* Zero. Here are the histories of each aircraft in order of their first appearance.

Canadian Car and Foundry Harvard Mk. IV
RCAF 20380 (N7757)

Mitsubishi A6M Zero replica
First episode: "Flying Misfits" (pilot, season 1, episode 0, September 21, 1976)
Total episodes: 31

This aircraft was delivered to the Royal Canadian Air Force (RCAF) as RCAF 20380 on August 19, 1952, and remained in service until October 12, 1967, having logged an incredible 8,000-plus hours. It was quickly snapped up by 20th Century Fox on June 24, 1968, registered as N7757, and converted to a Zero at Cal-Volair. After filming and storage in Long Beach, this was one of the two Zeros (the other was then-N296W) purchased by Ed Schnepf's (1930–2014) Challenge Publications (publisher of *Air Classics*) at the February 1971 auction at which 20th Century Fox tried to sell them outright. The auction was only moderately successful. Word at the time was that no one wanted anything to do

with the highly modified aircraft. In the July 1976 issue of *Air Classics*, Schnepf spoke of the auction: "Frank Tallman was also at the auction and after he vehemently described the vicious flying characteristics of the Tora birds, I had a hunch the old fox knew something I didn't. Once the auction started, I noticed Tallman's paddle was in the air with every bid. I began raising mine too and an hour later we left the auction, each the proud owner of five of the highly suspected machines."

While N296W was made airworthy rather quickly, N7757 was placed in storage at Van Nuys Airport (KVNY), where the Challenge fleet was based. When Challenge sold Niner Six Whiskey on December 22, 1973, N7757 was removed from storage and restored by Nelson Knuedeler and it remained very active with Challenge for the next 13 years, logging more than 300 hours on the airshow circuit.

Just prior to "Flying Misfits", this Zero appeared on *The Six Million Dollar Man* episode "Nightmare in the Sky" (season 4, episode 2, September 26, 1976), which starred Farrah Fawcett-Majors (1947–2009) and, coincidentally, Dana Elcar as Larry Stover.

Challenge sold the Zero to the Chino-based American Aeronautical Foundation on July 15, 1984, where it remained for two decades. On September 16, 2004, it was acquired by an owner from Senoia, Georgia, who operated the aircraft until December 7, 2015, when it was acquired by Lost Aviators of Pearl Harbor in Bellingham, Washington, an organization that was formed for the purpose of researching the eight American civilians, three of whom were killed, and aircraft that were airborne over Oahu when the Japanese attacked Pearl Harbor.

Of the five Zeros flown on *Black Sheep*, N7757 is the easiest to identify on screen, especially in "Flying Misfits", where it featured bold markings consisting of a red arrow running the length of the fuselage; squared red wingtips, which were original Harvard pieces because round tips were stolen when the aircraft was dismantled after the auction; yellow leading edges; and U3-757 on the vertical tail between two horizontal red stripes. However, these markings were short-lived, as they seemed to disappear after "Meatball Circus" (season 1, episode 6, November 9, 1976), after which the only positive way to identify this Zero is by its square red wingtips.

Less than a year after it was retired from the Royal Canadian Air Force (RCAF), this Harvard Mk. IV was purchased by 20th Century Fox for use in *Tora! Tora! Tora!* In 1971, the aircraft joined the Challenge Publications fleet and remained there for 13 years. (*James Larsen*)

This aircraft, along with the Zero that was then registered as N296W, appeared, usually together, in 31 episodes. Since 2015, N7757 has been part of the Lost Aviators of Pearl Harbor organization in Bellingham, Washington. (*Kedar Kedarmarker*)

Canadian Car and Foundry Harvard Mk. IV
RCAF 20473 (N296W/N60DJ)

Mitsubishi A6M Zero replica
First episode: "Flying Misfits" (pilot, season 1, episode 0, September 21, 1976)
Total episodes: 31

The Zero known today as *TORA 101* was the seventh-from-last Harvard delivered to the RCAF when it was taken on charge on January 14, 1953. It was originally based with the First Flight Training Squadron in Penhold, Alberta, followed by a stint at Centralia, Ontario. Then on February 2, 1968, after 6,000 flying hours, 20473 was released through the Crown Asset Disposition Center.

On August 16, 1968, the aircraft was acquired by 20th Century Fox for *Tora! Tora! Tora!* After two years in the Challenge Publications fleet, the aircraft passed through several owners, including Texas resident William C. Childers, who owned the aircraft during the *Baa Baa Black Sheep* years. It was acquired by J and R Investments in July 1992 and three years later, Douglas R. "Hollywood" Jackson, the "J" in J and R, purchased the plane outright, and over the next quarter-century displayed *TORA 101* in nearly 500 airshows. Sadly, on April 22, 2018, "Hollywood" passed away at the age of 63; and when *TORA 101* was put up for sale, it was purchased by David Prescott, who appreciates the history of this replica, and was a huge fan of *Baa Baa Black Sheep* as a kid and remains so today.

In January 2019, Prescott, a Navy veteran, related, "My passion, like many people, started with *Black Sheep Squadron*. As a kid I remember watching the show with my dad and then building plastic model airplanes and the first one we built was a Corsair." Prescott's first warbird was a T-6, which was followed by an FG-1D he acquired from the Evergreen Aviation Museum. When the opportunity to purchase this piece of *Baa Baa Black Sheep* history presented itself, David could not pass it up: "*TORA 101* is kind of unique in that I live in Albany, New York, and it's connected to a prop from *Tora! Tora! Tora!* that is on display at the Empire State Aerosciences Museum. They have a 30ft-long motorized model of the carrier *Akagi,* which is the same carrier the real *TORA 101* launched from on December 7. I also wanted the airplane because of its role in *Black Sheep Squadron*," he related.

Challenge Publications purchased Zero N296W along with N7757 but sold it to William Childers two years later. During the series, this Zero was fitted with a tail camera to capture footage of a Zero chasing a Corsair as well as lights in the gun barrels. (*Mark Schafhausen*)

In closing, Prescott summarized the influence *Baa Baa Black Sheep* had on him and others of his generation: "Today, I have the ability to buy and invest in different warbirds, and I do not have any interest in Army Air Corps airplanes from the European theater. My warbird interests lie in what you see in *Black Sheep Squadron*. Here's the reality of the matter: there was a whole generation of people that got interested in aviation, especially Naval Aviation, because of that show, and you can't discount that, and you can't put it any other way."

In 1992, CAF Tora pilot Douglas Jackson, purchased N296W, re-registered it as N60DJ, and displayed the aircraft in more than 500 airshows. Today, the Zero, known as *TORA 101*, is under the care of *Baa Baa Black Sheep* fan David Prescott. (*Greg Morehead*)

Vultee BT-13B Valiant USAAF #42-9026 (N56867)

Aichi D3A Val replica
First episode: "Flying Misfits" (pilot, season 1, episode 0, September 21, 1976)
Total episodes: 11

This Val was a regular at mid-Atlantic airshows for more than a decade and is considered the most original of the Tora Vals. Long before it became BI-211 though, it was Vultee BT-13B Valiant USAAF #42-90263, which rolled out of the Vultee production plant in Downey, California, and was accepted by the United States Army Air Forces (USAAF) on March 11, 1944. The next day, it was flown to Long Beach Army Airfield (AAF), California, and turned over to the 6th Ferrying Group, which included a squadron of Women Air Service Pilots (WASP). Subsequent to that assignment, '026 served at Bakersfield AAF, California; Deming AAF, New Mexico; and finally, Marana AAF, Arizona, where it remained for the duration of the war. Its military career ended on September 12, 1945, when it was turned over to the Reconstruction Finance Corporation (RFC).

The Valiant entered civilian life on December 22, 1945, when it was purchased by Orville Carbaugh of North Hollywood, California, for $766.50 ($12,966 in 2024 dollars). The aircraft was registered as N56867, which it retains to this day. Carbaugh sold the Vultee to John Hubbard of Glendale, California, just two weeks later, and over the next 22 years the aircraft passed through no fewer than seven owners. On August 8, 1968, the trainer was purchased by 20th Century Fox and sent to Stewart-Davis in Long Beach, California, for its transformation into an Aichi Val replica.

On February 28, 1971, Tallmantz Aviation purchased the aircraft and during its time on *Baa Baa Black Sheep*, this Val can be identified by the red stripes on its wheel pants. On March 9, 1987, the aircraft was purchased by Val-Air of Hershey, Pennsylvania, a business arrangement between Ken Laird, Al Wenger, and Gene Fisher. It was during this time that Laird first became involved in the Tora airshows. In 1991, the Val was sold to a new owner on the West Coast, but after years of seller's remorse, Laird bought the Val back on August 1, 1996.

Upon bringing the aircraft back to his home in Pennsylvania, Laird once again became involved with the Tora group. In addition to those shows, he displayed the Val at other airshows throughout the country, sometimes as many as 18 per year. In 2003, Laird began to scale back his airshow involvement but remained a regular participant at the Mid-Atlantic Aviation Museum's WWII Weekend in Reading, Pennsylvania, the 1941 Historical Aircraft Museum Group's "The Greatest Show on Turf" in Geneseo, New York, and "attacks" on the SS *John W. Brown* Liberty Ship during its Living History Cruises.

For Laird, the *Brown* flights were enjoyable and satisfying experiences, for he continued to operate the Val in the same role it has performed in for nearly four decades, that of a flying history lesson that tells the stories of the greatest global conflict the world has ever known. In the waning years of his ownership, Ken was succinct in his feelings about the Val: "I consider myself as merely a custodian of the Val and feel a great responsibility to preserve and display the airplane." In March 2023, Ken ended his association with his beloved Val when he donated the aircraft the Mid-Atlantic Aviation Museum in Reading, Pennsylvania.

The first of two Vals to appear in the series was N56867 that was, at the time, part of the Tallmantz collection. The two Vals were nearly identical except for the stripes on their respective wheel pants, with this aircraft's being red. After many decades of displaying the Val, Ken Laird donated the aircraft to the Mid-Atlantic Aviation Museum in Reading, Pennsylvania. (*Greg Morehead*)

North American SNJ-4 BuNo. 27675 (N7062C)

Nakajima B5N Kate replica
First episode: "Flying Misfits" (pilot, season 1, episode 0, September 21, 1976)
Total episodes: 8

The overall gray Kate flown in the series began life as North American SNJ-4 BuNo. 27675, which was delivered to the US Navy at NAS Dallas on April 22, 1943. It seems to have remained in Dallas until that August, when it was transferred to Corpus Christi, where it would serve with three separate training squadrons throughout the duration of the war. Throughout 1946 and early 1947, the aircraft operated from Corpus Christi auxiliary fields Rodd, Cuddihy, and Cabaniss. In June 1947, the aircraft was transferred to Florida and spent the rest of its career training fledgling Naval Aviators at Pensacola and the outlying fields Saufley, Corry, and Whiting. When it was stricken in August 1956, it had logged 6,115 hours total time.

The SNJ's first civilian owner was San Antonio-based Ace Smelting, Inc., but it was saved by Downey, California, residents Boyd H. Bentley, Robert C. Fortune, and Charles W. Robertson on February 22, 1957. The assigned registration number was N7062C, which it retains today. Over the next decade, Six Two Charlie passed through four additional Southern California owners before it was purchased by 20th Century Fox on August 7, 1968. After *Tora! Tora! Tora!* the aircraft was purchased by M. Mayer and S. Bedford of Beverly Hills, and during their ownership the Kate was repainted to represent a Vultee Vindicator for the 1976 movie *Midway*. Shortly, thereafter Mayer and Bedford sold the Kate to Eagle Aviation of Tulsa, Oklahoma. Whether its time on *Baa Baa Black Sheep* was completed by then is unknown, but over the next 27 years, the Kate passed through five owners in four states and appeared on the 1988 TV mini-series *War and Remembrance*.

On March 18, 2004, the Kate was acquired by Japanese Bomber LLC, a three-way partnership between CAF Cols Alan Armstrong, Keith Wood, and Joe Broker, of the CAF Dixie Wing. In June 2018, the author spoke with Armstrong about the Kate, and the first thing he mentioned was an unusual entry in the aircraft logbook, which states, "This aircraft has been subjected to a 10-hour flight test regime and the weights and airspeeds are *believed to be accurate*." Armstrong said, "That will certainly get your attention, right? She's not exactly a nice-looking airplane. There are a couple of places where she looks…not bad…but a little rough, like you can see a few areas where metal got crimped. You can see where the transition is between what came from the factory and what was modified for the movie; but then again, they didn't have CAD machines back then. They modified these airplanes with pencils and slide rules. Of course, the plan was to fly them for 30 hours in the movie and trash them. I'm sure no one back then expected these airplanes to be flying 50 years later."

The Tora Kate (N7062C) that is currently owned by CAF Col Alan Armstrong and based with the CAF Dixie Wing in Peachtree City, Georgia, logged more than 6,100 hours in the Navy as an SNJ-4. During *Baa Baa Black Sheep*, this Kate appeared in mottled overall gray scheme and appeared in eight episodes. (*Mosley Hardy*)

North American SNJ-4 BuNo. 90654 (N6438D)

Nakajima B5N Kate replica
First episode: "Flying Misfits" (pilot, season 1, episode 0, September 21, 1976)
Total episodes: 7

Upon its acceptance by the US Navy on September 12, 1944, SNJ-5 BuNo. 90654 was delivered to training squadron VN3D8 at Whiting Field, Florida, where it remained until December 1945. After three months at Ellyson, it was moved to Pensacola in March 1946, then into a long period of storage at Houma and Litchfield Park. It was removed from storage on July 28, 1952, and returned to Pensacola for refurbishment and delivered to

NARTU Jacksonville on September 27, 1952. After flying a little more than 170 hours, 90654 headed north to Fleet Aircraft Service Squadron Three (FASRON 3) just before Christmas 1954.

In March 1955, it embarked aboard USS *Intrepid* (CVA-11) for six months during one of the carrier's shakedown cruises. When it comes to verifying whether or not a particular warbird was deployed aboard an aircraft carrier, it usually involves making an educated guess based on often-scant historical documents because photographic evidence is often impossible to come by. However, such was not the case with 90654's assignment aboard *Intrepid*. The author took a chance and contacted the Intrepid Sea, Air & Space Museum, and the inquiry was answered by aviation curator Eric Boehm, who did a deep dive into deck logs, cruise books, and photograph collections, both digitized and non-digitized, and came up with two photographs from the right time period – and they show a single silver SNJ on the flight deck. While these photos do not show a BuNo., this is about as close as one can get to conclusive evidence that this aircraft spent time aboard "The Fighting I." The SNJ's final assignment was to the Naval Air Basic Training Command at NAAS Barin Field, Florida, where it was stricken on June 14, 1958, with 2,242 hours.

The San Antonio-based Arrows Sales, Inc. purchased the SNJ on August 25, 1958, for just $358.87 ($3,774 today), and like all of its co-stars it passed through numerous owners before it was purchased by 20th Century Fox on July 30, 1968. During the film, Three Eight Delta was painted in a green-over-gray scheme, with pale yellow tail surfaces with red horizontal stripes on the vertical stabilizer and rudder.

Post-*Tora! Tora Tora!* the aircraft sat in open storage until it joined the Challenge Publications fleet in November 1971, at which time it had more than 3,200 hours. Other than the

The second Kate (N6438D) to appear in the series was an SNJ-5 that once embarked aboard USS *Intrepid* (CVA-11) during a six-month shakedown cruise in 1955. During *Baa Baa Black Sheep*, the aircraft was part of the Challenge Publications fleet. (*USS Intrepid Museum*)

deletion of the red stripes on the vertical fin and the addition of two vertical blue stripes on the aft fuselage, the paint scheme was relatively unchanged during the filming of "Flying Misfits" and subsequent episodes of *Baa Baa Black Sheep*. During its time at Indian Dunes, the Kate flew a little more than 90 hours. Shortly after *Baa Baa Black Sheep*, the aircraft was stripped to bare metal, except for the *Hi no maru*, and remained with Challenge until it was sold to John M. Horecky of Houston, Texas, on March 23, 1984.

Horecky's time with the aircraft was short-lived, as he sold the aircraft to Tennesseans Douglas A. Peoples, Ronald J. Grasso, and Donald I. Argall on July 15, 1987; and although partners changed over the years, the Kate was in Peoples' care for nearly 30 years. Naturally, the paint was freshened up over the years, but the overall scheme remained the same, except that the tail surfaces were painted to match the rest of the aircraft and it took on the identity of EII-301. The aircraft is currently in the care of Hiroyasu Takai of San Jose, California.

Challenge sold N6438D to a new owner in 1984, but three years later it was acquired by Douglas Peoples, who flew the aircraft for almost three decades. Unlike when it appeared on *Baa Baa Black Sheep*, the Kate now flies with a replica torpedo. (*James Larsen*)

Canadian Car and Foundry Harvard Mk. IV RCAF 20326 (N15799)

Mitsubishi A6M Zero replica
First episode: "Flying Misfits" (pilot, season 1, episode 0, September 21, 1976)
Total episodes: 29

This Harvard Mk.IV, RCAF 20326, was delivered on June 10, 1952 and struck off charge on March 12, 1968, after having been in storage in Saskatoon, Saskatchewan, since November 1965. This was one of six aircraft acquired by Gerald Weeks in the February 1971 auction. Weeks donated the aircraft to the CAF in 1972, where it has remained ever since. This Zero holds a special place in CAF/Tora history, as it was one of four Zeros that participated in the first Tora airshow flown by the group in Galveston, Texas, on June 25, 1972, with Bob Bunton at the controls.

In addition to *Tora! Tora! Tora!* and *Baa Baa Black Sheep*, this Zero, along with N15797 (AI-114), also appeared in *The Final Countdown* (1980), in which they famously engaged in a 2v2 with F-14A Tomcats from VF-84 *Jolly Rogers*.

Opposite: Since it was donated to the CAF in 1972, N15799 has remained with the organization and has been displayed in countless Tora airshows as AI-113. (*Glenn Watson*)

Below: One of the so-called "Green Zeros" was N15799, which made Tora history when it appeared in the group's first airshow on June 25, 1972. This Zero, along with the second "Green Zero" appeared in 29 episodes, including "Flying Misfits". (*Robert S. DeGroat*)

AI-113
NX15799
COMMEMORATIVE
AIR FORCE

Canadian Car and Foundry Harvard Mk. IV RCAF 20408 (N15797)

Mitsubishi A6M Zero replica
First episode: "Flying Misfits" (pilot, season 1, episode 0, September 21, 1976)
Total episodes: 29

This Harvard Mk. IV RCAF 20408 was delivered on October 2, 1952, and struck off charge on March 25, 1968, the same day as its future co-star, N15796. This aircraft was another of six acquired by Gerald Weeks in the February 1971 auction. Weeks donated the aircraft to the CAF in 1972, where it has remained ever since. Like N15799, this Zero was also a participant in the first Tora airshow in Galveston, Texas, on June 25, 1972, with Ken Ross at the controls.

In addition to *Tora! Tora! Tora!* and *Baa Baa Black Sheep*, this Zero, along with N15799, also appeared in *The Final Countdown* (1980), in which they famously engaged in a 2v2 with F-14A Tomcats from VF-84 *Jolly Rogers*.

Pictured here at Sun 'n' Fun 1987, N15797 was the second "Green Zero" in the series and like N15799, it appeared in the first Tora airshow, 29 episodes of *Baa Baa Black Sheep*, the 1980 United Artists film *The Final Countdown* and remains in the CAF to this day. (*James Larsen*)

Vultee BT-13A Valiant USAAF #41-22926 (N56478)

Aichi D3A Val replica
First episode: "High Jinx" (season 1, episode 3, October 5, 1976)
Total episodes: 8

This BT-13A 41-22926 rolled out of Downey's doors on October 9, 1942, and was delivered to Pecos AAF, Texas, which was a primary pilot-training field and home to the 38th Flying Training Wing, where it remained until the 3024th AAFBU was established at Marana AAF, Arizona, in May 1944, where it likely served alongside its co-star N56867. Later that year, this Vultee moved close to where it came from when it was assigned to the 3035th AAFBU at Victorville AAF, California. Its final two assignments were 3034th and 3033rd AAFBUs at Stockton and Gardner AAFs, respectively, in California, after which it was turned over to the RFC for disposal.

On December 17, 1945, the RFC sold the aircraft to Rankin Aviation Industries of Tulare, California, for $755.16. When it was manufactured three years prior, it cost the taxpayers $18,082. Rankin placed it on the register as N56478. On June 10, 1947, it was purchased by Tulare resident Ray Franks, who held on to the aircraft for only five months. Between November 1947, when Franks sold the aircraft, and August 1968, when it was acquired by 20th Century Fox, this Vultee went through ten Southern California owners!

After the filming of *Tora! Tora! Tora!*, this was the third aircraft acquired by Challenge Publications on February 28, 1971. On screen in *Baa Baa Black Sheep*, this Val can be identified by the blue stripes on its wheel pants. The Val joined the CAF when it was purchased by Gene Armstrong in 1983, and he went on to display it in hundreds of Tora airshows until he gave it to the CAF's American Airpower Heritage Museum in 2000 with Gene staying on as the aircraft's primary sponsor. Although Gene has retired from flying, his son, W.E. "Gooser" Armstrong continues to display the aircraft. In addition to *Tora! Tora! Tora!* and *Baa Baa Black Sheep*, this Val appeared in *Pearl Harbor* in 2001 and *Letters from Iwo Jima* in 2006.

Another of the Challenge-owned aircraft was Val N56478, which can be identified by the blue stripes on its wheel pants. Unlike the other Val, which first appeared in "Flying Misfits", this aircraft made its series debut in the third episode, "High Jinx". The aircraft became part of the CAF in 1983 and remains with the organization today. (*James Larsen*)

Canadian Car and Foundry Harvard Mk. IV RCAF 20225 (N15796)

Mitsubishi A6M Zero replica
First episode: "Trouble at Fort Apache" (season 1, episode 18, February 15, 1977)
Total episodes: 5

This Harvard Mk. IV was delivered to the RCAF as 20225 on January 24, 1952, and struck off charge on March 25, 1968. On June 20, 1968, 20th Century Fox purchased the aircraft directly from Canada and registered it as N15796. After filming, it was acquired by Tallmantz Aviation in the auction on February 28, 1971. The Zero remained in the Tallmantz collection until Forrest G. Fisher of Boiling Springs, Pennsylvania, acquired it on February 17, 1987. Throughout the 1990s, it passed through three different owners in California, Illinois, and Michigan until it was acquired by Brian Reynolds, president of the Olympic Flight Museum in Olympia, Washington, in 2001. In addition to *Baa Baa Black Sheep*, this aircraft also starred in *Shack* (1977 TV movie) and *Aces: Iron Eagle III* (1992).

The fifth Zero to appear in the series was N15796, which made its first of five appearances in "Trouble at Fort Apache" (S1, E18); it was part of the Tallmantz collection from 1971 through 1987. Today, it resides at the Olympic Flight Museum in Olympia, Washington. (*Zane Adams*)

North American SNJ-5 BuNo 90790 (N3375G)

Mitsubishi A6M Zero replica
First episode: "W*A*S*P*S" (season 1, episode 20, March 1, 1977)
Total episodes: 11

This sixth and final Zero replica to join the show, SNJ-5 BuNo 90790, was accepted by the Navy on October 12, 1944, in Dallas, Texas. Over the next three years, the aircraft served with a variety of units including VS-50, aboard USS *Yorktown* (CV-10), and several Carrier Air Service Units. After a period of maintenance in Pensacola, the aircraft was placed in storage at Glynco, Georgia, until July 1948, after which it served at Anacostia, Pensacola, Monterey, San Diego, Miramar, and Alameda. From January to October 1954, it was at Kwajalein for the atomic bomb tests, followed by a brief stint at NAS Barbers Point, Hawaii. The aircraft was struck off charge on January 26, 1956, with a total of 3,311 hours total time.

Acquired by The Air Museum in 1961, the Texan was restored to flying condition by Bob Nightingale and Bob Oltersdorf and registered as N3375G. For the first decade it averaged just 10 hours a year, but as the need to train new warbird pilots rose it was pressed into service as a trainer.

In the middle of the first season, the Planes of Fame modified its SNJ-5 N3375G into a Zero replica. Fitted with the windscreen and canopy from the museum's original A6M, it appeared in 11 episodes beginning with "W*A*S*P*S" (S1, E20). (*Scott A. Thompson*)

In 1977, the SNJ was fitted with the canopy from the museum's Mitsubishi A6M5 Zero and pressed into service late in the first season of *Baa Baa Black Sheep*. Planes of Fame president Steve Hinton told the author in January 2024, "Soon after *Black Sheep*, Frank Sanders was flying it when the engine blew. We had to leave it at Oxnard for a year before we had another engine to put on it."

By 1979, the SNJ had been returned to its standard SNJ configuration, but that didn't keep it from being used as a Zero in the television mini-series *Pearl* in 1979 and *War and Remembrance* in 1987. Its lone appearance as a trainer on screen was in the 1985 film *Space*.

Today, this television and three-time movie star, N3375G, continues to fly at Planes of Fame, where it has been housed since acquired by Ed Maloney in 1961. (*Scott A. Thompson*)

THE ALLIES: FLYERS

Curtiss TP-40N Warhawk USAAF # 44-47923 (N923)

First episode: "Flying Misfits" (pilot, season 1, episode 0, September 21, 1976)
Total episodes: 1

Ironically, the first warbird to appear on-screen in the two-hour pilot, "Flying Misfits," was not a Corsair, but a Curtiss TP-40N then owned by Tallmantz Aviation and flown by Frank Tallman. Built by Curtiss in Buffalo, New York, P-40N USAAF #44-47923 (c/n 33915) was accepted by the USAAF on November 2, 1944, but was not delivered until March 3, 1945. On March 20, it arrived in Niagara, New York, where it remained for nearly three months. This aircraft was one of approximately 40 Warhawks converted into dual-control TP-40Ns. After its conversion, it was attached to the 2539th Army Air Force Base Unit (AAFBU) at Foster AAF, Victoria, Texas. At the time, Foster had an Advanced Single Engine training unit and a Fighter Gunnery School, but with available records it is not clear as to which school the TP-40N was assigned, if any. Shortly after the war ended, this fighter was delivered to the storage facility in Walnut Ridge, Arkansas, on October 3, 1945.

Howard LaVerne Pemberton of Kalamazoo, Michigan, purchased the fighter for $1,250 ($19,532 today) on March 25, 1946. However, it appears that Pemberton never flew the aircraft, which was eventually registered as N923. When the Limited Airworthiness Certificate was issued on July 25, 1957, the Aircraft Inspection Report indicates that the aircraft had logged only 65 hours TT since it was delivered to the USAAF.

On November 5, 1958, Paul Mantz Air Services, Inc. acquired the aircraft, and one can only assume that the Warhawk was ferried from Kalamazoo to Mantz's home base at Orange County Airport in Santa Ana, California. Just over three years later, ownership was transferred to Tallmantz Aviation. While with Tallmantz, N923 appeared in *Death Race* (1973 TV movie) and *Tales of the Gold Monkey* (TV series, 1982–83), in which *Baa Baa Black Sheep* star Jeff MacKay appeared. While on the set of "Flying Misfits" in 1976, John Schafhausen took Super 8 home movies of Tallman beating up Indian Dunes with multiple low passes and victory rolls.

When the Tallmantz collection was sold in 1985, Kermit Weeks purchased the fighter and placed it in storage for more than a decade. Restoration to airworthy status began in 1994, and N923 took to the skies again in April 2004 and still makes occasional flights from Weeks' airfield. As of December 2023, the aircraft is still on the US register, and the current certificate is good until March 31, 2030.

The Tallmantz TP-40N N923 spent less than 12 months in the USAAF, having been placed in storage in October 1945. It entered civilian life in March 1946, and was part of the Tallmantz collection from 1958 to 1987. During this time, the fighter appeared in *Tales of the Gold Monkey* and the TV movie *Death Race*. Today, it is part of the Kermit Weeks collection. (*James Larsen*)

Douglas C-47B USAAF # 45-1059 (NC63250)

First episode: "Flying Misfits" (pilot, season 1, episode 0, September 21, 1976)
Total episodes: 25

Just as it was during World War Two, a Gooney Bird was very much a part of both seasons of *Baa Baa Black Sheep*, the first of which was C-47B USAAF #45-1059. This aircraft rolled out of the doors of Douglas' Oklahoma facility on August 17, 1945, and was delivered to the 6th Ferry Group at Long Beach AAF, California, three days later. On September 6, the aircraft was ferried over to San Bernardino AAF (later Norton AFB), where it was assigned to the 4126th AAFBU. Although it is not clear, the Individual Aircraft Record Card (IARC) seems to indicate that the aircraft spent time in Cincinnati while still attached to the 4126th, but what is clear is that it was ferried to Ontario, California, on March 1, 1946, and turned over to the Reconstruction Finance Corporation (RFC) for disposal.

On the 28th of that month, '1059 was purchased by Lawrence D. Pudney of Burbank, California. The 36-year-old Pudney was a commercial pilot who sat on the board of directors of Havenstrite Air Service, Inc. The President was Russell E. Havenstrite of Havenstrite Oil Company. Born in Lovell, Oklahoma, Havenstrite moved to Signal Hill, California, to drill for oil in the early 1920s. In 1932, then-36-year-old Havenstrite headed for Iniskin, Alaska,

and began drilling there in 1938. Just before the outbreak of World War Two, he struck pay dirt when he discovered oil in Newhall, California. After the war, as the company's operations expanded, Havenstrite needed an aircraft to conduct his business that would take him to the remotest areas of the globe.

Alfred J. Ghezzi, Jr., of Seattle, Washington, purchased Two Five Zero and a spare R-1830–75 engine on December 18, 1957. The aircraft was repossessed on January 20, 1960, and eventually acquired by Gerald Duby of Fremont, California. During Duby's and subsequent ownership of Heady Aircraft Company, it seems the aircraft flew very little, if at all. It was purchased by Trans National Airlines on August 23, 1973.

In July 1979, Two Five Zero was flown to Long Beach to receive modifications for a ferry flight from San Jose to Honolulu. Aircraft Associates installed a pair of 400-gallon collapsible fuel tanks in the fuselage, and to keep the tanks stable during the flight they were supported by "plywood structure and steel bands." In addition to the tanks, a temporary HF radio and LORAN were installed in the cockpit. This equipment was essential for the nearly 2,600-mile flight over the vast Eastern Pacific Ocean. The names of the pilot and co-pilot have been lost to history, but the crew departed Norman Y. Mineta San Jose International Airport (KSJC) on July 20, 1979, and vanished. The exact circumstances are not known, but the crew must have been in communication with controllers in Hawaii because the accident report indicates that the temporary LORAN system in the aircraft failed, and the crew was forced to ditch when it ran out of fuel.

Columbia Aircraft Corporation J2F-6 Duck BuNo. 33587 (N67790)

First episode: "Best Three Out of Five" (season 1, episode 1, September 23, 1976)
Total episodes: 4

This aircraft was one of 330 J2F-6s built by Columbia Aircraft Corporation, which operated out of a small facility in Valley Stream, New York. This facility was home to Grumman from November 1931 to November 1932. This particular aircraft was part of the second production batch of Dash 6 Ducks and was accepted by the Navy on June 9, 1945, and delivered to NAS South Weymouth, Massachusetts, a week later. After a two-month stint at CGAS Brooklyn, it was transferred to CGAS Port Angeles, California, in October 1945, and remained there until it was stricken exactly one year later. Frank M. Corbit of Sebastopol, California, quickly bagged the Duck for just $1,500 ($25,070 in 2024 dollars) on October 21, 1946, and it was placed on the US register as N67790.

Corbit had the aircraft ferried to San Francisco, where it was refurbished and returned to the sky in August 1954. It is believed that the Duck was operated from a Sausalito seaplane base while under Corbit's and two subsequent Bay Area gentlemen's ownership. A decade after it left Columbia's production line, the Duck was still essentially a brand new aircraft, having logged just 100 hours total time as of August 1955.

The next owner, Richard E. Packard of Phoenix, Arizona, acquired the Duck on March 21, 1961. In 1960, Packard had founded Aircraft Specialties, Inc, an air tanker operation based at Falcon Field (KFFZ) in eastern Phoenix. The fleet of more than 50 aircraft included six TBMs and two Trackers, but Seven Niner Zero was the only Duck. Desert Aviation Service, which was co-located on the field, installed a 300-gallon water tank and flaps on the lower wings. The big amphibian, now Tanker Charlie 07, was painted white with red trim, sported a cartoon Duck superhero on the vertical fin, and flew in the 1962, '63, and '64 fire seasons.

Shortly after the 1964 fire season, the Duck was purchased by Ernest L. Terry of Tucson, who apparently was in the US Air Force, for on May 9, 1966, there was a legal document written up by an Air Force lawyer at Tan Son Nhut AB, South Vietnam, naming Terry's wife,

The J2F-6 Duck made famous by Frank Tallman's aerobatic displays, served in the US Navy and Coast Guard during World War Two. In the 1960s, it was operated as a fire bomber before it joined the Tallmantz collection in 1970. The aircraft appeared in four episodes of *Baa Baa Black Sheep*, two in each season. (Steve Guilford)

Norma, Special Power of Attorney. Suddenly, two weeks later, the Duck was sold! Whether it was Ernest's intention to have his wife sell the aircraft is not known, but it spent the next four years with Hart Marine, Inc, where it was utilized for offshore oil rig support. Interestingly, all of the firefighting gear was removed, but it retained its air tanker paint scheme.

On January 9, 1970, Tallmantz acquired the Duck and immediately put it to work, along with J2F-6 BuNo. 36976 (N1196N), in *Murphy's War* (1971) starring Peter O'Toole.

After its four appearances in *Baa Baa Black Sheep*, Seven Niner Zero was flown in the 1977 TV mini-series *The Amazing Howard Hughes*, in which Tommy Lee Jones played the eccentric aviation pioneer. On April 2, 1985, Kermit Weeks purchased the Duck and donated it to the then-United States Air Force Museum in exchange for a Nieuport in March 1986. Today it hangs in the Cold War Gallery and represents an OA-12 from the 10th Air Rescue Squadron at Elmendorf AFB, Alaska.

Kermit Weeks purchased the Tallmantz Duck in 1985 and ultimately donated the aircraft to the National Museum of the United States Air Force, where it hangs in the Cold War Gallery. (*USAF*)

Stinson L-5G Sentinel USAAF #45-34950 (N6055C)

First episode: "Small War" (season 1, episode 2, September 28, 1976)
Total episodes: 10

The Sentinel that appeared in the show was accepted by the USAAF on July 24, 1945, at the Consolidated-Vultee facility in Wayne, Michigan, where it apparently remained until it made a cross-country flight to McChord AAF, Washington, for assignment to the 161st Liaison Squadron. During the 17 months the aircraft spent with the squadron it traveled to most of the airfields the 161st operated from, including Gowen AAF, Oregon; Alexandria AAF, Georgia; and Biggs AAF, Texas. In December 1946, the aircraft was transferred to the 72nd Liaison Squadron at Langley AAF, Virginia, and remained with that unit until June 1951, when it was assigned to the 3585th Pilot Training Wing at Gary AFB, Texas. This was its final assignment.

On May 7, 1956, the Stinson was acquired by the Idaho Wing of the Civil Air Patrol and placed on the US register as N6055C. On October 3, 1961, Edward Maloney purchased the aircraft from Idaho resident D.J. Wilkins, who had owned the L-5 for a mere month. Maloney "owned" the aircraft until 1997, when the ownership passed on to Planes of Fame.

During its ten-year career in the USAAF/USAF, the L-5G that is now with Planes of Fame operated from airfields in Michigan, Washington, Oregon, Georgia, Texas, and Virginia. The L-Bird appeared in ten episodes, five in each season, and has been part of the Planes of Fame since 1961. (*Frank B. Mormillo*)

North American B-25J-25-NC Mitchell USAAF #44-30801 (N3699G/N30801)

First episode: "Meatball Circus" (season 1, episode 6, November 9, 1976)
Total episodes: 5

Now flying as *Executive Sweet*, the Kansas City-built B-25J USAAF #44-30801 was delivered on February 27, 1945. Her initial assignment was to Moody Field, Georgia, for multi-engine pilot training, but soon after it went into temporary storage. In May 1945, it was transferred to Maxwell Field, Alabama, where it served with three units, including the 502nd Air University Wing where it was used for transport and utility duties. In December 1947, she was assigned to Randolph Field, Texas, to be used for Flight Surgeon proficiency and staff transport duties. It went through the Hayes modification program in August 1954 and was converted to a VB-25N, after which it returned to the 3rd Aviation Medical Unit at Randolph and remained there until May 15, 1957, when it returned to Maxwell and the 3800th Air University Wing. In December 1958, it was flown into storage at Davis-Monthan and declared surplus in March 1959.

During its long career in the USAAF/USAF, B-25J USAAF #44-30801 (N3699G) flew as a multi-engine trainer, proficiency aircraft, and executive transport. In 1960, Christler & Avery Aviation purchased the bomber and converted it to an agricultural sprayer. In 1970, it appeared in *Catch-22* as *Vestal Virgin*. (*Milo Peltzer*)

On September 9, 1959, the bomber was sold to Fogle Aircraft of Tucson, Arizona, and registered as N3699G. Christler & Avery Aviation of Greybull, Wyoming, purchased the aircraft in January 1960 with plans to convert it to an agricultural sprayer, but that conversion did not take place until August 1961. In February 1969, Filmways of Hollywood, California, acquired the bomber for the filming of *Catch-22* (1970), where it appeared as *Vestal Virgin*, with 6K on the tail. After filming it was briefly part of the Tallmantz collection, but in February 1972 it was purchased by Challenge Publications, put through an extensive restoration, and re-registered as N30801, which it retains today. In July 1985, Eight Zero One was purchased by the American Aeronautical Foundation, and remained in its care until its acquisition by the Liberty Foundation in October 2023.

By the time it appeared in its first of five *Baa Baa Black Sheep* episodes in 1976, N3699G was part of the Tallmantz collection. In 2023, after 38 years with the American Aeronautical Foundation, this bomber, long known as *Executive Sweet*, was acquired by the Liberty Foundation. (*James Larsen*)

North American B-25J-25-NC Mitchell USAAF #44-30423 (N3675G)

First episode: "Up for Grabs" (season 1, episode 7, November 16, 1976)
Total episodes: 7

The B-25J *Photo Fanny* that is now based at the Planes of Fame Museum in Chino, California, rolled out of North American's Kansas City plant on January 13, 1945, and was immediately put into storage for the duration of the war. In January 1946, she was recalled to service and modified at Dayton Field, Ohio, being redesignated an EB-25J and assigned to the 3171st Electronic Research and Development Group (ERD) at Griffiss AAF, New York. Between June 1952 and February 1956, this aircraft was based at Hanscom AFB, Massachusetts; Birmingham, Alabama, for maintenance; back to Hanscom; then down to Laurinberg Field, North Carolina, where she was redesignated a JB-25J. By 1957, she was redesignated a TB-25J and loaned to North American Aviation in Inglewood, California, for an unspecified test program. She was flown to storage in August 1958 and declared surplus in February 1959.

On July 30, 1959, she was sold to National Metals and registered as N3675G. In March 1960, she was sold to John Carter and John Jacobson of Rancho Cordova, California, and ultimately donated to the Air Museum in Ontario, California. During *Baa Baa Black Sheep*, Seven Five Golf wore a basic olive-drab-over-gray scheme with no markings other than national insignia.

From 1983, this Mitchell appeared on an episode of *Simon & Simon* (1981–89) and in feature films *1941* (1979), *Forever Young* (1992), and *Pearl Harbor* (2001), where it flew off the deck of USS *Constellation* (CV-64) and flew on both sides of the camera in the 2019 remake of *Catch-22*.

Originally built as B-25J USAAF #44-30423, the Mitchell now known as *Photo Fanny*, received a number of designation changes, including EB-25J, JB-25J, and TB-25J. Donated to The Air Museum (Planes of Fame) in 1960, the bomber (N3675G) wore an olive drab-over-gray paint scheme during its seven *Black Sheep* appearances. (*Frank B. Mormillo*)

Douglas DC-3 c/n 3278 (N28341)

First episode: "Divine Wind" (season 2, episode 1, December 14, 1977)
Total episodes: 10

To the casual viewer and perhaps even ardent fans, it appeared that the aforementioned C-47B USAAF #45-1059 was the only Gooney Bird flown in the show. This was true until the first episode of the second season, when a second DC-3, one of incredible historic value, made its debut. This aircraft, DC-3 c/n 3278 (NC28341) was the second of five DC-3s to be delivered to Delta Air Corporation, where it became Ship 41. The first aircraft, Ship 40, named *City of Atlanta*, was being used for pilot training, so Ship 41 became the first DC-3 to carry Delta passengers when it entered scheduled service on December 24, 1940.

In the early 1950s, Ship 41 received a major update, including an air stair door, the galley moved forward of the passenger door, the lavatory moved forward of the bag bin area, and the seating capacity increased from 21 to 25. The exterior received the new "white top" paint scheme that included Delta's Flying D logo.

In April 1958, Ship 41 was retired from Delta service and was purchased by Joel H. Carroll of Elmira, New York, and leased to North Central Airlines (later part of Northwest Airlines), followed by Galaxy Airlines in 1968. Its time with the latter was short-lived, as it was acquired by Boone Flying Service, Inc of Boone, Iowa, the following year. In April 1976, Joel R. Grundy and James P. Friedland of El Segundo, California, purchased the aircraft, but sold it shortly after *Black Sheep Squadron* was canceled.

In December 1981, Ship 41 headed south to Puerto Rico, where it became a freight hauler with Sixto Diaz Saldaña and Del Caribbean Corporation for the next 13 years. To facilitate the loading of cargo, the airframe was modified with a C-47-style cargo door in August 1982. The aircraft was also re-registered as N29PR, a change that could have easily hidden its historic provenance forever.

Thankfully, in 1990, a group of retirees led an effort to locate one of Delta's first five DC-3s to be the centerpiece of the future Delta Museum. It took several years, but the hearty retirees located Ship 41 in Puerto Rico, and Delta officially took possession of the aircraft in June 1993. Not only had the retirees located one of those first five DC-3s, but the only Delta DC-3 still in existence. It was carefully restored by a team of volunteers and Delta employees from 1995 to October 1999, to combine 1940-vintage style with modern avionics. No other DC-3 in the world has been restored with such attention to detail.

With its freshly applied paint scheme, DC-3 NC28341 awaits its first appearance in front of the Universal cameras in July 1977. This aircraft appeared in 11 of the 13 episodes during the second season. In 1940, this aircraft was the first DC-3 to carry passenger for Delta Airlines and is rightfully enshrined in the Delta Air Museum at Hartsfield-Jackson Atlanta International Airport. (*John Cassidy*)

Schweizer SGS 2-33

First episode: "Operation Stand Down" (season 2, episode 5, January 11, 1978)
Total episodes: 1

The glider that Bill Yoak flew in the second season has yet to be identified.

North American AT-6D Texan USAAF #42-85866/SNJ-5C BuNo. 90649 (N7976C/N101RF)

First episode: "The Fastest Gun" (season 1, episode 22, March 15, 1977)
Total episodes: 1

In addition to the sextet of Tora Zeros, there was a single episode in which a standard T-6 was featured, and it was one of the last aircraft I identified. The aircraft was originally built as AT-6D USAAF #42-85866, but next to the acceptance date of September 11, 1944, on its Individual Aircraft Record Card is a handwritten note "Navy to Fly" and thus became SNJ-5C BuNo. 90649. From that date until February 1946, it served as an intermediate and basic trainer at NAS Whiting & Ellyson and then went into storage at NAS Houma and Litchfield Park. In July 1952, the aircraft spent its last five years at NAS Anacostia and Seattle before it was stricken on October 22, 1957.

The SNJ went on the US register as N7976C in September 1958 and was lucky to survive the year, as its first two owners were a pair of Phoenix-based smelting companies. The aircraft was rescued by Rex G. Clemmer of Albuquerque on January 13, 1959, but he sold it five months later and over the next decade the aircraft passed through ten different owners. On January 2, 1973, it was acquired by Junior Burchinal of Paris, Texas, and he kept the aircraft for nearly a decade. After a short time with Courtesy Aircraft, it was sold to a pair of owners in Salem, Oregon, in 1982. Its registration was changed to N101RF in 1987, and it went through a few additional owners before it was acquired by the CAF's American Airpower Heritage Flying Museum in February 2012. It remains with the organization to this day.

Lockheed P-38L Lightning USAAF #44-26961 (N74883/N38DH/N6961)

First episode: "Hotshot" (season 2, episode 10, March 15, 1978)
Total episodes: 1

The P-38 flown by Lt Thomas Bishop (Richard Stanley) in "Hotshot" (S2, E10) was P-38L USAAF #44-26961, which rolled off the Burbank production line on April 16, 1945. Four days later, it departed Burbank for Lockheed's Dallas Modification Center for conversion to an F-5G. The conversion was complete by June 1945, after which it was flown into storage in Kingman, Arizona. In April 1946, this aircraft became one of 11 P-38s and F-5Gs acquired by

R.A. Wardell and Dick Martin. The former eventually hoisted the aircraft on to the roof of his gas station in Portland, Oregon, where it remained until Robert "Bob" Caren Forsblade, who was scouring the country looking for fighters for the Fuerza Aérea Hondureña (Honduran Air Force, FAH), purchased it for a reported $2,000 ($30,684.10 in 2024)! After having the aircraft checked out, Forsblade flew the Lightning down to Los Angeles and turned the fighter over to FAH pilot Capt Jorge Torres. After clearing customs in Brownsville, Texas, Torres delivered the aircraft to Toncontin Field in Tegucigalpa, Honduras, on October 1, 1948.

In FAH service, the fighter became FAH-504. Although a few P-38s allegedly saw action in the brief border skirmish with Nicaragua, it appears that FAH-504 flew very little while in Honduras. In August 1959, the FAH traded its four remaining airworthy Lightnings for a mixture of F4U-4s and -5s.

Perhaps the only warbird rarer than a Corsair in the mid-1970s was a P-38 and *Baa Baa Black Sheep* featured two flying examples in "Hotshot" (S2, E10), which premiered on March 15, 1978. This is P-38L USAAF #44-26961, which was converted to an F-5G and photographed shortly after it returned from its time with the Honduran Air Force. (*Dan Hagedorn*)

On December 18, 1961, this Lightning was purchased by noted warbird collector Bob Bean of Hawthorne, California, but it is unclear as to when the fighter actually came back to the United States. Although it was registered as N74883, it seems that Bean never flew the aircraft because it was later purchased by World War Two P-38 ace Laurence Blumer of Puyallup, Washington, on July 24, 1968, and the first A/W certificate was issued on August 2, 1968. The following year, Blumer had a more thorough restoration performed on the fighter, and when it emerged, it was painted to represent his wartime mount, P-38J-25-LO USAAF #44-23590, *SCRAPIRON IV*. It was in this aircraft on August 25, 1944, that Blumer became an "ace in a day" when he shot down five Fw 190s in a 15-minute dogfight.

Blumer sold the P-38 to Don Hull of Houston in 1975, and the following year the registration was changed to N38DH. After a year-long stint in San Diego, John G. Deahl of Denver, Colorado, acquired the aircraft on April 15, 1977, at which time it still had just 283 hours on the clock. In John Schafhausen's narrated home movies taken at Indian Dunes, he indicated that Deahl flew the Lightning himself. Sadly, on April 9, 1981, Deahl was killed in this aircraft when an engine failed on take-off from an airport in Salt Lake City.

From 1968 to 1975, this Lightning (N74883) was owned and flown by P-38 "ace in a day" Laurence Blumer. When the fighter appeared on *Baa Baa Black Sheep*, it was flown by owner John Deahl, who would sadly die in the aircraft in 1981. (*Ron Olsen*)

Lockheed P-38L Lightning USAAF #44-53097 (NX67861/N9011R/N7TF/N3JB)

First episode: "Hotshot" (season 2, episode 10, March 15, 1978)
Total episodes: 1

The second Lightning in "Hotshot" was Burbank-built P-38L-5-LO USAAF #44-53097, which was one of the last Lightnings built before the end of the war. It was accepted by the USAAF on June 18, 1945, and delivered two days later. On June 22, the aircraft was ferried to Dallas, with an overnight stop at Coolidge AAF, Arizona, where it was placed in storage. On August 4, 1945, the fighter was assigned to the 4127th AAFBU at McClellan Field, Sacramento, California, where it was converted to a P-38M-6-LO night fighter with AN/APS-6 radar and an elevated rear seat for a second crew member. Shortly thereafter, on November 9, 1945, this brand-new night fighter was declared excess and placed in storage in Kingman, Arizona.

Like its co-star, this Lightning served with the FAH, arriving in-country in January 1949. It was operated as FAH-503 and allegedly became a trainer, but as with FAH-504, little to no flight time had been recorded when Bob Bean took delivery of the fighter at Kelly AFB, San Antonio, Texas. Placed on the register as N9011R, it passed through four owners between 1968 and 1970, when Tom Friedkin bought the aircraft and requested special registration number N7TF. When John J. Stokes acquired the fighter in 1974, it had been re-registered as N3JB. In *Baa Baa Black Sheep*, it wore an overall silver

The second Lightning flown in "Hotshot" (N3JB) left the factory as a P-38L but was soon converted to a two-seat P-38M night-fighter. Though it spent nearly two decades in the Honduran Air Force, available records seem to indicate that it was rarely flown. (*Dan Hagedorn*)

paint scheme with the insignia of the 49th Fighter Squadron (FS) and a scoreboard of 25 Japanese flags that was reminiscent of the scoreboard on Maj. Thomas McGuire's P-38L *Pudgy IV*.

In December 1979, the Lightning was acquired by H&E Aviation in Canby, Oregon, but it remained there for only a few years, for in June 1983 it was purchased by Windward Aviation of Mesa, Arizona. It was during this time that the Lightning was converted to its original single-seat L-model configuration. Today, it is permanently grounded at the Museum of Flight in Seattle on pylons in the World War Two gallery. It is painted in the markings of P-38L USAAF #44-25930 Lizzie V, which was assigned to John E. Purdy of the 475th FG/433rd FS.

When Tom Friedkin purchased the fighter in 1970, he was the fifth owner in two years. The Lightning is easily discernible on screen because it retained its two-seat configuration. At some point in the 1980s, the fighter was returned to single-seat configuration and is currently on display at the Museum of Flight in Seattle, Washington. (*James Larsen*)

Static Aircraft

Curtiss P-40N Warhawk USAAF #44-7983 (N9950)

First episode: "Flying Misfits" (pilot, season 1, episode 0, September 21, 1976)
Total episodes: 1

For a long time, I believed that the first aircraft seen in the series was the aforementioned Tallmantz TP-40N N923, but in June 2023, Facebook friend and *Baa Baa Black Sheep* fan Jason Hodge pointed out in the pilot episode that a static P-40 appeared before N923 took off. The spinner was a different color and the sharkmouth was different as well. This P-40 appeared on screen for three seconds, but I still couldn't believe I missed these details.

This aircraft, P-40N USAAF #44-7983, rolled out of the Curtiss factory in Buffalo on October 16, 1944, and remained in service until August 1945. Unlike many P-40s, '983 escaped the scrapper and was stored in Stillwater, Oklahoma. In February 1946, it was one of the 90 P-40s purchased by Paul Mantz. Soon after the aircraft was disassembled and stored until it was purchased by David Tallichet and moved to his facility in Chino.

Over the next three years, various parts of this P-40N were combined with parts from other Warhawks and assembled into an airworthy aircraft. It was placed on the register as N9950 and received an Airworthiness Certificate on August 30, 1973.

On January 13, 1989, the fighter was acquired by Doug Arnold, Spitfire Hangar, Biggin Hill Airport, Kent, England. It was reportedly restored again at Chino by Aero Trader and shipped to England in a container and from that moment forward mystery surrounded this aircraft. It changed hands several times over the decades, but in all that time it has remained in a storage container somewhere in the United Kingdom.

Beechcraft C-45 Expeditor USAAF # Unknown

First episode: "Flying Misfits" (pilot, season 1, episode 0, September 21, 1976)
Total episodes: 1

Near the end of "Flying Misfits," an unremarkable Twin Beech was seen taxiing at Indian Dunes. It can be seen in the background of Schafhausen's home movies, but since the aircraft carried no serial number or registration number, its identity is a mystery.

Grumman F6F-5N Hellcat BuNo. 80141
(N80132/N100TF/G-BTCC/N467RL)

First episode: "Meatball Circus" (season 1, episode 6, November 9, 1976)
Total episodes: 1

This Hellcat was the first of two F6Fs to appear in the series as a static/background aircraft, and unlike the other aircraft that will be covered later, this Hellcat has a complicated and distorted history. Built in Bethpage as F6F-5N BuNo. 80141, the fighter was accepted on June 1, 1945, and served at air stations from Alameda and Cherry Point to Glenview and Key West over the next dozen years. It was stricken in 1961 with 1,812 hours TT.

After stints in museums in Illinois and Virginia, it was acquired by W.C. Yarbrough of Marietta, Georgia, in April 1971, followed by early warbird movement pioneer, Thomas Friedkin, four years later. The Hellcat received minor damage in a taxi accident in December 1976 and substantial damage in an off-airport landing after an engine failure over San Marcos, California in April 1979.

From that point, the history of the airframe becomes quite convoluted. After the latter accident, the aircraft was rebuilt by the Yankee Air Corps (now the Yanks Air Museum) in Chino, California, with the right wing and center fuselage section from F6F-3 BuNo. 08831 and various parts of F6F-3 BuNo. 40467, both of which were partial airframes acquired by the Chicago Vocational High School by collector Earl Reinhart of the Victory Air Museum in Mundelein, Illinois.

Once the rebuild was complete, the aircraft left the United States for The Fighter Collection (TFC) still bearing its original F6F-5 identity. While in England, through a flurry of paperwork and sleight of hand, TFC managed to have the Hellcat assume the identity of 40467, in which US Navy ace Lt Alex Vraciu claimed six of his 19 victories. The aircraft was purchased by Rod Lewis in December 2014 and sent for Ezell Aviation for a complete restoration.

The history of this aircraft has become even more complicated, because parts left over from the '80s have been incorporated into the restoration of F6F-3 BuNo 40467 at the Yanks Air Museum.

This Hellcat, which was seen in the background in "Meatball Circus" (S1, E6) left the Bethpage factory as F6F-5K BuNo 80141. Following an off-airport landing in 1979, it was rebuilt using parts from two different F6F-3s and now has a ridiculously confusing history. It is seen here at Duxford's Flying Legends with Nick Grey at the controls shortly before it returned to the United States in 2014. (Stephen Bridgewater)

Boeing (Douglas) B-17G-90-DL Flying Fortress
USAAF #44-83663 (N47780)

First episode: "Trouble at Fort Apache" (season 1, episode 18, February 15, 1977)
Total episodes: 1

Rolling out of the doors of the Douglas Long Beach facility on April 30, 1945, B-17G USAAF #44-83663 was accepted the following day and spent just five years in active service. In the spring of 1951, it became one of six Fortresses to be transferred to the Força Aérea Brasileira (Brazilian Air Force, FAB), where it made history as the first FAB aircraft to make a trans-Atlantic flight and was the last Flying Fortress to be retired from service.

In 1968, the aircraft was marked for preservation at the then-United States Air Force Museum but was loaned to David Tallichet's Yesterday's Air Force Museum (YAM) in Chino, California. Tallichet sent mechanics to Wright-Patterson to make the bomber ferriable, after which former USAF B-17 pilot Jim Appleby and Tallichet, himself a wartime B-17 co-pilot, made the uneventful flight from Dayton to Chino.

In 1983, with the bomber then in Clearwater, Florida, the Air Force canceled the loan agreement and took physical possession of the bomber and had it ferried to the Cleveland National Air Museum for display. Ultimately, '663 was disassembled and trucked to the Hill Aerospace Museum at Hill AFB, Utah, where it is displayed as the 493rd BG Fortress and wears the name *SHORT BIER*.

The B-17 that is now displayed at the Hill Aerospace Museum in Utah had a significant history with the Brazilian Air Force. It was the first Brazilian Fortress to make a trans-Atlantic flight and the last example to be retired from service. In "Trouble at Fort Apache", this Fort (N47780) was used as static only. (*James Larsen*)

Boeing (Douglas) B-17G-90-DL Flying Fortress
USAAF #44-83684 (N3713G)

First episode: "Trouble at Fort Apache" (season 1, episode 18, February 15, 1977)
Total episodes: 1

The second Fortress used in "Trouble at Fort Apache" was also used only for static and taxi shots. It emerged from the Douglas Long Beach plant seven days and 201 airframes after its above-mentioned co-star, and was just as historic. After five years in Texas, the aircraft was assigned to the Air Material Command, and was flown to the Middleton Air Depot at Olmsted AFB, Pennsylvania, to be converted to a DB-17G drone controller aircraft. From there, it was assigned to the 3200th Drone Group (DG) at Eglin AFB, Florida. In February 1951, the unit deployed to Eniwetok Atoll in the Marshall Islands to support the Operation *Greenhouse* series of hydrogen bomb tests. In August 1959, the Fortress was flown into storage at Davis-Monthan AFB, Arizona, as the Air Force's last Flying Fortress.

In 1959, the Air Force placed '684 on permanent loan to Ed Maloney's Air Museum, which had then moved to Claremont, California. Over the next decade, the bomber appeared on *The Dick Powell Theatre*, *12 O'Clock High* TV series, as *Piccadilly Lily*, the 1969 film *The Thousand Plane Raid*, and of course *Baa Baa Black Sheep*. For the last 40 years, the Flying Fortress has been displayed in front of the Planes of Fame Museum, but it is not necessarily destined to remain static. Planes of Fame gained formal ownership of the aircraft in 1999. In April 2019, when asked if this historic Fortress will ever fly again, Steve Hinton said, "There's always a chance, but it's on a strictly volunteer basis because we don't have the funding for it. We've pursued it for years, and we just haven't found the big number it needs. We've recovered the surfaces, and we completely gutted the interior, stripped it, and put all the wood floorboards back in and redid the cockpit. As far as flying? You never know. Someday it could happen, but only time will tell."

When the script called for a B-17 to taxi, the duty fell to the Planes of Fame B-17 (N3713G). During its time on active duty, this aircraft took part in the hydrogen bomb tests in the Marshall Islands in 1951 and was the last B-17 retired from active service in 1959. For the past four decades, it has stood as a gate guard at Planes of Fame. (*James Larsen*)

North American B-25J-10-NC Mitchell USAAF #43-28204 (N9856C)

First episode: "Trouble at Fort Apache" (season 1, episode 18, February 15, 1977)
Total episodes: 1

While the author was researching the aircraft seen on camera, noted warbird photographer Frank B. Mormillo, provided photos that showed a B-25 painted as a PBJ. Despite this photographic evidence, this aircraft was never seen on screen. Or was it? In the final editing of this book, the author re-watched "Trouble at Fort Apache" and finally, way in the background, the PBJ was visible for just a few seconds. The next objective was to identify the aircraft and, once again, Mormillo provided that critical piece of information.

The elusive Mitchell, known today as *Pacific Princess*, is B-25J USAAF #43-28204, which was completed on June 12, 1944, and delivered to a gunnery school in Kissimmee, Florida. The aircraft remained in Florida until 1949, when it was transferred to the 4th Air Force Headquarters at Robins Field, Georgia. In 1950, it was damaged when a crew from the

Seen in the distant background in "Trouble at Fort Apache" was B-25J USAAF #43-28204 (N9856C), which, in addition to its single appearance in *Baa Baa Black Sheep* appeared in three feature films including *Catch 22* (1970), *1941* (1979), *and Pearl Harbor* (2001). (*Frank B. Mormillo*)

USAF Medical School at Brooks Field, Texas, was forced to land when the nose and left main gear failed to lower and lock as a result of a failed hydraulic line. In December 1953, it was converted to a TB-25N and continued its service until it was flown into Davis-Monthan AFB, Arizona, in 1957.

The following year, the bomber was acquired by Blue Mountain Air Service of La Grande, Oregon. In 1959, the bomber, now registered as N9856C, was converted into a fire bomber, a role in which it operated until it was acquired by Filmways, Inc. of Hollywood, California, for use in the filming of *Catch-22* where it appeared as *BOOBY TRAP*. Over the next four decades, it appeared in the war comedy *1941* and led the formation of B-25s in a Missing Man formation to honor the 50th anniversary of the Doolittle Raid. Perhaps its biggest claim to fame is that it launched from the flight decks of three aircraft carriers – USS *Carl Vinson* (CVN 70) in 1995 to commemorate the 50th anniversary of the end of World War Two, and USS *Lexington* (CV 16) and *Constellation* (CV 64) during the filming of the movie *Pearl Harbor*.

In addition to its TV and movie credits, N9856C, known today as *Pacific Princess* and seen here off the coast of Honolulu in 1995, has the distinction of flying off the decks of three US Navy aircraft carriers, USS *Carl Vinson*, *Lexington*, and *Constellation*. (*Frank B. Mormillo*)

Curtiss SB2C-3 Helldiver BuNo. 19075 (N4250Y)

First episode: "Trouble at Fort Apache" (season 1, episode 18, February 15, 1977)
Total episodes: 2

Another Chino-based warbird that was used as a static background prop was Curtiss SB2C-3 Helldiver, BuNo. 19075. This aircraft was delivered to the Navy on May 4, 1944. Its whereabouts are unknown until it was assigned to VB-81 at NAS Cecil Field, Florida, on August 24, 1944. In October that year, this Helldiver found itself more than 4,000 miles to the west at NAS Barbers Point, Hawaii, where it was assigned to VB-17, VB-2, and VB-95.

At some point, the aircraft was purchased by Fox Movie Studios but was later saved by Ed Maloney in 1963. David Tallichet acquired the aircraft in 1978 for his Yesterday's Air Force collection. Restoration began during the '80s, but it was never completed. However, this Helldiver is currently undergoing comprehensive restoration at the Yanks Air Museum in Chino.

Filming at Chino meant there was no shortage of aircraft to serve as background props. Past owners of this Helldiver (N4250Y) included Fox Movie Studios, Ed Maloney, and David Tallichet. The Helldiver appeared in "Trouble at Fort Apache" and "Last One for Hutch." (*Frank B. Mormillo*)

Photographed in September 2023, N4250Y is undergoing a steady restoration at the Yanks Air Museum and will someday return to the sky. (*Adam Estes*)

Eastern Aircraft TBM-3E Avenger BuNo. 91264 (N7835C)

First episode: "Trouble at Fort Apache" (season 1, episode 18, February 15, 1977)
Total episodes: 2

The final aircraft to appear in "Trouble at Fort Apache" was another Planes of Fame aircraft, TBM-3E BuNo. 91264, which was delivered on July 19, 1945, and was assigned as a replacement aircraft aboard USS *Franklin* (CV-13). At the time, *Franklin* was in the Brooklyn Navy Yard undergoing extensive repairs from damage it received off the coast of Japan in March 1944. The war ended before repairs were complete and the Avenger was stored at several naval facilities including Weymouth, MA, Norfolk, VA, and El Centro, CA, until it was stricken from Navy records in 1950.

Less than a decade later, Ed Maloney acquired the aircraft and restored it to flight status in 1976. It has been a regular participant at PoF and other regional airshows ever since that time.

Like the Yanks Helldiver, the Planes of Fame TBM-3E appeared in "Trouble at Fort Apache" and "Last One for Hutch." It was photographed here during the filing of the latter. (*Frank B. Mormillo*)

Ed Maloney acquired the Avenger in 1960 and restored it to flying condition in 1976. Since that time, it has been a consistent performer at the Planes of Fame airshows. (*Wally Van Winkle*)

Beechcraft C-45 Expeditor USAAF # Unknown

First episode: "Poor Little Lambs" (season 1, episode 20, February 22, 1977)
Total episodes: 1

Like the previously mentioned Beech 18 seen in the pilot episode, the identity of the second Twin Beech that was seen briefly in "Poor Little Lambs" is also a mystery. Unlike the VIP aircraft that appeared in "Flying Misfits," this second aircraft featured a number of postwar modifications, including extended wingtips and a slightly longer nose. Be that as it may, this aircraft holds the singular distinction that no other aircraft seen on the show can claim. It was the only aircraft not to share the screen with the Corsairs or Toras, as "Poor Little Lambs" is the only episode that featured no Corsairs or Toras whatsoever.

Another B-25 seen in the background in "Last One for Hutch" was Ed Maloney's solid-nose B-25J USAAF #43-4030 (N3339G). Though not a combat aircraft, this Mitchell did serve as a VIP transport in the European Theater of Operations. Among those who flew aboard the aircraft was Allied Supreme Commander Gen. Dwight D. Eisenhower. Today, it is on display at the South Dakota Air and Space Museum at Ellsworth AFB, South Dakota. (*Frank B. Mormillo*)

North American B-25J-1-NC Mitchell USAAF #43-4030 (N3339G)

First episode: "Last One for Hutch" (season 1, episode 21, March 8, 1977)
Total episodes: 1

Shortly after this Mitchell was delivered on February 25, 1944, it was flown to North American Aviation in Inglewood, California, to undergo extensive modification to a VIP transport. After completion, the B-25 was ferried to the Eighth Air Force in England, where it served as Allied Supreme Commander General Dwight D. Eisenhower's personal, but not exclusive, transport. Upon its return to the United States, it continued its VIP duties in the Washington, DC, area until it was retired and placed in storage in December 1958.

On April 22, 1959, the bomber was acquired by Lanward Leasing Corp of El Paso, Texas, and placed in the US Register as N3339G the following July. After passing through four owners in five years, it was purchased by Newell Hayes of El Paso, Texas, in July 1965. The following year, Hayes donated the bomber to Ed Maloney's Air Museum and Maloney subsequently transferred it to the USAF Museum Program in October 1981. The aircraft has been with the South Dakota Air and Space Museum at Ellsworth AFB, South Dakota, since 1984.

Grumman F6F-5 Hellcat BuNo. 93879 (N4994V)

First episode: "Last One for Hutch" (season 1, episode 21, March 8, 1977)
Total episodes: 1

The second Hellcat to appear in the series, F6F-5 BuNo. 93879, was accepted by the Navy on June 26, 1945, and spent five years in the aircraft pools in San Diego, Santa Rosa, and Alameda. In September 1950, the fighter was transferred to the Marine Corps and attached to VMT-2 at MCAS El Toro, California. While it cannot be confirmed, there is a slim possibility that this Hellcat appeared in *Flying Leathernecks* (1951), starring John Wayne. Hellcats and Corsairs seen in the film came from VMT-2 and VMF-232 respectively.

In November 1950, the fighter was transferred to VC-3 at MCAS Moffett Field, where it remained until May 1951, after which it returned to Alameda and FASRON 8. The fighter was stricken on January 9, 1958, having logged 1,058 hours.

This Hellcat entered civilian life in 1958, when Ed Maloney acquired the aircraft, and it made a number of TV and film appearances before and after *Black Sheep*, including *Route 66* and *Close Encounters of the Third Kind*, where it appeared in the background posing as one of the Flight 19 TBFs. The fighter remained with the museum until it was lost in a fatal crash on October 8, 2005. On that day, Art Vance took off from Sevierville, Tennessee, on a VFR flight plan, and during cruise flight near Monterey, Tennessee, the Hellcat collided with power lines, fell to the ground, and burst into flames, tragically killing Vance.

During its military service, this F6F-5 was assigned to VMT-2 at MCAS El Toro, California, while John Wayne's *Flying Leathernecks* was being filmed in 1951. In addition to *Baa Baa Black Sheep*, it appeared in an episode of *Route 66*, and *Close Encounters of the Third Kind* (1978). (James Larsen)

North American P-51D Mustang USAAF #44-73856 (N5077K/N711UP/N7TF)

First episode: "The Hawk Flies on Sunday" (season 2, episode 3, December 29, 1977)
Total episodes: 1

This Inglewood-built Mustang, USAAF #44-73856, was accepted on April 1, 1945, and delivered to the 3428th Base Unit at Perry AAF, Florida, a week later. After assignments at Bartow and Hunter AAFs, it was placed in storage at Hobbs AAF, New Mexico, in November 1945 and Kelly AFB, Texas, in September 1947. In June 1951, it was pulled from storage and assigned to the Strategic Air Command's 131st Fighter-Bomber Wing (FBW) at Bergstrom AFB, Texas, followed by the 479th FBW at George AFB, California, in December 1952. In May 1953, the Mustang was transferred to the Air National Guard (ANG) and served with the 125th FBS, Oklahoma ANG for four months before heading north to the 109th FS, Minnesota ANG, where it would remain until it was retired in 1958.

The Mustang entered civilian life when it was purchased by Jim Jeffers of Stateline, Nevada, in 1963, and went on the US Register as N5077K. In 1965, James Fugate entered the fighter in the Harold's Club Transcontinental Trophy Dash (as Race 77) the year it was a 2,260-mile race from Clearwater, Florida, to Reno, but failed to finish. In 1967, the race started in Rockford, Illinois, and Fugate posted a time of 5:36.0 at 282.82mph, which was good enough for 4th place, but Fugate was moved down to 5th because he arrived late at the start. In closed-course racing Fugate posted 5th and 2nd place finishes in Heat 2 and Consolation races at 290.55mph and 306.43mph, respectively.

In the 1969 Harold's Trophy Dash, Charles Doyle piloted the Mustang, re-numbered as Race 0, to a 5th place finish at 279.88mph. Doyle had no intention of entering the pylon races, but when Mike Loening's Race 2 *Boise Bitch* had engine problems, Doyle loaned him Race 0 and Loening flew the aircraft to its one and only win in the Medallion Race at 319.48mph.

In August 1973, Tom Friedkin acquired the fighter, and it has remained with the family to this day. For decades it went by the name *Susie*, but in the mid-2000s it was repainted in its current *Double Trouble Two* scheme.

The P-51D that today carries the registration N7TF, once served in the Strategic Air Command and later Air National Guard units in Oklahoma and Minnesota. Tom Friedkin acquired the fighter in 1973, and it has remained in the Friedkin family's Comanche Fighters collection to this day. (*Minnesota ANG*)

Though it bears no evidence of it today, N7TF is a three-time participant in the Harold's Club Transcontinental Trophy Dash. In 1969, Mike Loening borrowed the Mustang for a single pylon race and took the win at 319.48mph. (*Wally VanWinkle*)

North American P-51D Mustang USAAF # 45-11582 (N5441V)

First episode: "The Hawk Flies on Sunday" (season 2, episode 3, December 29, 1977)
Total episodes: 1

The second Mustang to appear in the series was P-51D USAAF #45-11582, which was accepted by the USAAF at North American's Dallas facility on July 25, 1945. The following day, it was flown to Kelly AFB in San Antonio for three years of storage. In March 1948, it was assigned briefly to the 31st FW at Turner AAF, Georgia. Just nine months later, '582 was transferred to the 155th FS of the Tennessee ANG. In January 1951, the fighter headed to New England, where it was assigned to the 134th FS, Vermont ANG, the famous "Green Mountain Boys." In November 1952, the Mustang was assigned to the co-located 31st FIS. Finally, in August 1953, the aircraft was transferred to the 167th FIS of the West Virginia ANG. This would be its final unit.

In November 1957, Edward Maloney purchased '582 during the so-called "Great Mustang Auction" at McClellan AFB in Sacramento, California. A few days later the Mustang was flown to Cable-Claremont Airport, and later taken by ground to the Air Museum's first home in Ontario, California. It was registered as N5441V and is one of the longest continuously operated warbirds in the world today.

In its early years, the Mustang, which was long known as *Spam Can*, initially wore a generic 361st FG paint scheme, but over the decades it has worn a half-dozen different paint schemes, with the latest being of a 504th FG Mustang named *DOLLY*.

After spending a majority of its career in storage, P-51D USAAF #45-11582 went on to become a citizen-soldier, serving in the Tennessee, Vermont, and West Virginia ANG. Ed Maloney purchased the aircraft in 1957 and placed it on the register as N5441V. It has worn dozens of paint schemes and is one of the longest continuously operated warbirds in the world. (*Frank B. Mormillo*)

THE CAMERA SHIPS

Heroes Behind The Cameras

North American B-25J Mitchell, USAAF #44-30823 (N1042B)

The future Four Two Bravo rolled off the line at the North American Aviation plant in Kansas City and was accepted by the USAAF on March 1, 1945. It spent its first few years with various training units, eventually being redesignated as a TB-25J. That changed in 1949 when it was reassigned as a VIP transport, becoming a VB-25J. In 1958, having been upgraded and re-designated a VB-25N, this Mitchell was involved in a gear-up landing in 1958. It was declared unsalvageable and surplus.

The aircraft was purchased by Wenatchee Air Services of Wenatchee, Washington, for $855 ($9,014 in 2024) in 1958, registered as N1042B and set aside for a future conversion to an air tanker, but it was never completed.

In May 1962, Tallmantz Aviation purchased the bomber as a second camera ship for the Tallmantz fleet. Once the Mitchell was ferried to Tallmantz's Orange County base, it was overhauled as needed, after which the modifications to camera ship specification began. First and foremost was construction of the distinctive wraparound nose glass, which was performed by Potter Aircraft Services in Burbank, California. The nose, slightly longer than stock, incorporated a large hatch on the left side to assist in mounting cameras. The glass was specially formed as a cylindrical section with minimal optical distortion for filming. Although not quite as obvious, the waist and tail gun positions were also modified to accept camera mounts. The airplane was finished in an overall white scheme with red rudders and wingtips, and a black anti-glare panel forward of the cockpit. The engine nacelles were blue. A thin black cheat line extended from the cockpit to the aft fuselage. Extensive lettering was added to the nose, identifying the airplane's operator, and came to include a world map and a list of projects in which the aircraft was employed.

The new camera ship was quickly put to work, and it appears that the first film in which it was employed was *How the West Was Won* (1962), and by the time it arrived at Van Nuys to begin filming "Flying Misfits" in August 1976, it had already been flown on more than a dozen films, including the quintessential B-25 movie *Catch-22* (1969), which was the only movie in which it appeared in front of the cameras. The aircraft had also been modified slightly by that time. A bubble was installed in the former top turret location and wired for an intercom for an aerial director. The paint scheme was changed slightly as well, the overall white with blue nacelles was retained, but it gained the distinctive Tallmantz emblem on the vertical stabilizers, and the nose markings were updated.

When Four Two Bravo spent the summer of 1976 working on *Baa Baa Black Sheep*, it was flown by a number of Tallmantz pilots including Frank Pine, Tom Mooney, Junior Burchinal, James Appleby, and of course Frank Tallman himself.

When Tallmantz closed its doors in 1986, N1042B was sold to a Delaware corporation, Universal Aviation, and operated by Aces High out of historic North Weald Airfield, Essex, England, and employed, with Tony Ritzman at the controls, in the filming of *Memphis Belle* in 1989. In 1996, it was acquired by World Jet at Fort Lauderdale, Florida, and sent to B-25 guru Tom Reilly, where corrosion issues were addressed, and it lost its distinctive camera nose. It took several years, but the B-25 was finally sold to a new owner in September 2000. John Lister of San Antonio, Texas, operated the airplane for several years in polished natural metal with USAAC tail stripes and markings and the name *Top Secret*.

In November 2003, it was sold to Jim Terry of Cleburne, Texas, and based at the Vintage Flying Museum at Meacham Field in Fort Worth, Texas. The overall scheme remained the same, but the name was changed to *Pacific Prowler*. Scott Glover added the aircraft to his Mount Pleasant, Texas-based, Mid America Flight Museum in August 2013. Once again, the bomber retained the overall scheme, but the nose art and name were changed to *God and Country*.

Like so many warbirds today, the B-25J that became the famous and revolutionary Tallmantz cameraship N1042B led a mundane life in the military. As part of the Tallmantz fleet and beyond, it has been used in dozens of feature films and documentaries. (*Scott A. Thompson*)

In 1989, N1042B was used in the filming of *Memphis Belle*, which turned out to be its final film. Sadly, a few years later it was sold and converted back to its standard bomber configuration. The one saving grace is that the camera nose was saved. Today, the bomber is flown as *God and Country* by the Mid America Flight Museum in Mount Pleasant, Texas. (*Tyson Rininger*)

North American T-28-R2 Trojan, USAF #49-1587 (N9106Z/N28DS)

The second warbird camera ship used in the series was North American T-28A, USAF #49-1587, which rolled off NAA's Downey production facility on August 4, 1950. During its nine-year military career, the Trojan served at Vance AFB, Oklahoma, Kelly and Moore AFB, Texas, before being retired to the Boneyard at Davis-Monthan AFB, Arizona, where it was quickly acquired by Cincinnati-based American Compressed Steel, Inc. on December 31, 1959.

Five months later, it was purchased by another Cincinnati-based company and registered as N9106Z. On June 4, 1963, the Tucson-based Hamilton Aircraft Company acquired the

Identifying the T-28 in John Cassidy's photos proved to be a challenge, but it was finally determined that it was T-28A USAF #49-1587. In 1964, the aircraft (N28DS) was fitted with a 1,200hp Wright R-1820 and a three-bladed propeller as part of an apparent Hamilton conversion. With F4U-7 133693 in the background, aerial coordinator James Gavin is in the T-28 in this August 1976 photo taken in Van Nuys. (*John Cassidy*)

In this photo, which features FG-1D 92106 (foreground), F4U-7 133693, and the Duck, the modifications made to the canopy of the T-28 are evident. Note the tail surfaces are painted blue. (*John Cassidy*)

In the 1980s and '90s, N28DS participated in the Reno and Phoenix Air Races. On July 21, 2021, the Trojan was damaged in an off-airport landing and is allegedly for sale. (*Don "Bucky" Dawson*)

aircraft where it was presumably slated for conversion to one of two of Hamilton's T-28A models. The first was the T-28-R1, a trainer with dual instrumentation and flying controls, and hydraulically actuated rearward-sliding canopy. The T-28-R2 was a commercial conversion with two pairs of seats for four passengers that featured a fixed canopy and an entry door on the port side of the cabin.

When the Trojan was purchased by Cincinnati Air Taxi, Inc. on October 27, 1964, the bill of sale listed N9106Z as Hamilton T-28-R1 and carried serial number 10. The first production model flew in February 1962 and a total of ten were built and Zero Six Zulu was assigned serial number 10. However, it appears that Zero Six Zulu did not receive any of the R1 or R2 related airframe modifications save one. On November 10, 1964, an Application for Airworthiness Certificate was filed, and it indicated that the aircraft had been fitted with a 1,200hp Wright R-1820 model 704C9GC1 radial and a three-bladed Hamilton Standard 33D50 propeller, which was one of two engine/propeller combinations available for Hamilton T-28s.

The aircraft remained with the air taxi service until 1968, and after a brief stint with a Florida owner, it was acquired by Sherman Aircraft Sales in West Palm Beach on December 15, 1970. The following April, the registration was changed to N28DS. Over the next six years, the Trojan passed through four owners before it was added to Tom Friedkin's Cinema Air, Inc. on August 10, 1976, just in time to begin filming of season one.

Friedkin sold the aircraft in 1980, and by December 1982, it was in the care of Dwight Reimer of Bakersfield, California. In 1983, Reimer took the aircraft to Reno and qualified the aircraft, Race 26, in 28th and last place with a sedate speed of 263.51mph. Later in the week, Reimer not unexpectedly finished last in the two Special Added Medallion races with speeds of 227.16 and 232.80mph.

By 1995, the aircraft had been acquired by Bruce Wallace of Grant Pass, Oregon, who campaigned the aircraft at the Phoenix 500 air races as Race 206. After passing through an additional two owners over the next decade, the Trojan was acquired by Robert Dulany, of Fort Lauderdale on March 31, 2006, who operated the aircraft for more than 15 years. On July 21, 2021, the aircraft received damage in an off-airport landing near Iuka, Mississippi.

Subsequently put up for sale, it was purchased by Walter E. Bagdasarian of El Cajon, California, in the spring of 2023. It is interesting to note that over those two-and-a-half decades the aircraft's identity repeatedly changed back and forth between "T-28R-1" and "T-28R-2". Today, it is listed as the latter.

BIBLIOGRAPHY

Books

Abbott, Jon, *Stephen J. Cannell Television Productions: A History of All Series and Pilots* McFarland & Company, Inc. Publishers, 2009

Beck, Simon D, *The Aircraft-Spotter's Film and Television Companion*, McFarland & Company, Inc. Publishers, 2016

Boyington, Pappy, *Baa Baa Black Sheep*, Wilson Press, Inc., 1958

Brooks, Tim & Earle Marsh, *The Complete Directory to Prime Time Network and Cable TV Shows, 1946–Present*, Ballantine Books, 1979

Gamble, Bruce, *Swashbucklers and Black Sheep: A Pictorial History of Marine Fighting Squadron 214 in World War Two*, Zenith Press, 2012

Gamble, Bruce, *Black Sheep One: The Life of Gregory 'Pappy' Boyington*, Presidio Press, 2000

Gamble, Bruce, *The Black Sheep: The Definitive Account of Marine Fighting Squadron 214 in World War Two*, Presidio Press, 1998

Levine, Elana, *Wallowing in Sex: the New Sexual Culture of the 1970s in American Television*, Duke University Press, 2007

McClurg, Robert W, *On Boyington's Wing: The Wartime Journals of Black Sheep Squadron Fighter Ace*, Heritage Books, Inc, 2003

Hagedorn, Dan, *P-38 in Latin America*, Aviation Art & History, 2022

Reed, Robert T, *Lost Black Sheep: The Search for WWII Ace Chris Magee*, Hellgate Press, 2001

Thompson, Scott A, *Final Cut, The Post-War B-17 Flying Fortress: The Survivors*- Pictorial Histories Publishing Company, 1990

Walton, Frank E, *Once They Were Eagles: The Men of Black Sheep Squadron*, University Press of Kentucky, 1986

Magazines

Gault, Owen, "The Challenge Warbirds," *Air Classics*, July 1976

Stone, Tim, and Janczarek, J, "Baa Baa Black Sheep," *Air Progress,* December 1976

Allen, Dub, and Johnson, F," Colonel Gregory 'Pappy' Boyington," *Air Classics Quarterly Review*, Winter 1976

Walton, Frank E, "*Baa Baa Black Sheep* Is Pulling the Wool over Our Eyes," *TV Guide*, April 23, 1977

Davidson, Bill, "*Black Sheep Squadron* just won't play dead," *TV Guide*, July 15, 1978

Thompson, Scott A, "Hollywood Mitchells," *Air Classics,* September 1980

Margulies, Lee, "Can Universal Plug its Talent Drain?" *Emmy*, Fall 1980

Arden, Darlene, "Stephen J. Cannell: Millionaire Producer Took a Gamble That Paid Off," *Entrepreneur*, October 1982

Francis, Bruce, "The Case of the Reluctant Heir," *Entertainment Monthly*, January 1983

Fanning, Deirdre, "What stuff are dreams made of?," *Forbes*, August 22, 1988

Chunovic, Louis, VOP Interview, Stephen J. Cannell, *Variety's On Production*, September 1996

O'Leary, M, "Black Sheep Bent Wings," *WARBIRDS International*, March/April 2008

Keller, T, "A Remembrance – Stephen J. Cannell: 1941–2010," November/December 2010

Newspapers

"2 From S.A. Named On Group," *San Antonio Express*, 5-C, December 8, 1967

"Stuntmen Hit Hard by Anti-Violence Rules," *The Orville Mercury Register*, 11 and 14, October 12, 1968

"Citizens Committee for Broadcasting Formed," *The Oakland Tribune*, 18, October 21, 1968

Gould, J, "National Citizens Committee For Broadcasting Stands Ready To Challenge Status Quo In TV," *York Daily Record,* 1, 1968, December 14

Gould, J, "TV Watchdog Group Losing All Its Bite?," *The Courier Journal Sun*, E-1 & E-9, February 22, 1970

"Wild Wild West" Target of Anti-Violence Suit, 6-E, November 15, 1970

Peterson, B, "It's Back to Leaping For Robert Conrad," Detroit Free Press, 4-B, July 10, 1972

"TV Notes," *Fort Lauderdale News*, 32F, December 1, 1972

Kenion, J, "Actor Learns by Doing," B6, October 21, 1973

Witbeck, C, "Pappy Boyington's Ace-High Series," *The Sacramento Bee*, 2, June 6–12, 1976

Margulies, L, "New Tactic is Battling Violence on Television," *The Times and Democrat*, 12–A, August 8, 1976

Kleiner, D, "Baa Baa Black Sheep: Conrad's Fifth," *The El Paso Herald Post*, 7-C, September 3, 1976

Witbeck, C, "Keynotes: Ace Boyington's story didn't begin as series," *The Morning Call*, 42, September 8, 1976

Henninger, P, "Robert Conrad's Black Sheep Take To The Air Tuesday," *Fort Lauderdale News*, 14D, September 17, 1976

Lawler, S, "*Baa Baa Black Sheep* not just for the kiddies," *The Morning Call*, 34, September 21, 1976

O'Brien, K, "Pappy Boyington Brings 'Clean' Violence To TV," *The Tampa Tribune*, 1-D, September 21, 1976

Woods, S, "*Black Sheep* premise, action enough to make show work," *The Miami News*, 7B, September 21, 1976

O'Connor, J, "TV: Series on Pappy Boyington," *New York Times*, 21 September, 1976

"Survey lists television violence," *The Tampa Times*, 11-A, September 22, 1976

Morrison, B, NBC's "*Black Sheep* Blah Blah," *The News and Observer*, 27, September 23, 1976

Martin, B, "Dirk Blocker no 'Black Sheep' of the family," *Independent Press*, 1, September 26, 1976

Carter, B, "*Baa Baa Black Sheep*'s only appeal is action, which seem to be enough," *The Sun*, B 4, October 5, 1976

Brown, L, CBS attacks "Baa Baa, Black Sheep," *Globe-Gazette*, October 6, 1976

"Home grown critics review new TV shows," *The Miami News*, 5 B, October 18, 1976

Adams, V, "CBS accepts 'Black Sheep' into the fold," *Daily News*, 67, October 19, 1976

Freeman, D, "Sour grapes at CBS over *Baa Baa Black Sheep*?," *The Lowell Sun*, 6, October 24, 1976

Press, R, "TV Violence Protest Grows," *Albuquerque Journal*, A-15, November 14, 1976

Cooke, M, "Who says we were black sheep?," *The Honolulu Advertiser*, C-1, November 22, 1976

Scott, V, "Acting Part Of Whitmore Family's Heritage," *The Latrobe Bulletin*, 10, November 26, 1976

"Robert Conrad Sharing Hero Role With Canine," *The Latrobe Bulletin*, 10, November 26, 1976,

"Pappy Boyington's 'Misfits' Are Doing All Right Now," *The Evening Sun*, B-1, December 10, 1976

Deeb, G, "Video study reveals sponsors of violence," *Forth Worth Star-Telegram*, 8a, December 21, 1976

Hemby, L, "Pappy's Black Sheep: 'Aloha' After 30 Years," *The Tennessean*, 16, December 21, 1976

"Jeff MacKay: Big Breaks On *Baa Baa*", *The Sunday News*, 40, January 30, 1977

"TV Viewers' Forum," *The Tampa Tribune*, 45, May 22, 1977

Shales, T, "Cure for TV violence: Boycott the sponsors!," *The Ithaca Journal*, 26, March 5, 1977

"Robert Conrad, *Black Sheep* star, goes to war to save his NBC series," *Rapid City Journal*, V-11, July 1, 1977

Woods, S, "*Black Sheep* shot down, then revived," *The Miami News*, 3 and 15, July 16, 1977

"Ex-'Black Sheep' Says TV Show Is an Insult," *The Atlanta Constitution*, 18, August 23, 1977

Mermigas, D, "Conrad fights for his *Black Sheep*," *The Herald*, 6, August 25, 1977

"Conrad successful in fight for *Baa Baa Black Sheep*," *San Antonio Express*, 2-C, August 30, 1977

Biggers, B, "Sheep Not Lamb", *Emporia Gazette*, 3, September 10, 1977

Butler, R, "Tulsa TV Actor Due for Golf, "A17, September 10, 1977

"*Black Sheep* nearly shot down," *The Evansville Courier*, 4, December 6, 1977

Woods, S, "Conrad goes to war to get *Black Sheep* shown in Miami," *The Miami Press*, 78, December 12, 1977

Parker, C, "Conrad battles to keep sheep," *The Valley News*, 8, December 13, 1977

Henninger, P, "*Black Sheep* to Fly Again, *Lancaster News Era*, 31, December 13, 1977

Wister, E, "Pop Dan helped but Dirk did rest," *The Charlotte News*, 11A, January 18, 1978

"Jeb Adams joins the *Black Sheep* unit," *The Tampa Times*, 36, February 17, 1978

Sharbutt, J, "Four Stunning Damsels Join *Black Sheep*," *Honolulu Advertiser*, 7, February 26, 1978

Frisch, N, "Behind the Scenes," *The Jordan Valley Sentinel*, 9, March 23, 1978

"DuBarry is a lady and she's a lamb," *The San Bernardino County Sun*, 14, April 2, 1978

Shepard, R, "TV: Silverman Starts by Hiring Irwin Segelstein," *New York Times*, 46, June 10, 1978

Hughes, M, "'Court' opened new world for Larroquette," *Press & Sun-Bulletin*, 2E, November 2, 1990

Arkush, M, "Hollywood loses a Vietnam," *Los Angeles Times*, F25A-B, November 9, 1990

Interviews

Aresco, Joey, March 31, 2022

Armstrong, Alan, June 18, 2018

Bellisario, Donald, November 26, 2019

Bowman, Chuck, June 18, 2019

Cassidy, John, June 28, 2020

Chung, George (Byron), October 3, 2020

DuBarry-Hay, Denise, July 11, 2018

Ellsbury, Fred, July 1, 2018
Flach, Richard, February 10, 2019
Friedkin, Thomas, 2012
Hinton, Steve, 2012 and April 14, 2019
Johnson, Susan and Kenny, March 8, 2019
Leary, Brianne, November 29, 2018
Manetti, Larry, June 30, 2018
Prescott, David, January 16, 2019

Price, Frank, November 3, 2019
Rosenberg, Steve, 2012
Sagansky, Jeff, October 18, 2019
Sanders, Dennis, February 22, 2019
Tyler, Nelson, November 3, 2020
Walker, Michael, November 4, 2020
Whitmore Jr., James, June 11, 2019
Yoak, Bill, 2012